STORIES I TELL

A Comic's Random Attempts to Make Some Sense Out of Nonsense

by
Paul J. Murphy w/a Paul D'Angelo

STORIES I TELL

*A Comic's Random Attempts to Make Some Sense
Out of Nonsense*

Paul D'Angelo
Wakefield, MA 01880
pdangelocomic@aol.com
www.pdangelo.com
copyright © August 2014 Paul D'Angelo

ISBN 13: 978-0-692-29435-2
ISBN 10: 069229435X

(also available in eBook format)

For my mother - a small woman with an enormous heart

TABLE OF CONTENTS

- The Belt
- The Last Man in the World
- 'The Nostrilizer'

CHAPTER 3: ANOTHER NEW CHAPTER

- The Interpreter, Part I
- The Interpreter, Part II
- Christmas Dinner
- First Downer
- Authentic Mexican
- The Lonely Diner
- City of Fallen Angels
- A Real Lu Lu
- World Traveler
- Clothes Shopping with Mom
- Sex Education
- Inauspicious Beginnings
- Courtship
- Eva and Adolf

CHAPTER 4: A TOTALLY DIFFERENT CHAPTER

- The Interview
- Have It Your Way
- Alley "Oops"
- Lunch With Dad
- Timthy's Party
- Spooky Stories
- Cause for Alarm
- The Accident
- Man O' War
- Father and Son Moment

INTRODUCTION:
Paul D'Angelo, Comedian-at-Law

The Lawyer

People often ask me, "Paul, why did you decide
to become a lawyer in the first place?"
I tell them that, actually, when I was just a little boy,
my father took me aside and said,
"Paul, your mother and I have been talking and we think
you'll make a good lawyer when you grow up."
I beamed with pride and said,
"Because I'm intelligent and analytical?"
He said, "No, because you're a little sneak
who takes money off our bureau."

Paul D'Angelo

The Comedian

When I was a small child, I once announced to my mother,
"Mom, when I grow up, I want to be a stand-up comic!"
My mother answered, "I'm sorry Paul,
you can choose to grow up,
or you can choose to be a comedian,
but you can't do both."

adapted by Paul D'Angelo

The Result

It isn't work unless you'd rather be doing something else.

Peter Pan

"I wasn't looking for heaven or hell,
Just someone to listen to stories I tell."
Toad the Wet Sprocket

I suppose I should start by telling you something about my-self and how I got to where I am now.

I was born Paul J. Murphy and grew-up in the town of Wakefield, Massachusetts, a nice, suburban community located twenty minutes outside of Boston in an area referred to as the North Shore.

For the first fourteen or so years of my life, I grew up in a house that my grandfather built when he emigrated from Sicily. It was located in a predominantly Italian section of town affectionately known as "The Gulch." (A nickname often preceded with a slang term for Italians.)

I lived with my Italian grandparents, my Uncle Vito, my parents, Jack and Frances, and my younger siblings . . . my brothers Jay and Chris (who were known to my dad as "Dummy #2" and "Dummy #3") and my sister Shauna, over what had been my grandparents' general store many years before. Looking at faded photos of the 'J. Longo and Sons' sign, circa 1931, I discovered they sold everything from meats and deli products to shoes, fine clothing, washing machines, refrigerators, and even linoleum, before eventually phasing that business out and establishing one of the country's first open-air drive-in movie theaters. The Meadow Glen Twin Drive-In Theater in Medford, Massachusetts was the brainchild of my Uncle Paul, a brilliant visionary who tragically died in a restaurant fire when he was only thirty-nine years old, a couple of years before I was born.

I had a great childhood and the best family in the world. My father and Uncle Vito were my first comedic influences. When I was a little boy, my dad, over my mother's protests, would get me out of bed every Sunday night to watch the comedians on *The Ed Sullivan Show* and I 'borrowed' my uncle's Bill Cosby albums and played them over and over again. But, it was really their live performances that made the biggest impression on me. My Sicilian uncle was a great storyteller, animated and dynamic like Roberto Benigni on a double espresso, and nobody told a joke better than my father, a jovial Benny Hillish Irishman who was one of the funniest people I have ever known.

The General Store of Paul's Grandparents
Wakefield, Massachusetts (circa 1930)

As I neared graduation at Wakefield High School, I had no idea what I wanted to do with my life. For some reason, I finally decided that I would become a dentist . . . that reason being that it would give my mother the chance to proudly brag to her friends about her oldest son, the dentist.

I was accepted at Tufts, planned on taking pre-med courses and even met with their football coach about possibly playing as a walk-on . . . even though I pretty-much sucked as a football player. For example, I missed two games my senior year because of chapped lips.

I had the deposit check in a stamped envelope, sitting on my desk and waiting to get mailed, when those plans abruptly fell through after a fateful visit to my dentist.

I used to talk to my dentist all the time about his profession and asked an endless series of questions about med school and anything else dental-related. He knew how enthused I was about becoming a dentist, so I'll never know if my dentist did what he did inadvertently, or on purpose, but it dramatically changed the course of my life in an instant.

I had to have a filling and it was the first time I ever had nitrous gas as an anesthetic. I was high as a kite . . . too high, actually . . . and I left the chair disoriented with the spins. My dentist whipped out an illustrated book about oral surgery and began showing me photos of people missing various parts of their heads — blown off by a hand-grenade in Vietnam; eaten away by cancer; lost in a car accident; an oral surgeon sticking his hand through an empty eye-socket to get to an upper jaw — Gross!

I almost lost my lunch, then immediately bolted out of the dentist's office and ran down the street, vowing to myself over and over, "No way, baby . . . No fucking way!" . . . and I kept going all the way home, ran up the stairs to my bedroom, two steps at a time, then tore up the tuition deposit check into a million pieces.

I adamantly concluded, "Nope, that ain't for me!"

Once I made that important decision, it immediately gave rise to my next big dilemma, which was, "Now what?"

I thought for about a minute, no more than that, then envisioned myself wearing an impressive suit, carrying an impressive briefcase, impressively talking to hordes of news reporters as I walked down the impressive marble steps of the impressive marble courthouse with impressive marble pillars . . . and pronounced to myself, "That's what I'll be! I'll be a lawyer!"

Just like that.

Of course, I knew nothing about the profession other than what I saw on a couple episodes of *Perry Mason*, but it sounded good . . . not necessarily to me, you see, but for my mother who would now be able to smile and proudly boast to her friends about her son, the lawyer.

More than anything or anyone in the world, I wanted to please my mother and father. I loved and respected them dearly and constantly sought the approval of parents who were often reluctant to give approval . . . done for all the right reasons, of course. That's what motivates people to set high goals and always endeavor to better themselves . . . or just give up trying to satisfy people who can't be satisfied. It's all up to the individual.

And, believe me, I never thought that I'd ever be able to please my mom.

I used to tell my friends that, even if I was elected to be the President of the United States of America, I could still picture my mother, at lunch with her friends, who are all gushing and excited and saying to her . . . *"Oh Frances, you must be soooo proud of your son, Imagine, he's the head of the most powerful nation in the whole wide world!"*

And my indifferent mother responding half-heartily, *"Yes, of course I'm proud of Paul but, between you and me girls, he's no Abe Lincoln."*

Now all I had to do was break the news to my dad, Jack "Tiger" Murphy — the ex-Marine, Golden-Gloves winning heavyweight boxer, big football star and all-time legend at Holy Cross College — that I wanted to attend school at the Cross' hated archrival, Boston College.

Of course my dad was furious and thought I was doing it just to be rebellious, but the truth was that BC had a School of Management and I had now decided that I was going to be a corporate lawyer because I rationalized that my mother would be even *more* proud if she could refer to me as, "My son, the *corporate* lawyer." This, of course, was a decision made with as much forethought and consideration as my decision to be a lawyer in the first place . . . relatively none.

My dad finally relented, but warned me that, if I didn't get straight A's at BC, he'd pull my ass out of school and I'd be *"digging ditches for the rest of my life."* I was motivated to study hard because I wanted to prove to my dad that I'd made the right choice, even though the truth was that the only time my father and I ever agreed on anything was when I admitted I was wrong, which didn't happen very often.

I attended plenty of keg parties, but missed enough of them so that I graduated *magna cum laude* as a member of the Beta Gamma Sigma honor society (the equivalent of Phi Beta Kappa for management) near the very top of my class.

Now for law school. I needed to take time off to build up some money for grad school. I had outstanding grades, so I got a bunch of offers and ultimately took a job at a high-tech company that made satellite receivers on the Route 128 belt in Burlington, Massachusetts. My plan was to work for one year, get their health plan to pay for the removal of my aching wisdom teeth, and then tell them I was leaving to go to law school.

6

That year happened to provide me with of the most important lessons in my entire life . . . and not because I learned what I wanted to do. More importantly, I learned what I *didn't* want to do.

I discovered three valuable things about myself that affected the way I looked at my career path from that point forward:

#1: I learned that, if you don't love your job . . . if you look at the clock all day; if you can't wait to leave; if you don't think about your job when you're not there; when you don't want to work extra and do whatever it takes, you will never really succeed at it. To be the best, you had to love your work so much that it didn't feel like work.

#2: I was too independent to work in this corporate environment. When I took the job as a production control manager, the guy whose old job I was moving into was in charge of teaching me the ropes. He was a resentful redneck from New Hampshire and he made my life miserable while he did his best to make me look bad. I vowed that I wouldn't put myself in that vulnerable position again. I also concluded that I was not the type to keep my mouth shut and/or kiss ass to get ahead, and those traits seemed to be a prerequisite for success in the corporate environment.

#3: If you are a creative, imaginative person, you can't be happy working at a systematic, methodical job. If you do, you will go nuts with frustration absent some kind of outlet for your creativity.

Those lessons served me well when I eventually found out that life as a corporate lawyer encompassed everything I hated about that other job.

What now? I thought, I don't have a problem speaking in front of people, maybe I should be a trial attorney . . . and what better place to get trial experience than at the district attorney's office? So, after getting my Juris Doctorate from the Suffolk

University School of Law in Boston and clerking for several judges at the Middlesex Probate Court in Cambridge, I took a job as a prosecutor with the Essex County District Attorney's Office in historic Salem, Massachusetts — home of the infamous witch trials. I started at $18,500 a year and my salary wouldn't even cover my substantial weekly bar-tabs, so every month I'd have to raise extra cash by bartending; or designing stuff for an advertising company; or collecting insurance money when someone hit my car, so I only planned on staying three years, max, then taking a job with a law firm as a trial attorney.

It sounded like a plan . . . finally.

It was about this time that I first started attending live comedy shows. Boston was a hotbed of comedy featuring some of the best stand-up comics in the country and I especially loved watching the brilliant Steven Wright perform, but I never dreamed of doing it myself.

That was until my best friend's bachelor party.

Bobby Ogan, who I met on my first day of orientation at Boston College, was getting married, and the guys he grew up with planned on roasting him after a sit-down dinner in a rented room at Jimmy's Allenhurst function facility. Evidently I must have already had a reputation for being funny because I was the main attraction, and everyone anticipated that I'd be giving Bobby a good 'ol ball-bustin'.

I didn't let them down. I prepared for weeks, got pretty shit-faced on Scotch beforehand, and delivered what amounted to be a 45-minute, mostly-original comedy show to a bunch of happy drunks.

After my presentation, many of the attendees asked about hiring me for one occasion or another, but I told them that this was a one-time performance and I had no intention of repeating it . . . however, the seed had been planted.

When I subsequently went back to watch live comedy, I

returned with a different perspective. Instead of being a non-participating spectator, I watched the show as a critic, contemplating, "Can I do that? I think I can be funnier than this guy . . . I wonder if I could get up there." Then I went home with newfound inspiration and started writing like crazy.

I knew that, if I attempted to be a stand-up, I couldn't go through the obligatory phase of sucking for a while because I was a good lawyer and I just imagined everyone getting on my back going, *"Are you crazy? What the hell is wrong with you?"* — especially my parents who I'd always wanted so much to impress. At that point I had already prosecuted over a hundred bench and jury trials, so I wasn't worried about my presentation, but knew that I needed to come up with some decent material.

Over the next several months I literally filled dozens of legal pads and manila folders with jokes, concepts and ideas, vowing to create twenty minutes of usable material before I signed up for my first five-minute set at an open-mike night, which I eventually did at Stitches Comedy Club on Commonwealth Avenue next to Boston University, early in 1985. (Coincidently, it was the very same night that my extremely successful friend, Louis C.K., also debuted as a comedian.)

To be honest, I wasn't really sure if my boss, Essex County District Attorney Kevin Burke, would approve of his Assistant DA moonlighting as a comic, so I thought it was best to use a different stage-name. Because of my Italian look and my overwhelmingly Italian upbringing in an overwhelmingly Italian neighborhood, my friends at Boston College used to call me "Angelo," so I decided to sign in as "Paul D'Angelo."

To get up the nerve, I started with Bloody Marys at 10 a.m. and continued drinking steadily throughout the day, only to arrive at Stitches and be surprised by twenty-or-so of my close friends, along with my father and mother . . . just to add a little more pressure to my debut. I waited anxiously for my turn in the back of the showroom when I heard the emcee announce, "Ladies and gentlemen, please welcome our next comedian to the stage, Paul Murphy."

My confused friends said, "I thought you gave them another name?"

I said, "I did, but they must have screwed it up," and proceeded to run toward the stage when an enormous guy waddled onstage, took the microphone and said, "Hi, I'm Paul Murphy" . . . and he was *awful!* My friends just about pissed their pants laughing.

"Ha! You changed your name and now people are going to think this terrible comic is you!"

That pretty much sealed the deal with my pseudonym, later to be reinforced when I did several shows in front of paroled ex-cons who I had put in jail under my real name.

Anyway, I finally got my chance, got a great reaction, and the host actually had to physically pull me off the stage by my arm at the end of my set because I didn't want to get off.

I was psyched, but I'll never forget the motivational words of encouragement I got from my mother after the show: "I'm glad you got *that* out of your system."

But I hadn't . . . and, even though I only did another dozen or so open mike nights before I quit doing comedy under pressure from my family and the guilt of not focusing on my legal career, my head was filled with ideas, so I never stopped writing material.

It eventually came time for me to make a major career decision. After several interviews, I was offered jobs with a couple of mid-sized Boston law firms and I told them I needed some time to make a choice. Then I went out and bought a little, red Mazda RX-7 sports car that I couldn't possibly afford on an ADA's salary to force me into leaving the district attorney's office.

I only had one problem. Once again, I realized that working for one of these law firms represented everything I loathed about the high-tech job I endured before attending law school. They told me I would be working long hours and weekends; my A.D.D. and I would have to do tedious research and paperwork for several years before they would let me try cases; and I would have to "play the game" and kiss-up to get anywhere in the firm.

When the deadline approached for my decision, I panicked. Instead of accepting a job as an associate in a law firm, I impulsively called Boston-based booking agents Mike Clarke of Five Star Comedy and Barry Katz (later to become the manager of comedy superstars Dane Cook, Dave Chappelle and Jay Mohr and the producer of *Last Comic Standing*) and lied about my credentials as a comic, reading off a print-out list of New York City comedy clubs that I had never actually performed at. They both agreed to give me an audition and I showed up with a bunch of new material and my guitar, with which I performed song parodies and sang like artists who couldn't really sing, such as Neil Young and Bob Dylan:

"How does it feel, to call Bedrock your home . . . your whole world's made out of stone . . . you use a shell for a phone . . . your next meal is a bone . . . 'cuz you're Fred Flintstone."

Fortunately for me, it was the beginning of the end of the comedy boom of the mid-to-late '80s and comedy clubs were popping-up everywhere, so there was a big demand for talent. Both Mike and Barry agreed to start booking me as a headliner and, from that point on, I started working anywhere from three to seven nights a week, every week — including dates in Boston; Providence, Rhode Island; Portland, Maine; Hartford, Connecticut; Springfield, Massachusetts; Manchester, New Hampshire and everywhere in-between — while remaining at the DA's office.

In addition to many comedy clubs, I also performed in Chinese restaurants, Mexican restaurants and pizza joints; I performed at a bachelor party where the guest of honor was puking into a trash barrel three feet in front of me; I did a show at a college frat house where a huge melee broke out in front of the stage; I had a drunk throw his prosthetic leg at me on stage; I did shows into a PA system from the front of a moving bus; I was tackled onstage by a crazy woman in the middle of a football routine: I performed on a cruise ship in front of 800 passengers — none of whom spoke English. Hell, at the first (and one of the last) house parties I ever did, the hosts introduced me minutes after the entire audience watched a routine groundball go through Bill Buckner's legs and essentially blow the 1986 World Series against the Mets. Throughout my entire act, I had to put-up with the intermittent interruptions of frustrated Red Sox fans who would spontaneously scream out, "*FUCK!*" or "*SHIT!*" . . . Like a rare strain of Tourette's syndrome.

These examples are just the tip of the iceberg, but it's said what doesn't kill you just makes you stronger and I learned from every experience. I dropped the guitar portion of my act after a couple years, but it was instrumental (*rim shot!*) in getting my comedy career off the ground.

For more than seven years, I kept that busy nighttime schedule at the same time I was supervising several of Massachusetts' busiest DA's offices, including Haverhill and Lynn District Courts, the Salem 6-man jury session and the Peabody District Court Jury Session. I was always exhausted, but they were the best years of my life. I even spent all of my vacation time performing on cruise ships and working the road . . . on stops that included Las Vegas, Atlantic City, etcetera.

Over those seven-plus years I had the privilege of hosting

my own weekly show at Boston's hottest comedy club at the time, Nick's Comedy Stop, located in the theater district near the infamous "Combat Zone." I also had the opportunity to open for many international recording artists such as Ray Charles, Aretha Franklin, The Four Tops, The Temptations, Patti LaBelle, Huey Lewis and the News, Jerry Lee Lewis, The Doobie Brothers, The Beach Boys, Chicago, The Righteous Brothers, Hall & Oates; Lyle Lovett, Tony Bennett, Englebert Humperdinck, George Carlin, Joan Rivers and Dennis Miller.

There eventually came a time when I needed to make another move and, after almost eleven years, I left the DA's office at the end of 1993 with the intention of moving to Los Angeles in order to concentrate on my comedy career, but once again, things didn't happen as I had planned.

I spent a couple weeks in Hollywood, California with my comedian friend, Patty Ross, and put a deposit on an apartment near hers but, before I could make the move, I accidentally became a criminal defense attorney.

One night, as I was returning from a show in New Hampshire, a lawyer who was a close friend of mine made a desperate call and asked if I could appear at an arraignment the next morning in Lowell District Court. My friend assured me that the client I was to represent had been mistakenly identified as a third co-defendant in a case he was involved with and my guy would be exonerated in a matter of days. Piece of cake.

Yeah, right.

I showed up in court with a hangover and was unexpectedly met with a myriad of cameras, intense TV coverage and a throng of reporters because my friend had conveniently failed to mention that it was a controversial and highly publicized incident.

When I got home I was met with an answering machine filled with messages asking me what the hell I was doing. Well, it took me over a year and a half to resolve that case and, in the process, I reluctantly developed a practice as a defense attorney and had to delay my move to the West Coast as a result.

I became successful, but unhappy. I was no longer the good guy. I had to discredit cops on the stand who were my friends to win cases for defendants that I suspected of being guilty as sin. I had to grovel to DAs and clerks to get my cases called. I had the intense pressure of trying to preserve someone's precious freedom, even though they may have deserved to go to jail. The last straw was a motor vehicle homicide case where a high school honor-roll student got run down by one of my unrepentant clients. I felt a little sleazy and a bit compromised, but I was lucky enough to have another option available to me.

In 1996 I stopped taking new cases and moved to an apartment building on Hollywood Boulevard. Convinced that I would be "discovered" within a year, but realizing that the transition was necessarily going to suck for a while, I started writing a diary that I titled *L.A. Misérables*. I figured that it would make a best-selling chronology of my guaranteed success. Six 300-page diaries later . . . nothing, but my time spent in L.A. was the "struggle" that I never had to go through when I rose so quickly in the Boston comedy scene and it helped me to grow immeasurably as a writer and performer. After six years I eventually moved back to Boston and have been busier than ever . . . and happy that I was home with the people who are most important to me.

I am still a lawyer and I always will be . . . it's kind of like being an alcoholic. I go to L.A. meetings (Lawyer's Anonymous) and sometimes — when I drive past a courthouse — I get the shakes and think, "Maybe I'll just take one case" . . . but you can't. Sure, you think you can stop at one case but, next thing you know, you're working nights and weekends, becoming serious, developing ulcers, and before you know it, you're a full-blown lawyer again.

I'm fine with my decision. Why? For starters, I love what I do and thank God every day for the way my life turned out. Also, when I was a lawyer, I never did a trial in Las Vegas or in the Caribbean; I never finished a closing argument and had someone say, "Great job! Would you like a cocktail and a lobster?" and, as a lawyer, I never, ever had a 45-minute work-day.

I am known as a prolific writer who is constantly updating and complementing his material, but there are many comedy routines, true stories and humorous anecdotes that I don't usually have the opportunity to include in most of my live performances.

For that reason, I've compiled many of these eclectic musings in a random collection, the subject matter of which ranges from true courtroom stories, to the dilemma facing an unhappy Eva Braun as she contemplates breaking-up with Hitler; from a stand-up comic's life in Hollywood, to being attacked by a great white shark in my own water-bed; and from satirical commentary on contemporary society, to my awkward attempts at conversation while having lunch with Jesus.

I had so many good stories I couldn't even fit them all in. After all, how many people can say that they have been kissed by the reigning Middleweight Champion of the World (Marvelous Marvin Hagler); got sucker-punched in the gut and had the wind knocked out of them by legendary Penn State football coach Joe Paterno; and actually beat-up a well-known, former television child-star in their Hollywood apartment (He deserved it!) . . . But those are all tales for another time.

Have fun.

Photo from aborted *People Magazine* feature

CHAPTER 1:
THE FIRST CHAPTER

Socratic Method

The first year of law school can be very intimidating.

Many people were introduced to the intense competition, tremendous pressures and resultant insecurities of first year law school by watching the movie *The Paper Chase* and its spin-off TV series back in the '70s.

The main character was a highly-respected, but greatly feared, contracts professor named Charles Kingsfield Jr., played by John Houseman who won an Academy Award for Best Supporting Actor in that role.

Professor Kingsfield used the Socratic Method of teaching, which basically means that the professor instructs a class by arbitrarily calling on anxious students and grilling them with insightful questions, hoping to move the debate towards incrementally self-solving a case or legal issue. It's effective because you learn through fear and stress . . . and sometimes total humiliation.

I had a teacher just like that.

He was probably one of the best professors I ever had, brilliant and one of the country's most esteemed experts in the field of torts (negligence), but we were all scared shitless of him, especially after he had a few cocktails.

I didn't notice it myself, but a couple of my classmates pointed out that they could tell the days when the professor had been hitting the bottle because he would hold on to the lectern at the front of the class for dear life . . . which was fine by me, because that meant he wouldn't be stalking the aisles of the big amphitheater and randomly picking on hapless students to torture.

When he singled you out and asked you a question in front of the class, no matter what answer you gave him, it was usually wrong . . . even if it was right.

He'd walk up the steps of the big auditorium and suddenly point . . .

"YOU! What rights does the plaintiff have in the case we're discussing?"

"Well, to begin with . . . "

And he'd bark, "You're an idiot! What are you doing in law school? You should be working in food service! That's all you'll amount to!"

A few more steps up or down the stairs then, unexpectedly . . . "YOU!"

"Yes?"

"What damages can the plaintiff sue for?"

"Under federal law they have a right to . . ."

"How did you ever get accepted here? You have no idea what you're talking about! You're a disgrace to the legal profession! I'm disgusted with this class, every damn one of you!"

Well, one day, the professor's nose was glowing Rudolph-red and he was in a particularly foul mood as he went up and down the aisle, putting people on the spot and throwing one student after another out of his class.

He'd yell, "You're useless! Get out of my class! I can't stand to look at you! Get out, NOW!" and point to the door located way down at the bottom of the amphitheater, upon which the

18

humiliated student would collect their books and papers and walk out in shame, several of them in tears.

One by one, he terrorized the class as each one of us prayed silently that we could somehow become invisible for the next hour.

"I'm fed up with this class! There isn't one of you who has the aptitude to be a decent lawyer! All right, let's see if you can redeem your sorry selves. Here's the scenario . . . a tiny midget is lonely and has no future, so he runs away and joins the circus. While working in the circus, he meets the love of his life, another midget just like him, and the two of them get married. One day, while the show is going on under the big top, a careless patron drops a lit cigarette into a trash barrel that starts a fire. The crowd panics and starts to flee from the tent, spooking the elephants and causing a stampede that crushes the midget's beloved wife to death . . . What remedies does the midget have?

"YOU!"

The young woman he was pointing at answered, "The midget can seek damages based on . . ."

"Did you even bother to read the materials? Get out of my class! You're embarrassment to yourself and your classmates! It's not too late to apply to trade school! In fact, I recommend it! Out! NOW!"

"Yes, sir," she said, and she took her books and ran down the stairs sobbing.

He pointed at another frightened student.

"YOU! What recourse does the midget have?"

"Well, the midget can file a lawsuit to . . ."

"Another moron! Doesn't anyone have a clue in this class? Is there no hope?"

Now he walked up the stairs menacingly, looking for his next victim as every intimidated student avoided making eye contact and slouched in their seats, trying to make themselves as small as possible.

"YOU!"

I wondered who the unlucky bastard was this time, but I didn't hear a response, so, fearing the worst, I sheepishly raised my eyes and saw the shaking finger pointed right at me.

"Me?"

"YES, YOU! What is the midget's course of action?"

"Huh?"

Seething, he reluctantly repeated . . . in a much louder voice, "DIDN'T YOU HEAR ME? I SAID, WHAT IS THE MIDGET'S COURSE OF ACTION?"

I thought for a moment, then looked into his bloodshot eyes and said . . .

"Small claims court?"

No reaction.

Stillness.

Absolute silence . . . You could have heard a butterfly fart.

Like death . . . or, more accurately, impending death.

Nothing . . . from either the professor, who appeared stunned, or the students, who were *waaay* too scared to laugh.

You could have heard the proverbial pin drop as everyone in the class waited for the violent explosion that was sure to follow . . . But there was none. The professor just stared at me for what seemed like an eternity, yet it was probably only a few seconds, then he ever so slowly turned around, calmly walked down the stairs to his desk, gathered his belongings, picked-up his briefcase and walked out the door without saying a word.

No one dared to move or utter a word for maybe five minutes.

Finally, one of the students in the front row got up enough courage to get up, open the door, and peek into the hallway.

He looked back at us with an astonished expression on his

face.

"He's gone."

"Are you sure?"

"Yeah, he's not here, he's *gone*."

The entire auditorium broke into cheers and I was mobbed by my relieved classmates as if I had doused the wicked witch with a bucket of water.

Ding-Dong, the wicked old witch is dead!

The next class, the professor began his lecture as if nothing had happened, but it was too late, for irreparable damage had already been done . . .

I really loved the feeling of making a room full of people laugh.

Boston Accent

People tease me about my thick Boston accent.

I can see why. When I talk to people, the word "car" sounds like "*cahh*," the word "Boston" sounds like "*Bahsten*" and the word "no" sounds like "What are you, fuckin' kiddin'?"

My Boston accent has actually gotten me in trouble before.

Once, I was working on a cruise ship and I was having dinner in the formal dining room with a nice couple from New York.

At one point, the husband apparently got up from the table to go to the bathroom and, as he left, I asked his wife, "Where is John going?"

She answered, "He's going to the potty" . . . meaning the toilet.

I thought she said he was going to a "party" . . . you know, with balloons and dancing and cocktails . . . so I got all excited and exclaimed, "Oooh, I want to go too!"

She shot me a puzzled look and said, "Why would you want to go with him?"

I bubbled, "Because, if it's a big one, I don't want to miss it!"

They avoided me the rest of the week.

Still Single

I'm sure that one of the reasons I never got married was that, for most of my life, my little Italian mother didn't like any girl I went out with until *after* we broke-up.

I'd come over to visit and walk-in as my mom would be stirring her homemade tomato sauce on the stove with a wooden spoon.

"Hi, mom."

(With anger and contempt.) "Are you with that pig? That *puttana!* . . . pooh . . . I spit on her! She is the devil! She's no good, I tell you. You'll see! She will be the ruination of you! pooh . . . no good *puttana!"*

"Relax, ma, we broke up."

(Sweetly, with compassion.) "Awwwww, that's too bad. I always liked her. She was such a nice girl."

Great White Hype

I don't know who to believe anymore. Everybody lies now. Who can you trust?

The media? Are you kidding? No one is worse than the media.

You can't believe anything you watch on television or read in the newspaper anymore.

Journalists get caught plagiarizing articles that they claim as their own.

Trusted news anchors like Dan Rather get caught using forged documents about President Bush's National Guard record.

Newsweek magazine runs a story about U.S. soldiers flushing Korans down the toilet at Gitmo without first verifying whether it was true or not.

Formerly esteemed newspapers such as *the New York Times* don't report the news so much as forcing their political agendas down your throat.

You find out a lot of reality TV is actually staged.

Everything is sensationalized. It's all about selling newspapers or boosting TV ratings

There's no integrity. The truth just doesn't matter anymore.

Here's what I mean . . .

I once had a large great white shark's tooth on a chain that I used to wear around my neck.

It was very pointy, sharp and serrated.

Well, one night, while I was sleeping, I guess I must have rolled over the wrong way and the pointed end of the shark's tooth stuck into my neck.

It hurt enough to wake me up and actually broke the skin and drew a little blood.

Now let's exaggerate a little and imagine that I was having a really bad dream, causing me to toss and turn even harder, and the shark's tooth somehow nicked my jugular vein. Now suppose that I thought I was falling into a deep sleep, while I was actually bleeding to death in my own bed.

Can you imagine the media frenzy when they found my lifeless body the next morning . . . in my waterbed . . . with a big, great white's shark's tooth sticking out of my bloody neck?

You just know that the press would blow the story totally

out of proportion.

I can envision the TV coverage . . .

"BREAKING NEWS! . . . A man is attacked by a great white shark in his Wakefield apartment. Report at 11."

"News Center 5 begins NOW!"

"Tonight's top story . . .

"A Wakefield man was apparently attacked and killed by a giant, man-eating great white shark while sleeping in his water bed, twenty miles from the nearest ocean.

"Let's go, LIVE, to the scene of that gruesome tragedy."

Reporter at the scene . . .

"The mangled, half-eaten body of stand-up comedian, Paul D'Angelo, was found lying in a pool of his own blood this morning.

"The only evidence the killer left behind . . . a large, razor-sharp tooth lodged in the victim's throat.

"That tooth has now been identified as belonging to a 10 to 15-foot man-eating great white shark.

"The shark was no longer on the scene when police finally arrived, however we interviewed our local shark expert, a Mr. Quint from the beach resort of Amity, to give us his opinion."

"It sounds frightening, Mr. Quint, but is it possible that a giant great white shark could actually get into someone's home and eat them?"

"Aye, a Great White gets hungry enough she'll swim up-stream and make her way up the sewer system through the pipes . . . get into the home through a faucet or shower head. . . even a ice-cube maker or dishwasher during the rinse cycle. From there it's just a short hop over to the water bed."

"Really?"

"Aye, mate . . . See? . . . water goes in the water bed . . . shark goes in the water bed . . . *comedian* goes in the water bed . . . then it's *Farewell and adieu to you fair Spanish ladies, farewell and adieu to you ladies of Spain* . . .

"See this scar?"

Quint rolls up his sleeve and reveals his forearm.

"Eight foot mako come through the ball-washer at the local golf course . . . grabbed me arm . . . ruined me swing."

"I'm sorry, but we are now going to break away for a press conference with Chief Martin Brody of the Wakefield Police Department."

The chief clears his throat and steps to the podium.

"Thank you. It appears that we have a rogue great white shark loose in our community.

"As a safety precaution, all the water mains going in and out of the city have been blocked off and we are urging all residents to stay out of their swimming pools and Jacuzzis until we can catch this indiscriminate killer.

"Citizens are further advised to turn off their lawn-sprinklers and water-picks, and we strongly urge any men using a public restroom to stand a safe distance away from the urinals for obvious reasons.

"I've seen such a shark once before and, bottom line is, I think we're gonna need a bigger Wet-Vac!"

BULLETIN!

"This just in . . .

"It now appears that the panic caused by the sighting of two large fins moving slowly through Kenmore Square was nothing more than an older-model Cadillac driving by.

"News Center 5 will keep you informed as this story develops . . . Now, in related news . . .

"Greenpeace is mobilizing its members to protect the shark.

"The National Rifle Association is urging its members to *shoot* the shark . . .

"The IRS is working to find a way to tax the shark for using the public works . . .

"The American Bar Association has filed a defamation lawsuit against the shark for impersonating a lawyer . . .

"New York's Mayor Bloomberg has banned the shark from eating any jumbo-sized residents weighing over 300 pounds . . .

"And Governor Deval Patrick welcomes the shark to Massachusetts and has already started the paperwork to get the shark food stamps and a driver's license.

"In other news tonight . . ."

God help us.

Photo of an original painting by Paul

My First Time

I'll never forget the first time I had sex.

It was late at night and my girlfriend and I were in the front seat of my father's car, way in the back of an empty parking lot.

I had absolutely no idea what I was supposed to be doing, but I seemed to be doing it pretty well . . . at least I thought.

I was so into it that I didn't see the police cruiser pull up right next to us.

Suddenly, the interior of the car was illuminated by the bright spotlight mounted on the police cruiser as the cop announced over the loudspeaker . . .

"OK, LET'S MOVE IT IN THERE!"

My girlfriend stuck her head out the window and yelled out, "Thanks officer. Maybe he'll listen to you!"

Sacked!

I've heard a lot of horror stories about comedians having skirmishes with audience members, but that rarely happens to me because I'm not confrontational in my act.

Still . . .

One night I was headlining a comedy show in the packed function room at Kitty's Restaurant in North Reading, Massachusetts, accompanied by my good friend, singer Billy Pezzulo.

I was scheduled to do a 50-minute set and leave immediately thereafter to perform at a corporate event being held in a big hotel at Logan Airport.

Knowing I was on a tight schedule, I looked at my watch and realized I only had about five minutes left so, as I was finishing-up one routine, my mind was simultaneously searching through my repertoire of jokes to pick out a closing bit for the finale. It was then that I recalled Billy specifically requesting that I perform my "John Madden" routine, which I had so far neglected to include in the show.

In a nutshell, the basis of that routine is that, if you go out with someone long enough, at some point that person will inevitably say something so incredibly stupid . . . so illogical . . . so irrational . . . so preposterous . . . so absurd . . . that, upon hearing it, you will immediately look around you in the hopes of finding a witness, or a corroborator, or a stenographer . . . or maybe a loaded hand-gun . . . "Give me the gun, I'm gonna shoot her!"

I proceed to tell the story of my girlfriend in Los Angeles who, upon learning of her promotion at work, celebrated by drinking way too much and then, when I offered to help in any way I could, made it very clear that she was miserably sick and just wanted to be left alone . . . which she emphasized by storming out of the room and shutting herself in the bathroom.

Of course, when I did leave her alone as she demanded, she eventually left the bathroom and proceeded to admonish me for leaving her alone.

"I can't believe you left me alone! I could have been dead or passed out and you wouldn't have even known because you don't care!"

"But, honey, you told me to leave you alone."

"You know I didn't mean it! You are so selfish! I can't be-lieve you left me alone! What an asshole!"

It didn't make any sense and that's when I suggested that, in these circumstances, I really could use demonstrative football commentator John Madden to explain what just happened, the same way he dissects and analyzes a complex football play through the use of diagrams on a chalkboard.

With a pointer in my hand, I mimic an animated John Madden on stage as he explains, "You two go into a huddle over here. Your girlfriend says she doesn't feel good and goes into the single-wing 'Leave me alone!' formation in front of the bathroom toilet while you split wide to the right, lining up on the living room couch, thinking you've done everything you possibly could . . . Boy, were you in for a big surprise!

"Now, while your girlfriend was alone in the bathroom, a crazy idea started running through her mind. This foolish thought dodges common sense, fakes out the facts, and then shoots through a big gap in her logic . . .

"She almost gets a hold of reality for a moment, but she fumbles it when she gets hit with emotion or some female hormone shit, *even I* can't explain to you . . ."

On and on for about two or three minutes.

Well, I was almost through the football routine . . . and my set . . . without incident, when I saw a rather large woman approaching the right side of the stage.

I figured that she was just on her way to the bathroom, so I didn't think anything of it and continued miming Madden as he diagrammed my girlfriend's convoluted thought process on an imaginary blackboard.

The next thing I knew, I was leaving my feet . . . the victim of a perfect form-tackle that Hall of Fame linebacker Lawrence Taylor would have been proud of . . . literally flying through the air and landing with a solid thump on the ground to the left of the stage. (Witnesses claimed that, as I was airborne, I had the presence of mind to scream "WHAT THE FUCK?" into the microphone, but I honestly can't recall.)

While I lay on the floor, several patrons came to my rescue, prying the offending woman off of me and escorting her out the backdoor of the establishment.

I don't know if she was really drunk, completely out of her mind, or a combination of the two, but those customers told me, when asked what the hell she was thinking, the woman replied, "It was a football bit. I thought it would be funny!"

Fortunately I was unhurt, but it could have been much worse.

I got to my feet and astounded audience members yelled up, "Was that part of the act?"

Incredulous, I replied, "Part of the act? Yeah, I'm willing to risk spending the rest of my life confined to a wheelchair for a cheap laugh at Kitty's. Are you fucking nuts?"

Someone yelled to the patrons who ushered the crazy woman out to the parking lot, "Did you get her number?"

I interjected, "I'm not sure, but I think it was 63!"

Not only was I shaken up, but this bizarre incident made my next gig even tougher because I was starting out that show deep in the hole with a 2nd and 17 and an obvious passing situation.

Mrs. da Vinci's Son

I can only imagine how history may have been changed if some famous people had *my* mother and father as their parents.

To Michelangelo . . . (Yelling up at the scaffolding in the Sistine Chapel in Rome)

"How long does it take to paint a ceiling? All our friends are asking when you're going to be done and I don't know what to tell them. And, by the way, just so you know, Mrs. da Vinci's son Leonardo has already invented the helicopter and *painted the Mona Lisa since you started."*

To Albert Einstein . . .

"Comb your hair, you look like an idiot!"

To Thomas Edison . . .

"Go to sleep and turn off that damn light!"

To Elvis Presley . . .

"Stop doing that thing with your lip, it's annoying."

To Napoleon Bonaparte . . .

"You may have conquered most of the world but, when you're in our house, you're going to help clear the table like everyone else."

To Paul McCartney of the Beatles . . .

"I don't care how the other kids are cutting their hair, you're getting a crew-cut."

(An actual quote from my mother.)

To the Wright Brothers at Kitty Hawk . . .

"Yeah, that's great . . . and what are you going to do when this doesn't work out?"

(An actual quote from my father.)

To Sigmund Freud . . .

"You may think you're a genius, but we saw you grow up. . . we

30

know the truth."

(An actual quote from *both* of my parents.)

To George Washington, as he leaves for Valley Forge . . .

"Wear a hat."

<u>Big Plans</u>

When I was a kid growing up, people would often ask me, "Paul, what are you going to be when you grow up?"

And I always had the same answer . . .

"I don't know what I'm going to do with my life, but whatever it is, my goal is to be a millionaire by the time I'm thirty years old. I'm definitely going to be a millionaire by the time I'm thirty."

Well, let's see how that prediction worked out . . .

As of right now, I am twenty-eight years late and approximately one-million and twenty-five-thousand-dollars short of my goal.

Ooooh, soooo close . . . just missed it.

What did I know? I was young, naïve and inexperienced and, as a result, still very optimistic.

And, when I fantasized about becoming a millionaire, I would naturally imagine the things I could buy with all that money.

One of the luxuries I coveted most was a classic 1958 Corvette. I could picture the exact model I wanted . . . a black convertible with silver accents in the side panels and lipstick-red leather seats. Wow, what a beautiful car.

The dream lived on for many years, until one day . . . in the midst of struggling to make my car payments, cover my insurance bills, make rent and keep up with a mounting credit card balance . . . reality bitch-slapped me into the sobering realization that I'm probably never gonna own that 1958 Corvette that I always wanted.

Face it, Paul, it just ain't gonna happen.

Then, one afternoon . . . coincidently not too long after adding the vintage Vette to my ever-expanding list of broken dreams . . . I was flipping through a magazine and saw an advertisement for a Franklin Mint 1/24th scale-model replica of a black 1958 Corvette convertible with silver accents in the side panels and lipstick-red leather seats . . . just like the one I always wanted . . . for $120.

I started thinking, "That model's really nice, but I don't know, $120 is a lot of money," . . . until I read a little further and saw the words 'or 4 easy payments of $29.95' . . . and concluded, "Oooh, I think I can afford that!"

So I dialed the 800-number on the ad, purchased the 1/24th scale-model, black 1958 Corvette convertible with the silver accented side panels and lipstick-red interior, *just* like the one I had always dreamed of owning, and proudly put it on prominent display right in the middle of my living room bookshelf above my TV.

And that's where it sits today . . . serving as a constant reminder that I am approximately 1/24th as successful as I once thought I would be.

How tragic . . . I have become my own Mini-Me.

By the way, another good call, Nostradamus.

Calling-In Sick

When I worked at that high-tech company after college I hated my job and I didn't want to be there, so I used to call in sick to work all the time.

I used every excuse I could think of.

I would tell them I had a stomach ache . . . or food poisoning . . . or Irritable Bowel Syndrome . . . or I had a bad cold, the flu, scabies, scurvy and kidney stones . . . I came down with the measles, chicken pox, the mumps and dyslexia . . . I got toothaches, headaches and earaches . . . battled Hepatitis A through C . . . had my tonsils out (again). . . suffered a severe case of halitosis . . . contracted the bird flu, the swine flu and Mad Cow Disease . . . had my appendix taken out (again) . . . got shingles . . . anthrax . . . gonorrhea . . . dementia, a mild case of leprosy and even Sickle Cell Anemia.

I called in sick so often, I was running out of excuses . . . and diseases.

One day the boss answered the phone at work, "Hello."

"Yeah, hi . . . (cough) This is Paul . . . (looking through a medical encyclopedia) I'm sorry but (cough) I don't think I'm gonna be able to make it in today."

(Rolling his eyes.) "What is it now, Paul?"

"Now . . . Uh, I (cough) I don't feel good because I have (running my finger down the page) ummm . . . (cough) let's see . . . um, I have Scarlet Fever."

"You have *Scarlet Fever?*"

"Yes, Scarlet Fever."

"Well I don't care. Get your ass in here."

"But, didn't you hear me? I have Scarlet Fever!"

(Doing his best Clarke Gable impression.) "Frankly Paul, I don't give a damn."

No Deposit, No Return

Another true story . . . I'm embarrassed to admit.

Many years ago, my sister Shauna worked as a bank teller in Woburn, Massachusetts.

One day she told me, "There's a really nice guy who always comes into my bank and he says that he knows you. He's a comedian too."

I was curious. "Really, what's his name?"

She said, "His name is Dave Andrews."

I thought for a moment, but the name didn't ring a bell.

"Dave Andrews? I'm sorry, but I don't know who that is."

"He says he knows you, Paul. You must know who I'm talking about, he always asks me to say hello to you for him."

I said, "I'm sure I've met this guy somewhere, sometime, but I meet a lot of people. That name doesn't sound familiar to me, but don't let him know that. Just tell him I said hi."

It seemed that, every week or so for as long as my sister worked at the bank, she would bring him up.

"That guy came into the bank again and asked for you. He insists that he knows you."

I stressed, "Shauna, I told you a hundred times, I'm sure we worked together before but I honestly have no recollection of meeting him. I'm sorry, but I'm sure I'll run into him again someday and maybe then I'll recognize him."

My sister eventually moved on to another job and I never gave it another thought until several years later when I was doing a show at Stitches Comedy Club in Providence, Rhode Island. I was the headliner, so I walked in while the show was in progress. The opening act was on stage and I asked the manager, Dana, what comic was going on before me. She told me that the feature act was Dave Andrews and pointed to a guy sitting at a table under one of the loudspeakers, but I didn't make the connection at the time.

I walked over to the table to introduce myself and, as I approached Dave, I put out my hand, leaned in, and said into his ear, "Hi, I'm the headliner, Paul D'Angelo. It's nice to meet you."

He said, "I know, we've met before," but his answer was drowned out by the loud volume of the speaker hanging directly over our heads, so I cupped my mouth with my hand and said loudly, "EXCUSE ME? I CAN'T HEAR YOU."

Dave spoke up and repeated in a loud voice, "I SAID, WE HAVE ALREADY MET," but I still couldn't hear him.

"HUH?"

He had to yell louder, "I SAID, WE HAVE MET BEFORE."

I yelled back, "REALLY? WE DID? I DON'T RECALL."

Shouting over the noise, he said, "YA, I USED TO BANK WITH YOUR SISTER."

A look of horror came over my face and I inquired angrily, "WHAT DID YOU JUST SAY?"

Dave repeated, "I SAID, I USED TO BANK WITH YOUR SISTER."

Next thing you know, I was lunging at him and had a hold of his throat as I screamed, "YOU SICK SON OF A BITCH!" while the poor guy yelled back, "I WENT TO THE BANK WHERE YOUR SISTER WORKED! THAT'S ALL I DID, I SWEAR TO GOD!"

I immediately let go of him, put my hand on his shoulder and said with great humility, "I AM SO, SOOO SORRY! PLEASE ACCEPT MY APOLOGY . . . I THOUGHT YOU SAID THAT YOU *USED TO BANG MY SISTER.*"

Dave offered, "OH MY GOD! SHIT, EVEN IF I *DID*, I WOULDN'T HAVE *TOLD* YOU!"

We've been good friends ever since.

First Impressions

Comedians can be a strange bunch . . . some more bizarre than others.

I have a very dear friend named Bob Seibel, who is now in his '70s. Bob is truly a unique character who defies description in a short passage but, suffice it to say, if you saw him thumbing a ride on the side of the road, you would be much more likely to punch the gas pedal than pull over and pick him up . . . but just the sweetest and funniest human being there is.

A fellow comic, Steve Bjork, tells of his first encounter with Bob.

Steve was a new comic when he was booked for his first paying gig, a milestone for any aspiring comedian. He asked the show booker who he would be working with and he was told that the headliner that evening would be none other than the highly esteemed comedic icon, Bob Seibel.

Steve was all excited, thinking to himself, "Wow! I get to work with Bob Seibel! That guy is a legend of the Boston comedy scene! He's one of the comics I admire the most! That is so impressive! I can't wait to meet him!"

On the day of the show Steve was understandably very anxious and arrived at the comedy club a full two hours before show time. When he got to the almost deserted venue, Steve walked into the men's room only to find "The Legend," Bob Seibel, standing completely naked, holding a pair of soaking wet pants up to the electric hand drier on the wall.

Steve, stunned by this bizarre sight, remarked, "What the hell are you doing?"

Bob, *The Legend,* looking over his shoulder as he dried his trousers, answered . . .

"I had an accident!!! . . . *I thought it was a fart!"*

The Blizzard

A big blizzard in New England can be either a blessing or a curse, depending on who you are snowed in with.

If you are snowed in with someone you love, there is nothing more romantic.

"We're snowed in. The roads will be closed for days!"

"That's all right. We'll make hot cocoa, watch old movies and snuggle . . . giggle, giggle."

But if you are snowed in with someone you can't stand, there is nothing worse. You'll be outside with a soup spoon and a hair dryer trying to clear a path out of there.

It happened to me once.

Many years ago my friends set me up on a blind date. The plan was for the girl to come over my house for Chinese food and a movie.

I was kinda excited and I was looking forward to meeting someone new.

"I hope she's nice . . . I hope she's good looking."

DING-DONG.

The doorbell rang and I got all nervous.

I opened the door in anticipation aaaand . . . *Ewwwwwwww* . . . Uh-uh . . . Ugh! . . . Nooo Good . . . "Danger, Will Robinson!" . . . Oh boy.

But it went both ways. She wasn't thrilled with me either.

We had absolutely nothing in common. We weren't attracted to each other. There was no chemistry whatsoever between us . . . The date *sucked* . . . It was a total disaster, big mistake, extremely awkward and, to be honest, I couldn't wait for it to be over.

In fact, I was so anxious for the date to end, while we were watching the movie, every time she got up to go to the bathroom, I would stay on the couch, hit the remote and fast-forward the movie.

She came out of the bathroom, "What happened?"

"Don't worry. You didn't miss anything. Sit down and finish this movie with me."

The ending credits weren't even over when I was helping her on with her coat and shuffling her out the door.

"Thank you very much, I had a wonderful time. That was really nice . . . sorry to see you go."

Then I opened the door and learned that, while we were watching the movie, a couple feet of snow had fallen and the wind was howling.

We were in the middle of a big blizzard, and we didn't even know it.

That's when she said, "I can't drive home in this weather."

I said, "Are you sure? Don't you have 4-wheel drive? It *IS* New England, you know?"

"No, I don't."

"Do you at least have *front*-wheel drive?"

"No."

"How about good tires? Do you have good tread on them?"

"Huh?"

"How about a cell phone and a couple flares?"

I put-up my finger to ask for complete silence and cupped my ear.

"Wait! I think I hear a snowplow in the distance . . . You should give it a shot. See how far you can make it . . . I'll be here if you need me."

She said, "No. Let's wait a while, maybe the storm will slow down."

We waited an hour, but the storm got worse and worse.

Before you know it, there were snow-drifts as high as my chest around my house . . . We were buried in snow . . . You couldn't see the tops of the cars anymore . . . The end of the driveway was a solid mountain of heavy ice and slush.

She said, "I'm gonna have to stay over tonight."

Shit.

I was standing there in a daze, when I snapped out of it and said, "Look, would you like a drink? Huh? How about I make us a couple of drinks? Good idea?"

So I made us a round of drinks.

We got along OK.

Then I made a second round of drinks.

We had a couple laughs.

Then . . . I made a *third* round of drinks . . . and, by the third round of drinks, I have to be honest with you, I was looking at this girl a little bit *differently*.

I started thinking.

I looked at her . . . then I looked outside at the snow.

I looked at her again . . . then I looked outside at all the snow.

And I said to myself, "Hey, we're stuck together. There's a raging blizzard outside. No one's going anywhere for a while and there's really nothing we can do about it . . . What the hell, Paul . . . *make the best of a bad situation*."

I don't want you to think I took advantage or anything but, the next thing you know . . . one thing leads to another . . . and *whatever* . . . and then, what's that phrase they use?

"Shit happens."

And, it wasn't long after that that she started giving me that little disclaimer that men have heard women give a million times . . .

"Paul, I don't know what kind of girl you think I am . . . But I need you to understand one thing, and this is very important to me.

"Paul, I need you to know that I have never, *ever* . . . done anything like this on a first date before."

I yelled to her, "YA, I BELIEVE YOU . . . JUST KEEP SHOVELING!"

Opening for Michael Bolton
Waldof-Astoria main ballroom - New York City

In trial mode as an assistant district attorney

CHAPTER 2:
THE VERY NEXT CHAPTER

Doomed To Irrelevance

The time I spent in Hollywood was similar to the advertisement for a furniture sale.

"Six years . . . Zero interest!"

I arrived in Hollywood full of hope, but I realized that I had absolutely no chance to get noticed the first week I moved there, and I vividly remember the moment I had that epiphany.

I was driving down Sunset Boulevard, stuck in traffic at a major intersection during the afternoon rush hour, when I looked over at the curb next to the traffic light and saw a dwarf wearing a ten-gallon hat, pink leather chaps with fringe, and cowboy boots with spurs on them, pushing the button to cross the street.

And nobody was looking.

It didn't get a second glance from anyone else, as if there was nothing unusual about this bizarre scene.

In any other city in the country, there would be screeching brakes and near rear-end collisions as stunned drivers exclaimed, "Holy shit! Did you see that little fucking dwarf with the huge hat?"

Not in Hollywood.

Ho-hum . . . Routine . . . Borrrrrring . . . Nothin' to see

here, move along . . .

As if to say, "Hmmm. No big deal . . . I've seen a smaller dwarf with a bigger hat."

Diddler on the Roof

How many times have you seen a criminal get arrested for some heinous crime and declare that they're innocent of the charges against them; or insist that they've been unjustly arrested; or swear that they were a "victim of circumstance" who just happened to be "in the wrong place at the wrong time?"

I was a prosecutor for years, so believe me when I say that most every time the accused is totally full of shit, but there were some circumstances when you would go, "Hmmm, I'm not so sure about this one."

I can see how it could happen.

One time, I was on a six-hour flight from Los Angeles to Boston.

I was sitting way in the back of the huge airplane, in an aisle seat on the right-hand side of the plane.

There was a mother and father with four young children on the same flight with me. The parents were sitting in the seats directly across the aisle from me, to my left. Three of their kids were able to sit with them but their fourth child, a cute little boy who was no more than four or five years old, had to sit in the seat right next to me, to my right-hand side.

About an hour or two into the long flight they began showing the in-flight movie and the passengers were asked to draw their shades as they turned off all the cabin lights, plunging the entire airplane into darkness.

Well, right in the middle of the movie, the little boy sitting next to me got a visit from the Sandman, dozed off and, in his sleep, he rolled over toward me, wrapped his tiny, little arms around my arm, put his miniature head down on me . . . and started cuddling.

Oh oh. Not good . . .

Needless to say, it was an extremely awkward situation.

I kept trying to wake the kid up while, at the same time, I kept glancing nervously across the aisle at his dad . . . but it was no use, the child was in a deep coma.

Under my breath, I kept going, "Hey kid, wake up." Nothing . . .

"Rise and shine, little buddy." Nothing . . .

"Nap time is over." Again, nothing . . .

"Wake the fuck up you little bastard! Now! You're gonna get me in trouble!" But he didn't respond.

I tried clearing my throat real loud . . . "AHEMMM . . . " but it didn't work.

I tried kicking his little legs as they dangled off the seat, but the child just moved them onto the cushion as he slept and buried his small face closer against my stomach.

I gave the kid a chicken-wing with my arm, attempting to jolt him awake with a nudge, but he kept right on snoring through it all.

That kid could take a punch!

It was no use, he was out like a light, and every time I tried to pry his tiny little hands off of my arm, he grabbed onto me even tighter.

I was thinking, "Ohhh, this is *not* good. Definitely not good . . . on any level . . ."

All I needed was his father to check-up on his son at that moment and look over at the two us, snuggling in the darkness.

Thank God the little kid finally woke up.

I could just picture myself, knocking on doors in the old neighborhood that I grew up in . . . where I knew everybody and their families, and had so for years and years . . . and my mother and father knew their families too . . . and even my grandparents before that . . . working hard, minding their own business, and building up an impeccable reputation through decades of honesty, integrity and philanthropy . . .

"Uh, good morning, Mrs. Cresta, it's me Paul, Frances' oldest son. How are you? It's very nice to see you too. How's the family? Good . . . good. Um, look, I'm really sorry to bother you, but I am required by law to inform you that I am now a registered sex offender and . . . "

(Making the sign of the cross and expressing horror.)

"Jesus, Mary and a Joseph."

"No, no, you don't understand, Mrs. Cresta, I'm not a pedophile, I swear to you, I was minding my own business on an airplane and this little boy fell asleep and . . ."

"Get outta here, you pervert!"

"I swear to God! I would never, ever do anything like that . . . I'm not into kids, I like divorced women with some mileage on them! You can ask around. Everyone knows . . . You can even check out my browsing history, it's mostly MILF sites, honest! Please, believe me!"

"GET OUT! *YOU SICK SON OF A BITCH!*"

"OK, OK, I'm sorry, I'm sorry, I'm leaving, I'm sooo sorry . . . Good bye and, ah, oh, by the way, my mother says hello. You should really give her a call, maybe go to lunch . . ."

"OUT!"

"I know, I know. I'm going, I'm going . . . "

No Leg to Stand On

My friend met a girl that he fell head-over-heels in love with, and it wasn't surprising because she was very pretty, had a tremendous body and a great disposition. She liked my friend too and they were together all the time, getting along great.

Before they had sex for the first time, this picture-perfect, All-American looking girl said to my friend, "Before we make love, I need to ask you something and it's very important to me."

He was taken aback . . . "Huh ? . . . W-What is it?"

She asked him, "I need to know if you would still find me attractive if I lost a leg?"

"Huh?"

"You know . . . Would you still like me if I was missing a leg? You know, if I had a wooden leg . . . if I was somehow, uh, defective . . . would you still feel the same? Would you still want to go out with me?"

My friend, not one to squander an opportunity, even if it meant taking a risk or telling a lie to get laid, answered, "Of course I would!" (As he alternately eyed each of the beautiful girl's pant legs for any sign of a fake limb or a stumpy nub).

He gushed, "It wouldn't matter to me, honeybunch. I'm crazy about you! Nothing could stop me from loving you! Nothing! What's a leg?"

She said, "Well . . . I'm not missing a leg . . . I have herpes."

"Oh."

I asked him, "What happened then? What did you do? Was it a deal-breaker?"

He said, "Well, actually, we talked it over and it's not gonna change anything. We're both madly in love and we'll just have to live with it, that's all."

I told him, "Man, I respect you. You're so much more un-selfish than I am . . . so much more of an adult than I would be under the circumstances."

He asked, "Why, what would you have said, Paul?"

"Truthfully? If she asked me if I'd still go out with her if she had a wooden leg, knowing me, I probably would have stuck my foot in my mouth and said something stupid like, 'Sure, I'd still go out with you if you were missing a leg because I suppose it could be worse . . . you could have herpes.'

"Then she would have got upset and said, 'Paul, why is having herpes worse than having a missing leg?'

"And I would have answered, 'Because, at least you can't catch a missing leg!

" 'I mean, if you sleep with someone who has no leg, you don't have to worry about waking up in the morning and going, 'OH MY GOD! WHERE THE HELL HAS MY LEG GONE?!?! I REMEMBER I HAD IT WHEN WE WERE HAVING SEX LAST NIGHT!!! IT'S GOT TO BE HERE SOMEWHERE . . . I CAN'T BELIEVE I LOST A LEG!!! HELP ME LOOK FOR IT!'

"Then she'd storm off and I'd never see her again."

My friend and the girl broke up the next week.

I hope I didn't have anything to do with it.

Driving Erotically

This is the actual testimony of a police officer during a hearing in Salem District Court.

Judge: " . . . and officer, why did you pull this driver over?"

"He was operating erotically, your honor."

"Erotically? . . . Officer, don't you mean he was driving 'erratically?' "

"No, your honor, I DO mean erotically . . . The defendant was having sex with his girlfriend while he was driving."

(Incredulous) "And how on earth do you know that, officer?"

"When I pulled the driver and his female passenger over, the only thing they had on was the radio."

Disjointed

My friend, attorney Neil Hourihan, (who has since been appointed to a state judgeship) once represented guy who was arrested for allegedly masturbating in public.

Apparently, a woman passerby accused his client of touching himself while he sat behind the wheel of his Corvette because she saw him doing something with his hands near his lap.

He told Neil, "This is a bogus charge! I wasn't masturbating when she walked by, I was cleaning the seeds out of some pot that was on a magazine resting on my lap."

Neil told him, "Well, it's this way . . . you're going to have to admit to one joint or another."

Shell We?

When you are booked to do a comedy show, you can occasionally get some pretty unusual requests from the clients who are signing your check.

Once I was hired by a Jewish organization as the opening act for the legendary singing group The Four Tops in a nice theater. Just before the show, the two women who contracted with me knocked on my dressing room door and asked if they could speak to me about the content of my show.

I told them, "Oh, there's nothing to worry about. I know it's a mixed crowd with some older people in the audience so I didn't plan on using any profanity."

They said, "Well, that's not what we're worried about. We know that won't be a problem but, you see, when we saw you do your act one time you did a routine about a lobster and we have a handful of very strict, Orthodox Jews in the audience, so we'd prefer it if you didn't mention shellfish in your act."

I was more than a little surprised. "I know that Orthodox Jews can't *eat* shellfish, but don't you think it's a little extreme that I can't even *talk about* shellfish in my show?"

"Well, I know it's a little weird, but we don't want to take the chance that we would offend anyone and we'd really appreciate it if you could leave that bit out of your set-list for tonight."

I said, "That's no problem at all, I wasn't planning on using it anyway . . . but now you better go tell the Four Tops that they can't sing 'Sugar-Pie Honey-Bunch' because there could be some diabetics in the crowd."

They laughed and said, "Yes, I know it's silly but you've made your point."

Nothing surprises me anymore.

Oil's Well That Ends Well

Thankfully, we are all more aware of preserving and improving the environment around us now, but it wasn't always that way.

It's not a valid excuse but, even back when I was a kid, people just didn't know any better.

For example, as a teenager I sometimes used to change the oil in my car.

Why do it myself? Well, first of all, because I had no money and I needed to save a few bucks but, also, because I was becoming a man, and that's what men did.

My reasoning back then was, "Why should I pay some place that specializes in oil changes $17.95 to do a complete oil and filter change in fifteen minutes or so while I wait in an air-conditioned office reading magazines and drinking free coffee when I, Mr. Goodwrench, can waste an entire afternoon, damage my driveway; wreck my engine so that it never, ever runs the same again; track oil and grease onto my mother's new white carpet; ruin the outfit that I was wearing; permanently stain my hands; sear my flesh; scrape my knuckles; get rust in my eye; piss off my neighbors when I borrow their tools and come up with swears that I never even heard before and save roughly four dollars and change by doing it myself?"

Then, when I was finished changing the oil, I had no idea what to do with the old oil that I had drained out of the engine.

So I would choose to do what many others did back in those days . . . either pour it down the storm drain . . . "I have no idea where this goes . . . maybe China?" . . . Or bury it in the backyard.

And, I must confess, as ignorant as it sounds, I did actually bury the used oil at the edge of the woods in our backyard a couple times.

Sure, it sounds stupid now, knowing what we do about pollution and introducing toxins to the earth, but back then we looked at it as an early form of recycling. You'd reason, "It came from the earth, I'm just sending it back where it belongs" . . . without any appreciation for the consequences, whatever they may be.

Then you'd go back to visit your old neighborhood, many years later, and knock on the door of your old house.

"Hello, can I help you?"

"Yes, my name is Paul. I'm sorry to bother you, but I actually grew-up in this house until I was a teenager. I was in the neighborhood and thought I'd stop by and see how things have changed."

"Well thanks for stopping by. We love it here. It was a great place for our kids to grow-up. They had the big backyard to play in and they spent a lot of time in the woods behind the house."

"Really?"

"Hi dad! I'm home!"

"And here's my son now, home early from the traveling carnival . . . Have you met Timmy? Or you might know him by his stage name . . . 'Lizard Boy.'"

"Woof!"

"Woof!"

"And that's our two-headed dog, Skippy."

"Ohhhh . . . Mister, I am soooooo, so sorry."

Childproof Cap

I was trying to open a bottle of mouthwash and I wasn't having any luck because the bottle had a complicated, child-proof, safety top on it. If I can recall, I believe you had to line-up the arrows, squeeze the sides together, then push down on the cover real hard while you twist it counterclockwise at the same time you are putting your right foot in, doing the Hokey Pokey and turning yourself around while repeating the words "Open Sesame!" three times during a waning moon . . . or something ridiculous like that.

I mean, is this necessary? Are we getting too paranoid?

Seriously now, is some little kid really gonna overdose on minty fresh Scope?

I can see it now . . .

Flashing strobe lights from police cars, fire engines, and an ambulance light up the neighborhood as emergency medical personnel race up the steps of a home leading to the upstairs bathroom.

Within moments an EMT is on his knees, giving an unconscious kid mouth-to-mouth resuscitation . . . an empty bottle of mouthwash lying at his side, while the boy's mother cries out in anguish, "Oh my God, is my little Johnny going to make it?"

The EMT stops, turns to the mother and says, "I don't know lady but, I gotta tell ya, his breath is *fantastic!*"

Ride, Drive, Repeat

I made an interesting discovery.

I realized that the prevalent manner of transportation used throughout the life of a boy/man evolves and goes through a distinct cycle that repeats itself.

Let me explain . . .

When you're a young boy, what is the first mode of transportation that you take on a regular basis?

Right, the school bus.

You ride the yellow bus to school every morning.

"Boy, this sucks."

You finally get your license and save up for your first car.

Your first car is usually a shit-box.

"I know it's a piece of junk, but I don't care, at least I have a car."

Then you start working and begin earning some decent money, so you splurge and buy yourself a little red sports car.

Zoom . . . "Look at me go, baby!"

Then you go through a phase where you get more involved in your job and you are working all the time, so you don't even need a car because you usually take home the company van.

When you get married and have kids, you need to buy a station wagon so you can yell at your kids in the back seat while you get yelled at by your wife in the front seat.

Then you get divorced and you have to start all over again.

Your ex-wife takes you for everything you have.

She gets the house and the car, and you end-up riding on

the bus again.

"Boy, this sucks."

Then you get back on your feet again and scrape-up a few bucks to buy yourself a shit-box to get around.

"I know it's a piece of junk, but I don't care, at least I have a car."

A few years later you go through your mid-life crisis and buy a little red sports-car like the one you had when you were young, but now it costs 10 times more than you originally paid for it.

"Look at me go, baby! I feel young again!" Zoom . . .

You get older and they put you in a retirement community where they give you rides in a senior citizen's van.

The last ride you ever take?

In a station wagon.

Thank you!

Physical Fatness

It puzzles me that some people will lift heavy weights for an hour and a half, three times a week, but they won't help their friends move.

It puzzles me that some people will walk on a treadmill for a half-hour, but they will drive around a parking lot ten times to find the parking space that's closest to the entrance.

It puzzles me that some people will do a hundred floors on the Stairmaster, but will always take the elevator if given the choice.

It puzzles me that some people will do two hundred sit-ups a day, but won't get off the couch to change the channel if they can't find the remote control.

It puzzles me that some people will run with weights in

their hands, but they buy luggage with wheels on the bottom so they don't have to carry it.

These people need to be more honest with themselves . . . like me.

My own weekly physical fitness program consists of . . .

2 sets:	dodging responsibility
2 sets:	pushing my luck
3 sets:	stretching the truth and running off at the mouth
3 sets:	wrestling with my conscience
3 sets:	jogging my memory
3 sets:	jumping to conclusions and sidestepping issues
3 sets:	running from commitment
2 sets:	lifting people's spirits
1 bag:	cheese curls
2 bars:	Nestlé's Crunches
2 sets:	climbing the walls
3 sets:	pulling my pud
1 set:	exercising my right to abstain from exercising
3 sets:	doing squats . . . oops, that's a typo . . . it should read "doing squat"

The Belt

It's hard to believe but, before the advent of video games, kids used to actually go outside and play.

When I was a young boy, I spent much of my time playing baseball, basketball, hockey and football in the backyard with my friends . . . with my parents' blessing. However, after breaking several windows in the garage, I was told by my parents that there would be no more ball-playing allowed in the driveway and, if I disobeyed their order and broke another window, there would be hell to pay.

Of course, I ignored them.

One day my friend and I were playing catch with the base-ball in the forbidden driveway when I let one get away from me, right through the pane of glass that my father had recently replaced. My mother found out and admonished me, "I thought we made it clear that there was to be no ball-playing whatsoever in that driveway" and then uttered those dreaded words that every kid fears, "Wait until your father gets home and I tell him what you did!"

Uh oh. I knew exactly what that meant . . . the belt.

See, for egregious offenses, my brother Jay and I were sub-ject to the occasional whipping with a leather belt. It was a very unpleasant experience but, in the long run, I'm sure that the rather severe punishment made us more disciplined and better for it. Unfortunately, by the time my youngest brother Chris was old enough to warrant the belt, corporal punishment was no longer acceptable and frowned upon, to the total dismay of his two older brothers.

When we knew Chris had a good beating coming, Jay and I would make a bowl of popcorn, set up chairs in the living room, and anxiously wait for the main event but, when my fa-ther would instead tell Chris, "Go to your room" Jay and I would go berserk.

"No way, Dad! That's not fair! You have to give Chris the belt, just like you did to us! It's his turn! Pleeeease hit him . . . Just a couple good smacks. Come on! We've been waiting years for this! Don't let us down, Dad. Come on! It's his turn! Pleeeease!"

And my personal favorite plea . . .

"Dad, if you don't give Chris the belt, it will hurt *us* a lot more than it does him!"

But my Dad would banish Chris to his bedroom and, as he

climbed the stairs, Chris would make sure to taunt me and Jay with a big, shit-eating grin on his face.

But that was then . . . and this was, well, before then.

I heard my father's car in the driveway and immediately looked for a place to hide. My grandmother had a queen sized bed and I knew that my father couldn't reach me if I hid underneath it, way back against the far wall. So I dove under the bed, wriggled my way back, laid prone on the hardwood floor amongst a flock of dust-bunnies the size of tumbleweeds . . . and waited.

I heard the back door open and, before my father could even get his coat off, my enraged mother began ranting and raving about my misbehavior, her stream of words sounding much like an adult in a Charlie Brown special, "Paul wah wah wah! . . . and then Paul wah wah wah! . . . and I told Paul wah wah wah!"

I heard the belt come off and my irritated father say, "Where is he?"

He went from room to room while I lay silent and motionless, hoping that my father would eventually give up and all would be forgotten.

Yeah, right . . .

I saw my father's shoes on the other side of the bed.

(Sternly) "I know you're down there, Paul. Come out from under the bed."

(Scared shitless) "No, dad! You're gonna give me the belt for breaking the window."

"No, I'm not."

"Yes, you are! You're going to hit me for breaking the window cuz you told me not to play in the driveway."

"I am *not* going to hit you for breaking the window."

"You promise?"

"Yes, I promise I will not hit you for breaking the window."

"Swear to God you won't hit me with the belt for breaking the window in the garage, even though you told me not to play there?"

"I swear, I will not hit you with the belt for disobeying me and breaking that window."

Relieved, but still unconvinced, I reluctantly crawled out from under the bed.

WHACK!

"OWWWWWWWW! (sob) Dad, you promised you weren't gonna hit me for breaking the window! (sob) You lied!"

"No, I didn't . . . That was for hiding under the bed."

Paul and his dad, Jack 'Tiger' Murphy

The Last Man in the World

I was at a wedding and I was talking to a girl who I have known for years and years, but has never been anything more than a friend of mine

After a couple of cocktails I was joking around, just being a wise-guy, and I asked her, "All these years that we've known each other, have you ever fantasized about . . . uh, you know. . . fooling around with me?"

She doubled-over and laughed out loud.

"Ha ha ha! Oh come on, Paul. Seriously! You're *the last guy in the world* that I would ever think about having sex with . . . The *LAST* guy! . . . Ha ha ha."

And I laughed along with her . . ." Ha, ha, ha . . . right, the last guy in the world . . . ha ha ha . . ." but, the more I thought about it, the more insulted I became.

If I was the last guy on the *ENTIRE PLANET* that she would have sex with, who were all the other men who she would rather have sex with than me?

Who am I less desirable than?

Who is she more attracted to?

If I was in a line to have sex with her, stretching across the planet, who would be in line ahead of me?

"Hey, aren't you her grandfather?"

(Shrugs his shoulders.)

The Elephant Man would shuffle over, tap me on the shoulder and mumble, "Mind if I cut in front of you, Paul?"

"Go ahead, everyone else has."

I became obsessed thinking about the possibilities.

I would think to myself, "You mean that she would rather hump an Eskimo who lives in an igloo, smells like raw fish, chews whale blubber and picks her up in a dog-sled, than have sex with me? That's outrageous!"

A while later, I'd suddenly stop and contemplate, "Is she saying that, if it was a choice between boinking me or a pygmy headhunter from the jungles of Africa, she'd say, 'Hmmm, OK, that's easy . . . I think I'll go with the cute little guy with the bare-feet, blow-gun, bone through his nose and the big plate in his lip who might eat my poodle when he's done having his way with me.' "

MEATLOAF!!! . . . That disgusting, sweaty singer . . . She'd would do him before me? . . . Is she telling me that she'd prefer to have a conjugal visit with Charles Manson or gang-bang a pair of Siamese Twins than do the nasty with me?

Yes, she was.

She'd rather make love to a Sumo wrestler . . . No! Better still, what about the 2,000 pound guy on the Discovery Channel who sat on his couch for so long without getting up that his body actually *GREW INTO* the fabric of the couch? Talk about a 'Sofa With a Secret!'

She would rather be with him and *work around* the furniture than touch *my* body.

"Hey baby, want a piece of this? You know what they say, the bigger the cushion, the better the pushin'!"

Her girlfriends will ask . . . "Ohh, you broke-up with Sofa Boy? What happened? I'm surprised, you were such a good couple."

"Oh, we got along fine but then, one day, I realized that he didn't really go with my coffee table. He's Colonial and my living room is contemporary. I had to redecorate."

But he's still more desirable than me.

Or, how about that other unfortunate guy on the TV special I saw who was afflicted with a rare and terrible condition called "Hidden Penis Syndrome." Now, to be honest with you, I never watched the show. I only read about it in the guide because I really didn't *need* to watch the program. Pretty much everything I needed to know about this disease is right there in the title, which is fairly self-explanatory and leaves very little to the imagination.

Let's put it this way . . . if this girl had to make a choice between doing the Horizontal Hokey-Pokey with me and the guy with the Hidden Penis Syndrome, she'd prefer to go searching for it with a coal miner's hat, a magnifying glass and a pair of tweezers.

She would rather play Whack-A-Mole with his shy little cocktail wiener than to ever take a chance with me.

"I'm gonna put some crackers on your leg, honey, and see if we can lure it out."

"Peek-a-boo!"

"Damn! Not quick enough. I almost had it!"

I was totally preoccupied.

I'd watch a National Geographic special featuring a guy in Africa with the tropical disease called Elephantiasis that made his testicles grow so big, he had to carry them around in a wheelbarrow and think, "She would actually share a bed with him and his two giant, swollen, beach-ball sized mega-nuts before she'd even look at me naked!"

It bothered the hell out of me for the longest time.

Six months after she told me that, I'd be walking down a crowded street and abruptly blurt-out, in a loud, angry voice, "WEBSTER! THE LITTLE BLACK MIDGET FROM THAT TV SHOW! HOW COULD SHE? . . . IS GILLIGAN STILL ALIVE? SHE CAN SCREW HIM TOO FOR ALL I CARE!"

People around me would point and go, "Whoa. That weird guy's talking to himself. What's with him?"

I'd snap and yell, 'WHAT ARE YOU STARING AT? . . . WHY DON'T YOU MAKE A BOOTIE CALL TO MY FRIEND? SHE'LL DO YOU! . . . SHE'LL DO ANYONE BUT ME! . . . AND DON'T FORGET TO BRING YOUR HUNCHBACKED, INCONTINENT, NINETY YEAR OLD UNCLE WITH YOU! . . . mumble . . . mumble . . . mumble . . . "

Still perturbs me from time to time.

'The Nostrilizer'

The United States of America is the greatest country in the world.

Our economic success has raised the standard of living to the point that over 99% of Americans have at least one television set, while over half of all families own three or more, and most people who are considered poor still have air-conditioning and a cell phone.

You wonder why people around the world hate us?

Because freedom and capitalism has made us prosper.

We are prosperous . . . and they are jealous.

Many of these other cultures have been around for thousands of years longer than our country, yet they still live in mud huts, have hot and cold running sand, a two-donkey garage and have to shit in a ditch.

And it's a good thing they don't have television sets because, if they ever watched TV, they'd be even more discouraged to learn that even the Flintstones are more advanced than they are.

Let's put it this way . . . in the United States, our progress can be defined as being somewhere between the Flintstones and the Jetsons . . . actually much, much closer to the Jetsons.

For those people, the Flintstones *ARE* the Jetsons.

No wonder they're pissed.

But you really don't get a sense of how spoiled and lazy we have become until you start going through a *Sharper Image* catalogue and see luxury items for sale such as a 'Robotic Floor Vacuum Cleaner' or a 'Laser-Guided Pool Cue' or a 'Heated Pet Bed with Faux Suede Lambskin Liner' or even a 'Cordless, Temperature-Controlled Butter Dish' with a thermostat and climate control system and low-battery alarm "that warms or cools two sticks of butter to your preferred temperature to insure consistent spreading."

How did we ever live without that necessity?

But, my personal favorite . . . for only $59.95 is the new Turbo-Groomer Cobalt Personal Nose-Hair Trimmer featuring dual-rotary cutting heads of stainless-steel blades with titanium cutting edges and a ½ horsepower motor and "blades that whirl at an impressive 6000 RPMs to gently and effectively trim nose hair down to 1/16th of an inch."

That is one *smooth* nostril, my friends.

And it only costs $59.95.

First of all, how severe is your nose-hair problem that you can't combat it armed with just a pair of sharp scissors and now need a specialized power tool to keep-up with the growth? It has to look like Troy Polamalu and Don King are trying to crawl out of your nostrils headfirst. For more irony, I've seen the people who live in these backwards countries I spoke of and, if anybody in the world needs a nose-hair trimmer, it's them.

All for only $59.95.

By the way, this device also features a straight-edge clipper that is "perfect for trimming eyebrows and the edge of your ears."

Hmmm, I don't know about that.

I had been thinking of letting the hair on the edge of my ears grow-out . . . you know, just let it go wild . . . and then combing the long strands of ear-hair over the top of my head to hide my bald-spot.

Wait, there's more!

For your $59.95, it also has two super-bright LEDs to make it easy to see exactly what you are doing, and "to help to eliminate shadows so that grooming is complete . . . every time!"

It's good to know that, if someone else's finger is blocking the nostril, you can flash them the high-beams and get them to pull-out and pull-over.

And, get this . . . the LED headlights last 110,000 hours "for several lifetimes of nose-hair trimming" pleasure.

Fantastic . . . won't your family members be psyched to learn that you'll be able to pass that little baby on in your will!

"And to my grandson Butchie, I leave my prized possession that I have been using faithfully for thirty-five years . . . my Nostrilizer-2000 Personal Nose-Hair Trimmer."

"Ahhhh!"

"Between me, my father and my father's father we have had these clippers lodged up our noses for no more than maybe 60 or 70,000 hours, so there's still a lot of life left in that sucker."

"Grosssss! That's disgusting!!! I got screwed, I wanted the Rolex!"

And, for only $59.95, it comes with a one year warranty . . . just in case your nose gets the best of the device. I imagine they will provide roadside service . . . and, I'm pretty sure that, if you join the N.H.A.A. (Nose Hair Association of America) and your nose-hair trimmer has to go into the shop, the dealer will give you a loaner trimmer to get you through the day without tripping over your unkempt ZZ-Top-length nose-hair.

Why not? Turbocharged? Headlights? Horsepower? Those are all automotive terms. This thing sounds more like a Buick than a personal hygiene device.

I can see the advertisements now . . .

"The Bush-Buster Hemi-GTX . . . It's *SNOT* your father's Nose-Hair Trimmer!"

Guys will start to customize their nose-hair trimmers . . . beef-up the engine . . . add horsepower . . . maybe a fancy paint job with flames on the side.

And wait until Hollywood catches on to the craze.

You can imagine the programming . . . *Pimp My Nose-Hair Trimmer . . . Nose-Hair Trimmer Overhaul . . . Nose-Hair Trimmer*

Build-Off . . . gives a whole new meaning to *Orange County "Choppers"* who'll be building a custom nose-hair trimmer with an extended front-end, a kick-starter and straight pipes coming out the sides, so loud that it sets-off car alarms in the neighborhood when you start it up. Bubububub-Bubububub (as opposed to the Japanese-made nose-hair trimmers that sound like a swarm of bees . . . Bzzzzzzz-Bzzzzzzz)

Your teenage son will want to borrow the nose-hair trimmer for the high school prom. And that means you'll be waiting at home, late at night, worried sick . . . nervously pacing the floor, constantly looking out the window and checking your watch . . . not really giving a shit about the safety of your son, but really just hoping he doesn't have an accident with the nose-hair trimmer . . . a worst-case scenario playing-out in your mind in which your son lends the nose-hair trimmer to a drunk friend with a hooked nose . . . he uses it recklessly, the out-of-control trimmer can't make the bend, there is a horrible crash, and the cops find the boy wandering on the side of the road, dazed with a bloody nose and a deviated septum . . . lawsuits to follow.

And for only $59.95!

Who NOSE where we can buy one?

SINUS up for that deal!

This is how the Roman Empire fell. The people got soft, complacent and entitled, and it rotted from the inside.

I'm sure Julius Caesar had his own personal nose-hair trimmer too.

Of course, it was probably a half-naked, teenage boy with a pair of golden tweezers.

"Bring me the royal nose-hair trimmer!"

(With a pronounced lisp) *"Coming Caesar!"*

with Improv founder Budd Friedman

with Steven Wright

CHAPTER 3:
HERE'S ANOTHER NEW CHAPTER

The Interpreter. Part I

When I was a prosecutor, I once had an unusual trial scheduled in the Peabody District Court in front of Judge Santo Ruma, one of my favorite jurists.

The facts were that two Portuguese men, best of friends ever since childhood, were drinking at the local Portuguese Club all day and were highly intoxicated by the time the club closed, late at night.

Apparently, the two shit-faced friends were taking a leak against the side of the building when one of them made fun of the other guy's penis. His buddy responded by taking out his jackknife and slicing-off his best-friend's dick.

Really . . . It's true. I couldn't make this shit up.

Well, the cops arrested the guy and charged him with assault and battery with a dangerous weapon and mayhem. Now the case was scheduled for trial, but I wasn't expecting it to go forward because, incredible as it sounds, I was told that the victim was refusing to testify against his best friend, the assailant, and wanted to drop all the charges.

That's right, forgive and forget. His friend just said, "No problem, buddy. Accidents happen. No hard feelings . . ." probably for the rest of his life, for that matter which, I would imagine, would make the "forget" part of that equation much more difficult to accomplish.

Wow . . . that is true friendship.

I love my friends, but I don't think I could be that forgiving . . . especially when my penis is involved.

For the record . . .

I would immediately file a criminal complaint if one of my friends placed *sharp cheese* next to my weenie.

I would call 911 if one of my friends made *pointed comments* anywhere near 'Mr. Happy.'

I would take out a restraining order if one of my friends let out a *piercing scream* in the general vicinity of my joystick.

If one of my friends drank a can of *Diet Slice* near my crotch, I would never speak to him again and if he cut in line, cut into a conversation or even so much as cuts the cheese within striking distance of my privates that would be it. Over. Done. *Finis. Arrivederci. Sayonara.* "Check, please!" Nice knowing you. Get lost!

Not this guy. His policy was indeed to forgive and forget . . . well, at least until the next time he needs to sit down like a woman when he takes a leak.

Anyway, we had all the witnesses there, ready for trial, just in case the victim changed his mind, but the judge informed us that it would have to be continued until another date.

I pleaded, "Why do we need to continue it, your honor? I have all the witnesses here and we are ready to go."

Judge Ruma said, "We need to put it over for another date because we don't have a Portuguese interpreter available."

I asked, "What do we need an interpreter for, your honor?"

The judge said, "Why, Mr. Murphy? Can you speak Portuguese?"

"No, I can't, your honor, but based on the facts I think I can translate the critical testimony, which is most likely,

'AGGGHHHHHHHHHH!' "

This was one of the many times this judge . . . and several other judges . . . would pound their gavel and admonish me by yelling, "Let me remind you, Mr. Murphy, that this is a court of law and *NOT* a comedy club!"

That's sometimes debatable.

The Interpreter. Part II *(an excerpt from L.A. Misérables)* Day 263 - November 30, 1996 - LA Miz II

One day I was filling in for another Assistant DA in Lawrence District Court. Lawrence is a large city north of Boston that has a population that is predominantly comprised of minorities, which causes some significant communications problems in their extremely busy courthouse.

An arrest was made late in the afternoon and the police brought the defendant in to be arraigned for breaking and entering a house. I watched the presiding judge arraign the Spanish-speaking defendant, who was held in custody and standing, handcuffed, in the prisoner's dock.

The colloquy went something like this:

"Sir, you have been arrested and charged with breaking and entering a dwelling during the nighttime which is a felony in the Commonwealth of Massachusetts. Do you understand, Mr. Ramirez?"

"No. I no understand. No speak Eengleesh . . ."

"Sir, I want to remind you of your right to remain silent. Anything you say in this court may be used against you in a later proceeding. Understand, sir?"

"I no speak Eengleesh . . ."

The judge continued. "You have the right to a trial by jury."

"I said I no understand . . . I no speak Eengleesh . . ."

"You have the right to an attorney. If you cannot afford an attorney, one will be provided to you. Are you going to get your own attorney?"

"I no understand . . . I no speak no Eengleesh . . ."

Frustrated, the judge turned to the clerk sitting in front of the bench. "Mr. Clerk, this man claims that he doesn't understand me. Do we have an interpreter to assist him in this arraignment proceeding?"

"No, your honor," said the clerk. "All of the interpreters are tied up in hearings and trials today. I suggest that we hold Mr. Ramirez in custody at the Lawrence House of Correction overnight and arraign him first thing tomorrow morning when we have an interpreter available."

"OK, remand Mr. Ramirez into custody and we'll hold this over until tomorrow."

Suddenly from the dock came a high pitched plea, "I SPEAK A LEETLE EENGLEESH!! . . . WAIT! I SPEAK A LEETLE EENGLEESH!!"

Christmas Dinner, 2005

There's nothing quite like dinner at my family's home.

I have recreated just a sample portion of the delightful conversation between me and my Italian Uncles, Vito (age 85 at the time) and Frankie (90 years old), as a lovely meal was being served.

[Paul] "How have you been feeling Uncle Frankie?"

[Frank] "Rotten. (His standard answer to everything.) I've been coughing-up thick, yellow mucus and phlegm for a week. . . . Can you pass the vegetables?"

[Paul] "Sure . . . there you go. Did you get a lot of vegetables from your garden this year?"

[Frank] "It was a great year. The secret is the shit I used for the fertilizer. You can't use just any shit, you know . . . The worms are good for the soil. Pass the butter."

[Uncle Vito] "Did you know that, in the Civil War they used to use maggots to clean the infected, rotting flesh from the wounds of the soldiers? . . . Can I have the ham?"

[Paul] "Uncle Frankie, are you using the mustard?"

[Frank] "I hate mustard, it reminds of that yellow baby shit when a kid has the runs . . . Can you get me the squash, please?"

That's when I had enough and turned into Dustin Hoffman, "PLEASE GUYS! I'M EATIN' HERE! I'M *EATIN'* HERE!"

First Downer

I was doing a show way out in western Massachusetts, right near the New York state border, on a Saturday night. My alma mater, Boston College, was playing in a very important football game with the ACC conference championship at stake and I was extremely bummed that I was going to miss it because of the long ride to and from the venue.

After my show was finished, I got an update on the score and found out that the game was tied-up going into the fourth quarter.

So I ran to my car so I could start driving home and listen to the end of the game on the radio. The only problem was that there was absolutely no radio reception that far out in western Mass.

I started driving east as fast as I could to try and pick-up a radio signal, but I went through the AM and FM dials and got nothing whatsoever.

I was so far west that all I was getting were New York channels and it was going to be at least an hour before I would get the game on the radio and, by that time, the game would be over.

So I called every one of my friends for an update and all I got were answering services because it was a Saturday and they were all out for the night.

I was getting desperate.

My only option left was to call my sister **who** knows absolutely NOTHING about football. She wouldn't know the difference between a first down and a goal post, but it was my only hope.

I called up and luckily she was there because, by this time, I was in a panic.

"Good, you're home . . . what are you doing?"

She said, "I'm watching a *Lifetime* movie, why?"

"Look, you gotta turn on the BC game right away and tell me what is going on . . . and hurry, it's really important to me."

She says, "What channel is it on?"

"I don't remember, use the guide."

My sister says, "How do you do that?"

I was incredulous. "You don't know how to use the fucking guide on the TV? That's basic! Three year olds can do that! It's not that hard!"

"What button do I hit for the guide?"

"Try the big orange button that says GUIDE on it . . . How do you not know this? Just hurry up!"

She said, "OK . . . I got the game on."

"Good, good. Now what are the guys doing?"

She answered, "They are just standing around."

I said, "Standing around *WHERE?*"

"On the field."

"I know, I know they are standing on the field . . . No shit!

I mean, what YARD LINE?"

"Yard line? What's a yard line?"

"You've got to be kidding me, right? Listen, look for a big white number painted on the field where they're standing"

She said, "OK, it says ten."

"The ten? Oh my God! Is it *OUR* ten or *THEIR* ten?"

"What's the difference?"

"*What's the difference?* Eighty fucking yards! That's the difference! Eighty fucking yards!"

I needed to figure this out. "Look BC is the visiting team so they will be wearing white. So tell me, which side are the players on who are wearing white?"

She says, "White shirts or white pants?"

"You're killing me! The pants don't matter!"

"Why not?"

"Why not? That's not important right now! Just tell me, where are the guys wearing white?"

She says, "The guys in the white are on the right side."

"Good, good, we're finally getting somewhere. Now find the number 20 on the field. Is the big number 20 to the left side or to the right side of the number 10?"

"The number 20 is to the left side of the 10."

"SHIT, THE BALL IS ON OUR 10 YARD LINE! . . . OH MY GOD! WHO HAS THE BALL? TELL ME, WHO HAS THE FUCKING BALL?"

"Nobody has the ball. It's just sitting on the ground."

"Remind me to strangle you when I see you. Never mind, just tell me what's happening right now."

"OK . . . OK . . . wait a second. They are all moving . . ."

"Yeah . . . and?"

"Now one guy is running away and all the other guys are running after him."

By this time, I was hysterical. "RUNNING AFTER WHO?

WHO IS RUNNING AFTER *WHO?*"

"I don't know . . . Everyone is screaming like a bunch of idiots . . ."

"SCREAMING WHAT? WHAT ARE THE AN-NOUNCERS SAYING?"

"He's still running . . . Look, this is stupid. I have my friend on the other line, I gotta go. Bye."

"NOOOOOOOOOOOOO!!!!!!! YOU CAN'T DO THIS TO ME . . . Hello? . . . Hello? . . . Hello?"

Authentic Mexican

Do you like Mexican food?

No, I mean *real* Mexican . . . *authentic* Mexican.

Well, I found the most authentic Mexican restaurant ever.

Extremely authentic.

So authentic, there is no parking lot at the restaurant.

They have a remote parking lot where you park your car, then they shuttle you to the restaurant in the back of an old pick-up truck with 23 other people.

Then, when you leave the restaurant, you have to climb through a hole in a fence, go through a tunnel and wade across a river.

The next week, you can get your entire family in for free!

Now *that's* authentic Mexican.

Lonely Diner

One time I was eating in a nice restaurant with my girl-friend when she leaned forward and whispered to me, "Don't look now Paul but, directly behind you, there's a man sitting at a table all alone, eating dinner all by himself. I think that's so sad. I feel really bad when people have to eat by themselves."

I started to turn around to see who she was talking about, but she immediately reprimanded me under her breath.

"What are the hell you doing, Paul? Didn't I just tell you not to turn around? What's wrong with you?"

"I want to see the guy you're talking about."

"You can't just turn around in your seat and look Paul, he'll know we're talking about him. Don't draw attention to us."

"Sorry."

Then, a little while later, I noticed that my girlfriend kept glancing over my shoulder and she brought it up again.

"Paul, I can't help looking at that poor man dining alone behind you. He seems so lonely, eating all by himself. I really feel bad for him."

Now my curiosity was getting the best of me and I needed to see what this guy looked like, but I didn't want to make it obvious so, using a cool trick that I learned from watching some old spy movie, I ever-so-subtly picked-up my soup spoon from the table, polished it up on my shirt, and held it up so I could look into the reflection on the back of the spoon to see behind me.

As I looked at the man's image reflected on the backside of the spoon, I solved the mystery of the lonely diner.

I said, "Well, I can see why he's alone. It's no wonder the guy has no friends . . . his face is all distorted and he has a piece of rice on his forehead the size of a football!"

Case closed.

City of Fallen Angels

I was living on Hollywood Boulevard, it was sometime in the early 2000's and my parents were concerned about me living in Los Angeles.

73

I'd be on the phone with my mom back in suburban Boston and she'd say, "Isn't it dangerous there? I watch the news on TV. There's a lot of crazy stuff going on in Los Angeles, Paul. That city's not safe. There are a lot of crazy people out there. I'm so worried about you. That's all I do, worry about your safety."

I'd assure her, "You're being silly, mom. Of course it's perfectly safe where I live, Ma . . . I'm fine here . . . There's absolutely nothing to worry about, trust me. No risk whatsoever."

With that in mind, a couple of months later, they decided to visit me. My father planned to rent a car so he called me from the airport to get directions to my apartment in Hollywood. (Of course, this was before GPS.)

This was the conversation with my dad, who was hard of hearing:

"You got a pen, dad? OK, write this down . . . After you leave the airport, you want to get on the 405 Freeway going north . . .

"Huh? No dad . . . north . . . (louder) NORTH . . . no, whatever you do, don't go south, because that will take you toward San Diego . . .

"SAN DIEGO . . . Yeah, remember where all those dumb cult members with the Nike sneakers thought they were gonna catch a spaceship or a meteor or something and killed themselves in the mass suicide? . . . All dead, every one of them . . . Right . . . Yeah, that's San Diego . . .

"So you don't want to go south, you want to go *north* past the site of the Rodney King beatings . . . Yeah, you remember when they had all the violence and rioting and looting and fires?

"Huh? What dad? . . . No, Rodney King was the black guy the cops roughed up. The guy you're thinking of is Reginald Denny, the white guy who got dragged out of his car in Los

Angeles and beaten senselessly by the civilians . . . right, right
. . . anyway, it all started right there.

"OK, listen up, so then you'll go up over an overpass on
the 10 Freeway . . .

"Yes, over the 10 . . . Do you recall us watching the news
when the ramp on the highway collapsed during that giant
earthquake and crushed all the helpless people to death inside
their cars a few years ago? . . . That's right. That's it, that's the
ramp, but they fixed it, so don't worry, it should be fine now.

"Anyway, then you'll drive through Brentwood . . .Right . . .
Brentwood . . . Yeah, *thhaaat* Brentwood, where OJ murdered
the two people with the knife and all their blood was splattered
all over the place . . . Yeah, not guilty . . . I know. I know, dad
. . . What can you do?

"Huh? . . . No, not Hernandez, Dad . . . Menendez . . .
MEN-EN-DEZ . . . Yes, I know the case. The two brothers
who slaughtered their parents . . . No, I don't know where . . .
Somewhere near there, I'm not sure . . . It's probably not that
far.

"Anyway, then you're going to take the Mulholland exit . . .
MUL-HOL-LAND.

"How do I explain this . . . OK. Do you remember when
Bill Cosby's kid got shot in cold-blood for no reason whatsoever? . . . Ya, right, right . . . well that was Mulholland Drive . . .
right . . . right . . . it happened right there . . . Terrible, terrible, I
know. Tragic.

"So, after you take that exit, now you'll drive down Mulholland past Benedict Canyon where Charles Manson butchered
all those innocent people in their home and wrote on the walls
in their blood . . . exactly . . . right . . . no, they tore the house
down . . . it's not there anymore.

"Now this part gets a little tricky . . .

"You want to take a left where Phil Hartman got killed by

his wife . . . then take a right where Robert Blake killed *his* wife . . . you know, Baretta . . . right . . . and go straight where Phil Spector killed a woman who played somebody's wife in some lousy movie.

"All right, you still with me? . . . Good . . . So now you'll be heading east . . . and if you look to your left you'll see the Valley.

"Huh? . . . The Valley . . . North Hollywood . . . Uh, remember when those two ruthless killers robbed the bank with the automatic weapons wearing the flak vests? . . . Yes . . . and they had the big shootout with the cops live on the TV? . . . Right . . . Studio City . . . That's where it happened, right there . . . small world . . .

"So now you want to take a right, over the Hollywood Hills and you're gonna end-up near the Chateau Marmont where John Belushi died in his own vomit from the drug overdose . . . Yeah, that's the place . . .

"Then you'll get to the intersection on Fairfax where Biggy Smalls got whacked . . . Huh? . . . Oh, he was a rapper . . . He was in his car . . . No, never caught them . . . Whatever . . .

"And then you'll pass through the intersection where Eddie Murphy picked up that hooker with the . . . um, the . . . How can I explain this? . . . the . . . the . . . Oh! With the Adam's Apple! That's it, the Adam's Apple.

"Next, you're going to pass two crack-ho's, three homeless people, one drug deal and a burning car . . . take the next right.

"OK . . . Now you're going to go a little farther up the road and you'll see a bunch of gang members standing on the corner.

"If they're Crips, that's good . . . That means you're in the right neighborhood . . . But if they're wearing red, they're Bloods and you've gone a little too far . . . You want to turn around and come back.

"I'm two blocks before you get to the bad section.
"OK, great . . . Be careful."
That should make them feel safe.

A Real Lu Lu

There are times when you have to laugh about things, or you'll cry.

Right after my dad passed away, my mother's house was filled with dozens of grieving friends and family members. For years my mom and dad had been very friendly with a couple named Sal and Lu Lu. Lu Lu had passed on a couple years earlier and her daughter Rose and Rose's husband were among the many mourners.

Everyone needs comfort and assurance that your loved one is now in "a better place" at times like this, and my family was no different, so Lu Lu's daughter gathered us together to tell us a story that would help put our minds at ease.

"I want you to know that my husband and I have lived in our home for over twenty years and, in all that time, we had never, ever seen a deer in our backyard. Not even one. Then, the *very* next morning after my mother died, I saw my first deer coming out of the woods behind our home and I thought, 'That's a sign from heaven! That's Lu Lu coming back to tell us that everything is going to be OK. That she's in a good place now.' "

My mother and siblings were entranced . . .

She continued.

"Well, this is just the strangest thing but, since that day, we have never seen another deer in our yard . . . nothing! . . . until, get this . . . the *very* next morning, right after your father passed away when there was not one but *TWO* deer standing together in our backyard! How about that! So what do you think? Two deer at the same time, this time. What do you suppose that means?"

Before anyone could answer, I interjected, "I hate to break the news to you, mom, but I think our father is running around with Lu Lu!"

World Traveler

Once, when I was living in LA, I was having dinner with some people that I had just met and really didn't know well at all. They were very nice people, but more than a little pretentious, so I just sat there and listened to them all talking about their extensive travels throughout Europe.

"Last week, I was in Amsterdam."

"Amsterdam? Really? I *adore* Amsterdam, but I prefer Paris."

"On my most recent trip abroad, I visited Paris for at least the tenth time, but then went on to Germany, Switzerland and Denmark."

"Personally, I favor Southern France . . ."

Then, all at once, these people must have felt like they were excluding me from their conversation, so they turned to me and one woman asked, "Paul, have you been to Europe?"

I hadn't traveled to Europe at the time, so I fibbed a little because I didn't want to feel like the only loser there who'd never been. Well, I didn't technically lie, I just kind of stretched the truth a little.

"Europe? Me? Why, uh . . . yes, certainly . . . of course I have."

I thought that would be the end of the conversation and they would be satisfied with my answer, but this rather snobby girl added, "So, what part of Europe did you visit?"

Oh-oh . . . "Um, actually, uh, I saw m-most of it."

"Most of it? Really? . . . Euro-rail?

Embarrassed, I said, "Uhhh, no . . . Epcot."

Clothes Shopping with My Mother

I gave up a lot when I moved to Hollywood for six years. It was embarrassing, at my age, to need to borrow money from my parents . . . It was even more humiliating to a man in his 40's that one time, when I was back home in Boston, my mother knew I couldn't afford new clothes and took me clothes shopping . . . just like I was in third grade again, picking out my outfits for the upcoming school year.

The only difference was that, this time, I *WANTED* to go with her.

And I found out that absolutely nothing had changed after all these years.

I saw some pants I liked in Macy's and my mother said, "Try them on in the dressing room and show them to me . . . I'll wait out here for you . . ." just like she did when I was a little kid.

And, as if almost forty years had never gone by, I was in the dressing room maybe all of two minutes when I came out in my new pants, looking around for my mother to get her approval.

I yelled out . . . to no one in particular . . .

"Ma? Maaaaaa? . . . Look at my pants! . . . Maaaaaa?"

And, *exactly* like it happened when I was a little boy, my mother had wandered off, looking around at the clothes, and was nowhere to be found.

This strange incidence of déjà vu continued as, once again I ended up wandering around the huge department store with no shoes on, wearing my new pants with all the tags still on them, tripping over the pre-tailored pant-legs, and yelling out, "MAAAAAAA! . . . WHERE ARE YOU? . . . MAAAAAAA!"

Next thing I knew, a security guard was handing me a lollipop and assuring me, "Don't worry, we'll find your mother."

A short time later, over the loudspeaker, my mother heard, "WE HAVE A LOST BOY AT THE FRONT OF THE STORE. HE'S FORTY-FIVE YEARS OLD, ABOUT SIX FEET TALL AND HAS A GOATEE. HE'S WEARING A BRAND-NEW PAIR OF DOCKERS AND ANSWERS TO THE NAME OF 'LOSER.'"

Sex Education

Once again there was a story in the news about some thirty-two year old female teacher having sex with one of her teenage students.

My girlfriend said, "Don't you think that's disgusting, Paul? These sick teachers are having sex with fifteen and sixteen year old boys. Isn't that just horrible?"

I don't know what the correct answer is, but I now know that the wrong answer is: "Depends. What does she look like?"

It's just another way that kids have it so much easier than we did growing up. Some of the teachers that these high school boys are having sex with are extremely attractive.

One of the teachers in particular looked just like a Playboy bunny!

Her name was Pamela Rogers. She was a married woman, twenty-nine years old, who had a sexual relationship with her thirteen year old student.

I'm telling you, she was very pretty, had long blonde hair

and a great body . . . a real hottie.

Even after she was arrested she sent the kid nude photos from jail and sexy text messages so they violated her probation and sent her to the slammer.

Then she was prosecuted for sexual harassment.

Sexual harassment? Really?

Come on. That's not sexual harassment, that's advanced biology lab!

That's a dream come true . . . that's a guaranteed 'A' . . . and that's a great way for a teenage boy to clear-up his zits!

Every day is a Pep rally!

Every week is spring break!

Girls Gone Wild the home version: *Teachers Gone Wild!*

Those are the best years of his life! A High School Honeymoon!

When this teacher says she's a head mistress she means it!

The kid will graduate *Magna Cum Often.*

That is a lot of things, but it is *not* sexual harassment.

You WANT to know what sexual harassment is?

My teacher's name was Miss Bazely.

My mother had Miss Bazely . . . and I'm pretty sure my mother's mother had Miss Bazely before that!

She was a great teacher, but she was also about 140 years old and as stern as a prison guard!

Now *THAT* would be sexual harassment

Can you imagine being kept after class?

"You feel the need to chew gum in my classroom? (Taking her teeth out, licking her chops and puckering up) Here are some gums you can chew on . . .

"Want to pass my class? Pick a wrinkle and go for it! Don't be shy!"

Inauspicious Beginnings

It is amazing that I eventually became a comedian, because one of my first recollections of attempted humor is not a particularly pleasant one.

I was a young boy, maybe ten or eleven years old, and physically beginning to turn into a young man, if you know what I mean.

With my hormones raging, I would anxiously look forward to the weekend nights that my parents went out for the evening because, as soon as I saw the taillights of my father's car disappear around the bend down the street, I would immediately run into his office and start rummaging through the pile of *Playboy* magazines hidden under his desk.

That was until one night when my parents must have forgotten something and returned home unexpectedly, only a short time after they had departed.

It was a humiliating experience that I will never forget.

My mother and father walked in on me as I was gazing at a centerfold with my eyes bulging out . . . awkwardly matching the state of affairs in the front of my pajamas.

My mom was horrified and became hysterical, my dad got angry that I was going through his stuff, and I was embarrassed beyond belief.

When she finally calmed down, my mother said, "Jack, I think it's time to have a discussion with your son." So my dad sat down next to me on the edge of their bed to have "that talk" and he was every bit as uncomfortable with the subject as I was.

I remember him saying, "Paul, I understand that you are at an age when your body is starting to . . . uh, you know . . . to, um, to go through certain changes and . . . uh . . . and you're . . . w-well, you're discovering girls now, so all this is new to you, but you'll eventually get over this stage and . . . well, what I'm trying to say is that I know that you're, uh, all excited about these dirty magazines and such but . . . uh, in time, you'll grow out of it because . . . uh . . . basically, son, the truth is, if you've seen one breast, you've pretty much seen them all."

To which I immediately quipped, "If it's all the same to you, Dad, I think I'd like to see them all!"

WHACK!

Oooh, tough crowd!

When I was sent to my room as punishment, I remember thinking to myself, "If all naked women are really the same, then why does my dad have a three-foot-high stack of smut in his office?" . . . but I prudently decided that this was a question best left for another day.

Courtship

My father and I had a mutual friend, David, who was an attorney. Very nice man. My dad had him on our boat several times and we'd hang out on occasion.

One day David proudly announced to my father that he was going to be appointed a judgeship.

My dad looked at him, puzzled, and said, "Wait a second, David . . . To become a judge in Massachusetts these days, you pretty much have to be either a woman, black or gay. Well, you're not black . . . and you're not a woman . . . "

"Ta da!"

We weren't surprised because it wasn't anything that we didn't already suspect, so it made absolutely no difference to us.

One day, when I was working as a defense attorney, David called me and asked me to assist him in an important trial. A pedestrian was run down by his client and severely injured and, since David really wasn't a litigator and I had extensive trial experience, David wanted me to conduct the trial and he would second-seat me in the courtroom.

The trial took several days and it was held in a special session of Lynn District Court, a venue where I had once supervised the district attorney's office for a couple of years.

On the second day of the trial the judge declared a recess and David and I went out to the lobby of the courthouse to discuss the proceedings.

Before we did I said, "David, first I need to talk to you about something. You know I love you, you're a great friend, and I'm honored to be doing this trial with you, but you have to remember that this is a courthouse that I used to work in and I know everybody in the building, so would you please do me a really big favor?"

"Of course, Paulie, what is it?"

"Will you please stop calling me 'sweetie' in the courtroom?"

"Oh, I'm so sorry, Paulie. I didn't realize I was doing that. That will be no problem at all."

"Thank you for understanding, David."

"Of course! I promise you it won't happen again, darling."

"OK, see what I mean?"

Eva and Adolf

You think you have it bad? Suck it up . . . there is always someone in a much worse situation than you are.

Your car broke down? . . . There's someone who can't afford a car.

Your basement is flooded? . . . Another person lost their house in a flood.

You broke your leg? . . . Somebody else lost both their legs in Iraq.

Have you ever been trapped in a bad relationship? You might want to end it, but sometimes it's not that easy. You have to wait for the right moment. You don't want anyone to get hurt, so you hang in there longer than you should. You want to ease-out gracefully but the time is never right. Well guess what, someone else has been stuck in a much worse situation than you were.

I was watching the History Channel the other day and they had a show about the final days of World War II.

On the program they showed some rare home movies of Adolf Hitler up in his Eagle's Nest, located high up in the Bavarian Alps of Germany.

At that point the war was all but lost for Germany.

Hitler's 1,000-year Reich was crumbling around him, and the pressure and narcotic pills he was addicted to had transformed him into a complete lunatic who had lost his grip on reality.

And standing there behind Hitler was his brooding mistress, Eva Braun.

Her arms were crossed and she was pouting.

The narrator said that Eva had been unhappy with her relationship with the Fuhrer for the past couple years.

And I'm looking at this poor, sad girl and I'm thinking . . .

How the hell do you break up with Hitler?

Do you get a restraining order against him?

Would Eva go to the local courthouse . . .

"Can I help you?"

"Yes, I'd like to get a restraining order against Adolf Hitler."

"What?!?!"

"That is spelled H-I-T-L . . ."

85

"I know how to spell Hitler! . . . He's the Fuhrer! I'm not signing my name to this order!"

"But he has been constantly calling me and hanging up . . . I know it's him! And he keeps driving by my house in his panzer tank at all hours of the day!"

How do you break the news to him?

He screams, "IT'S NOT GEOBBELS, IS IT?"

"No, no, Adolf . . . there is no one else."

Slamming his fist on the table, "IS IT MUSSOLINI? I'LL CRUSH HIM LIKE A BUG!"

Can you imagine Hitler showing up at your house, late at night . . . shitfaced?

 "Adolf, it is not your fault . . . It is me, it's not d'you."

"What did you say?"

"I said, it is me, it's not d'you."

"Did you say you were a . . . *Jew?* . . . SEIZE HER!"

Would they go to couples counseling?

"What seems to be the problem, Eva?"

"He entered Poland . . . He entered France . . . Then he entered Russia . . . but I can't even remember the last time he entered me!"

Adolf barks, "IF YOU HAVEN'T NOTICED, EVA, I AM A LITTLE BUSY RUNNING A WORLD WAR RIGHT NOW!"

What if Eva hired a lawyer?

"OK, Mr. Hitler. We don't want this to get ugly. I think we can work something out.

"Eva wants the china and the silverware . . . You can have all the tanks, the U-boats and the Luftwaffe.

"She wants the Eagle's Nest . . . you can have all the bunkers, the concentration camps and the *Bismarck*.

"Eva also wanted Paris, but I guess we'll have to scratch that one off the list . . . "

He screams, "I VANT THE GERMAN SHEPHERD!!! . . . AND THE LOCATION OF HER FAMILY!"

Tragically, Adolf Hitler and Eva Braun were married in a bunker as the Russians closed in on Berlin, then they committed suicide immediately after the ceremony.

"Adolf, do you promise to love this woman until death do you part?"

(Looking at his watch) "WHICH IS IN *PRECISELY* TWENTY MINUTES!"

And you think your honeymoon sucked because it rained all week?

Don't you feel like an asshole now?

* * *

with Steve D'Addario, owner of Stevie D's

with **Gary Shandling**

**Co-stars of the Showtime movie, *The Godfathers of Comedy*:
Frank Santorelli, Paul D'Angelo, Willie Farrell, Rocky LaPorte
and John Camponera**

CHAPTER 4:
A TOTALLY DIFFERENT CHAPTER

The Interview

Here's a great story that didn't happen to me, but it's so funny I had to share it with you.

I have a buddy named Pete who lives in Cleveland. He told me about one of his good friends who was interviewing for an important job as a business executive. He had already impressed the corporation enough to make it through several stages of the interview process and it was now down to him and one other applicant for the opportunity of a lifetime.

His final interview was to be with the president of the company.

This was extremely important to his career so, understandably, the guy was very nervous about the interview and wanted to gain every advantage he could to make a favorable impression.

He thoroughly researched the organization beforehand; made a list of questions that he anticipated being asked; rehearsed his answers; and even did research on how to best present himself to insure a successful job interview. One of the hints that they strongly recommended was to look around the interviewer's office for anything of a personal nature that you may be able to make casual conversation about, so you can connect with the interviewer on an informal level.

It was the day of the big interview and this guy dressed in an expensive new suit he bought just for the occasion, got to the corporate offices early, and waited nervously in the lobby. Finally he was told that the president would see him and he apprehensively entered the very large and impressive wood-paneled office of the chief executive.

The president was on a phone call and motioned for the anxious job candidate to take a seat, which he did in a high-backed leather chair.

The whole atmosphere in the big office was very intimidating but, recalling the advice he was given, the first thing this guy did was look around the office to find something he could make small talk about in an effort to break the ice, cut the obvious tension in the room, and put the president at ease for their crucial meeting.

That's when he noticed the framed picture on the president's desk.

As the president was hanging-up the phone, a big smile came over this guy's face as he remarked, "Wow! Where did you meet John Madden? He's one of my all-time favorites! I *love* John Madden!"

The president looked at him inquisitively.

"John Madden?"

"Yes," he bubbled as he pointed excitedly, "That picture of you and John Madden on your desk. How did you get to meet him? Madden's awesome!"

The president glared menacingly . . . his face getting increasingly red . . .

"That is not John Madden in that picture . . . that's *my wife.*"

"*Check, please!*"

I was told that the guy stood up, said, "Thank you for your time," and just walked right out of the office.

You gotta know when to fold 'em . . .

Have It Your Way

I lived in Hollywood from 1996 to 2002. When I first moved there, it was still a time when people went to Blockbuster to rent VHS movies and Internet porn was just beginning to become popular.

Before I relocated to La La Land, I used to be embarrassed to rent a dirty movie at the video store in my hometown. I'd wait patiently until there was no one in the store, then I'd dash in, quickly pick something out, and pray that no one saw me when I left . . . but there was no such shame or modesty in Hollywood.

Why is that?

Did you ever watch a porno movie and wonder where they made things like that? Well, I'll tell you where . . . in my old neighborhood in Hollywood, that's where.

One time a crew was shooting porno movies in the apartment *right next to mine* and they were making a racket over there until real late at night.

I couldn't sleep so I would keep banging on wall and yelling, "KEEP IT DOWN IN THERE! KEEP IT DOWN!!!"

Then I would put my ear to the wall and listen to the frustrated actor complain to the director, "It's not my fault, dude! How can I keep it up when the guy next door keeps yelling, 'Keep it down!'? . . . I'm so confused, man . . . I need a latte and a Quaalude . . ."

Mission accomplished.

Anyway, after I moved I walked into a Triple X video store on Sunset Boulevard and the guy behind the counter said, "Can I help you?"

I had trouble making eye-contact with him and shyly said, "Yeah . . . I . . . um, I . . . uh . . . I'd like to . . . uh . . . rent a dirty movie."

Without embarrassment he chirped, "Do you want a prerecorded one off the shelf or do you want us to whip one up for you in the back room while you wait?"

I said, "Really? I can do that?"

"Hey, it's Hollywood, dude!"

"OK, I think I'm gonna go with the custom one."

I looked up and they had a big menu they had posted on the wall. It was like ordering a sandwich at a sub shop.

I contemplated the options then said, "Let's see . . . ummm . . . OK, I'll have the threesome . . . I'd like them to do it from behind . . . and could I have extra fellatio on the side?"

He said, "Would you like a lesbian scene with that?"

"No, thank you."

The guy yelled over his shoulder into the back room, "I NEED A TRIPLE-PLAY . . . OVER EASY . . . MAKE IT A DOUBLE-HEADER . . . HOLD THE CHICK-LICK!!"

Then he turned back and asked, "Do you want to add a black actor and Super-Size that order?"

Alley "Oops"

Many years ago I moved back into the house I grew up in when I was a little boy. It's a home that my grandfather built when he came to this country from Sicily and it is right in the middle of the Italian section of Wakefield, affectionately known to old timers as "The Gulch."

My apartment is on the second floor on one side of the house and there is an old, brick apartment building right across an alley, not more than twenty or thirty feet away from my unit.

For years, the apartment directly across from mine was occupied by a grouchy, old Italian man and his wife who used to fight all the time whenever he would come home drunk (which was often).

And it was worse than having adjacent apartments in the same building because, in an apartment building, at least there is a wall between you that provides some degree of privacy. Their window was right there next to mine and, on a hot, summer night, when all the windows were open, you could hear absolutely everything that went on next door.

It was like an early version of reality TV. When I had my divorced friends living with me, there were many times that we'd shut all the lights in my place, turn off the television, pour a couple Dewers on the rocks, and sit underneath the window listening to the long, screaming arguments next door.

It was very entertaining, to say the least.

Dinner theater in the rough.

"YOU'RE DRUNK AGAIN! YOU BUM!"

"YOU'D BE DRINKING TOO IF YOU WERE MAR-RIED TO YOU, YOU WITCH! GET OFF MY BACK!"

"WHY DON'T YOU STOP LYING ON THE COUCH AND DO SOMETHING AROUND HERE, YOU USELESS LUMP!"

"YOU SHOULD TALK. MAYBE IF YOU GOT OFF YOUR ASS ONCE IN A WHILE IT WOULDN'T HAVE GOTTEN AS BIG AS IT DID!"

"YEAH? YOU USED TO KISS THIS ASS!"

"THAT'S WHEN YOU LOOKED LIKE A CHEER-LEADER, NOW YOU'RE BUILT LIKE A LINEBACKER!"

I made my share of noise too.

Sometimes, I'd come home late after a comedy show with a good buzz on and I'd plug in my electric guitar in and crank-up the amplifier to practice. I have to admit that, back then, I was still learning and wasn't all that good, but I really didn't give a shit.

The grouchy, old man across the alley would yell out the

window at me, at the top of his lungs, "HEY, KEEP IT DOWN OVER THERE! . . . AND BY THE WAY, YOU *SUCK* AT THE GUITAR!"

And I'd yell back through my window, "OH YEAH? HOW'S YOUR MISERABLE MARRIAGE? YOU DON'T THINK I CAN HEAR YOU FIGHT? I HEAR EVERY-THING! JUST BUY HER THE DAMN BLUE DRESS SHE WANTS AND SHUT UP ABOUT IT!"

And this guy would keep it going.

"I WOULDN'T MIND SO MUCH IF YOU WERE ANY GOOD. BUT ALL YOU DO IS MAKE NOISE!"

So I'd yell back, "OH YEAH? HAVE ANOTHER SIX-PACK, MR. HAPPY . . . HOW ABOUT SOME DEEP PUR-PLE? DO YOU LIKE DEEP PURPLE?"

Then I'd launch into the classic beginner-guitar riff from "Smoke on the Water."

BA BA BA; BA BA BABA . . . BA BA *BOINK.*

"OOPS, I MADE A MISTAKE! . . . GOTTA START OVER!"

And on and on it would go.

Those were good days.

Lunch with Dad

My parents were extremely generous and couldn't do more for me and my siblings when we were growing up.

That's why I'm glad that I got to buy lunch for my dad be-fore he passed away.

We were out at a local pub and my dad went for his wallet, like he always did, but I grabbed his arm and stopped him.

"Put your money away, dad. This one's on me."

He was shocked.

"Are you serious? You've never paid for anything in your entire life."

"That's OK . . . the burgers and beers are on me, dad."

"What's the occasion?"

"No special occasion, dad. It's my turn to pay anyway because you picked up the last thing . . . you know, the . . . uh, you know . . . um . . . college."

Timthy's Party

My first Christmas in Los Angeles was much different than what I was used to. First of all, I had no family around, so I agreed to take a show at the Improv on Christmas Eve. I figured that the only reason they even asked me to be on the show was that they couldn't get anyone else to work that night, but it was OK by me because I desperately wanted the stage time.

The other reason I took the show was that I was invited to my hairstylist Timthy's home in West Hollywood for a Christmas party and I needed an excuse to bail-out if it got too weird which, knowing Timthy, was a distinct possibility. (No, I didn't spell it wrong. Timthy claims he had the 'o' surgically removed from his name.)

I went to the party with an open mind and I was having a pretty good time, mostly checking out all the strange people in attendance. At one point, I was talking to a . . . a, um . . . a man, or maybe a woman, or perhaps a man . . . or, could be a woman . . . or a man . . . wearing an admiral's uniform or something of the like, when Timthy approached me.

"Are you having a good time, Paulie?"

"Yes, I am, thanks for inviting me . . . Hey, Timthy, can I ask you, was that person I was just speaking to a man or a woman? We've been having a conversation for fifteen minutes but I just can't tell."

Timthy shot a glance in their direction and said, "To tell you the truth, I'm not even sure myself . . . Anyway, Paulie, come into the kitchen with me, I'd like you to meet some of my friends."

Timthy grabbed me by the arm and whisked me into the kitchen where he announced, "Hi everyone, I'd like you all to meet my heterosexual friend, Paulie."

"Hi, everyone."

"Hi, Paulie."

Timthy says, "Paulie, you're butch, could you open this bottle of wine for me?"

"Of course I will."

Timthy handed me one of those chrome corkscrews with the two arms on either side that rise up together as you twist the corkscrew into the cork.

As I was performing the simple task, I noticed that three of Timthy's obviously gay friends were watching me intently from the other side of the countertop, like I was inventing fire or doing something extraordinary. Not one to pass up the opportunity to entertain an attentive crowd, I removed the cork and asked, "Would you like to see me do an impression of someone walking alone through my neighborhood in Hollywood late at night?"

Puzzled, but intrigued, they all answered, "Sure."

I proceeded to hold the device upright and pull down on the corkscrew so that the two arms quickly shot up, looking like a person who was being held-up at gunpoint in a robbery . . . but they didn't get the joke.

A moment of awkward silence followed as the three of them stared at me with baffled expressions.

Suddenly, a look of recognition appeared on the face of the

one in the middle, and he threw his arms up in a theatrical manner and exclaimed, "Oh, I get it . . . you mean, like, *'FABULOUS!'?"*

I doubled-over laughing and not one of them had any idea why.

Spooky Stories

People love to be scared.

When you were a little kid, did you ever sit under a blanket in the dark with your friends and tell scary ghost stories?

I did. In fact I *loved* scaring the shit out of my friends.

The kids from the neighborhood would plead, "Paul, can you turn off the lights and tell us one of those spooky stories you make up! We want you to scare us! Will you scare us? Please scare us! Pleeeease!!"

And I'd go, "OK, get me a flashlight and shut all the lights."

The room would become completely dark as I held a flashlight under my chin to make myself look really sinister and evil, and I'd make-up chilling stories that would make my friends shake with fright.

"OK . . . This story is called *The Revenge of the Bus-Stop Butcher.*

"It was a dark and dreary Halloween night when the headless, rotting corpse of the deranged serial killer rose from the grave to seek out his next helpless victim . . . "

Then I'd let out a hideous laugh while the other kids held each other and cowered in terror.

"AGGGGGGHHHHHHHH!!!! Stop it, Paul, you're scaring us!"

I still like to scare my friends, but these guys all have jobs and homes and families now. Ghosts and witches and werewolves and zombies and vampires just don't terrify them anymore. They're over that.

Oh don't get me wrong . . . my friends and I are still afraid, but we are afraid of different things now, and I know just what it is that makes their hands tremble and their scrotums shrivel-up.

So, not too long ago, a bunch of the guys from my old neighborhood got together again and, after we all had a few cocktails, one of them said, "Hey, Paul . . . M'ember how you used to tell those spooky stories and scare us when we was little kids?"

"Yeah."

"Well I bet you can't do it again. In fact, I bet you *a hundred bucks* you can't scare us like you used to. You gotta remember, we're not kids anymore. We're adults now and we're all married with our own kids and we own houses and run businesses now. We don't scare so easy anymore."

I said, "A hundred bucks? Really? Cash? You're on. Shut all the lights and somebody find me a flashlight."

Then, just like when we were little kids, they turned off all the lights and I held a flashlight under my face to look creepy.

And I began in a hushed voice . . .

"This is a story about Joe. Joe was a really nice guy who was a hard-working, loyal, happily married, family man with a beautiful wife and three great kids who worked two full-time jobs to care for his family and build the dream house that he always wanted on a nice piece of land that his family handed down to him.

"One day Joe came home early from work and caught his wife in bed with his best friend!

"Even though he's a really nice guy, Joe was understandably upset and raised his voice . . . (pointing meacingly) just like any one of you guys probably would have done under the same circumstances.

"The next day Joe's wife went down to the courthouse and claimed Joe threatened her, so the judge kicked poor Joe out of *HIS OWN HOME!*

"Now Joe's ex-best friend is living in Joe's house . . . with Joe's wife and Joe's kids . . . sleeping in Joe's bed . . . and watching Joe's brand new 65-inch ultra hi-definition plasma TV with 7-channel home-theater surround-sound and Direct TV's NFL Sunday-Ticket Game-Day Package . . . THAT JOE IS PAYING FOR!!!

"While poor Joe . . . *WHO DID NOTHING WRONG!* . . . can only afford a tiny studio apartment with a lousy 27-inch television, basic cable and dial-up Internet and has to eat frozen TV dinners every night because every month a judge makes Joe pay for a big house Joe doesn't live in anymore . . . a nice car Joe doesn't drive anymore . . . three kids Joe hardly gets to see . . . and a pretty wife that Joe no longer sleeps with."

Cue the hideous laugh . . . *"EH EH EH EH EH EH"* . . . as my tough-guy, married friends recoil in absolute horror and scream like frightened children.

"AGGGGGHHHHHHH!!!! Stop it Paul, you're scaring us!"

"Take the hundred bucks! You win! You win!! Take it!"

Cause for Alarm

When was the last time you heard a car alarm going off and thought to yourself, "Oh my God, someone is trying to steal a car!"

No, it's more like, "Somebody shut that damn alarm off!"

It's the "boy who cried wolf" syndrome. False alarms are so prevalent that no one pays attention to them anymore.

There could be a car alarm going crazy while four teenage gang-bangers with baggy pants are trying to jimmy the door-lock of a brand-new Mercedes with a crow-bar and I'd walk by going, "Lock the keys in your car, boys? I hate when that happens. Have a nice day."

I lived on the second floor of a big apartment complex right on a very busy Hollywood Boulevard in Hollywood, California and every car that was parked along the street had a car alarm.

Each morning, when people were getting into their cars to go to work, they'd hit their remotes and it would sound like a bird sanctuary outside my window.

"Tweet, tweet."

"Chirp, chirp, chirp."

"Peep, peep."

It was just like waking-up out in the country, only these were the bird calls of Thunderbirds, Firebirds, Falcons and Skylarks.

There were false alarms from time to time, but there was one irritating car, in particular, whose car alarm went off constantly, at all times of the day and night.

On the average of two or three, even four times a day . . . afternoon, early evening, midnight, late at night, middle of the night, early morning . . . something would trip his alarm and this car would go nuts for a couple minutes, disturbing everyone in the building . . . and it was an obnoxious alarm.

"WHOOP, WHOOP, WHOOP . . . EII-OOOH, EII-OOOH . . . BUZZZ, BUZZZ."

The alarm did a variety of impressions like a bad Vegas lounge act.

"Rise and shine sleepyheads! Everybody up, its show-time! It's great to be disturbing you needlessly tonight. I just drove in from Detroit and boy, are my rear swing-arms tired. Do you like impressions? . . . As if you have a choice, ha-ha! . . . What if a car alarm sounded like an air-raid siren? I think it would go something like this . . . 'WHIRRRRR, WHIRRRRR' . . . Thank you very much. Next imagine, if you will, that an alarm clock and a fire engine had a baby. Their kid might cry something like this . . . 'BZZZZ, WOOO, BZZZZ WOOO' . . . Thank you, you're too kind. How about if a rabid water buffalo screwed a lighthouse? I imagine their orgasm would sound something like this . . . 'A-HOO, A-HOO' . . . Thank you, you've been a great audience! You can go back to sleep now."

The siren would blare continually, then it would whoop like an ambulance, then make an earsplitting buzzing noise. Next, it would make that obnoxious sound like a European police car, followed by a "whoop, whoop, whoop" like Curly on the *Three Stooges*, and perform a variety of three or four other repulsive sounds at deafening volume, culminated by some intimidating robotic voice admonishing the would-be car thief to "STAY AWAY! STAY AWAY!"

Then again, it could be saying "STAY AWAKE! STAY AWAKE!" I couldn't really tell because I was usually half-asleep and directing a torrent of swears at the car's inconsiderate owner when it went off.

I have no idea what was triggering the alarm. The motion detector was set so ultra-sensitive that it would go off if a mouse broke wind two blocks away . . ."WHOOP, WHOOP, WHOOP . . . EII-OOOH, EII-OOOH . . . BUZZZ, BUZZZ . . . STAY AWAY, STAY AWAY!"

It made no sense because I don't even know why there was an alarm on that piece of shit in the first place.

The asshole who owned the car was totally out of touch with reality. Did he think that car thieves just couldn't wait to get their hands on his beat-up 1992 Ford Fiesta with the faded shag-rug on the dashboard, mismatched replacement fender, body-rot and two missing hubcaps? The truth was that he could leave the car running with the keys in the ignition outside of a busy public bus terminal and it would run out of gas before someone would consider driving-off in that ugly shit-box.

All times of the day and night . . . 8:52 p.m. . . . 11:06 p.m. . . . 1:30 a.m. . . . 3:43 a.m. . . . 5:17 a.m. . . . 7:34 a.m. . . . "WHOOP, WHOOP, WHOOP . . . EII-OOOH, EII-OOOH . . . BUZZZ, BUZZZ . . . STAY AWAY, STAY AWAY!" . . . and it was really pissing me off and, I imagine, everyone else in the neighborhood.

"WHOOP, WHOOP, WHOOP . . . EII-OOOH, EII-OOOH . . . BUZZZ, BUZZZ."

Then, one morning after the alarm had gone off three or four more times in the middle of the night and woke-up everyone in the building, I went outside and saw the car being towed away. In the empty space where it was usually parked was a bunch of broken glass.

I overheard the owner of the car telling someone what had happened.

Apparently, sometime in the middle of the night, someone who was totally fed-up with being continuously woken up by that annoying alarm, finally had enough and they threw a big rock right through the windshield . . . then there was a downpour and the heavy rain ruined the interior of the car, so it had to be towed away for repairs.

To be honest with you, as much as I hated this asshole and his fucking car with the aggravating alarm, I have to admit that I kind of felt bad for the guy.

Why?

. . . I didn't know it was going to rain.

The Accident

When I was a defense attorney, I got a call from one of my brother's friends looking for help.

"Hey Paul. How you doin'?"

"I'm all right, what's up?"

"I need you to represent me. I got into a car accident."

"OK, tell me what happened."

"You know how the firemen sometimes stand in traffic and collect money in that big rubber boot for Muscular Dystrophy?"

"Yeah."

"Well I was pulling up in traffic to give the fireman some money when I got into an accident."

"You hit the guy in front of you?"

"Well, actually, to be perfectly honest, I'm not sure if I hit him or if he backed into me."

"How could you not know?"

"I dunno. It was a traumatic experience."

"Well, were you moving forward or did the guy in front of you back-up into you?"

"Well, you know, I was trying to get my wallet and I wasn't really paying attention, so he might have put his car in reverse and whacked into me . . . I don't know . . . like I said, I wasn't paying attention, but I'm pretty sure he backed into me."

"Was there a lot of damage?"

"Yeah, my whole front-end is all fucked-up."

"And the rear of his car is smashed-up?"

"Yeah, his rear *AND* his front-end too because he got pushed into the car in front of him."

"Wait a second. How is it possible that this guy could be pushed into the car in *front* of him if he was backing-up into you while he was in reverse?"

"Like I said Paul, I'm not really sure what happened . . . All I know is, when I slammed on the brakes, my front bumper got wedged underneath his rear-end."

"You slammed on the brakes? Why would you slam on your brakes if this guy were *backing* into you? . . . *Of course* you hit him, you dumb shit. Why are you lying to me? What do you think, I'm an idiot?"

"Yeah . . . Yeah . . . OK, OK, then maybe I did hit him . . . So, can we sue Muscular Dystrophy or the firemen for creating like a distraction or something? It's their fault!"

"Goodbye." (Click.)

Man O' War

Once, when I was working on a cruise ship, I went to Crane Beach in Barbados with some of my friends from the ship's band. While we were swimming in the surf, Steve, the trumpet player, suddenly let out a scream of pain.

"What happened?"

"I got stung by a jellyfish! I think it was a Man O' War!"

"Oh no! Those things are poisonous! What should we do?"

The guys started yelling, "HELP! . . . HELP! . . . THIS MAN'S BEEN STUNG! HE NEEDS HELP! HURRY! HELP!"

Steve was in obvious pain when a native finally responded to our cries for help.

"Thank God. You've got to help! Our friend's been stung by a Man O' War! You've got to help him!"

Steve was now in agony and, even though we were panicking, the native remained calm.

"There is only one way to counteract the poison," he told us in his thick island accent.

"What's that?"

"You must urinate on the bite."

"Excuse me?"

"Someone must urinate on the bite. Urine will disinfect the wound and counteract the effect of the venom."

"You're serious?"

"Oh, yes. It happens quite often on the island."

We all looked at each other while Steve writhed in pain at our feet on the beach.

"Well guys, I guess we need some urine . . . I don't have to go, do you?"

"I just went when I was swimming . . . How about you?"

"I don't need to pee . . . John?"

"Don't look at me."

"Come on, *someone's* gotta have to take a piss . . . for Steve."

No one said a word.

We stood there in silence for a moment, pondering the situation . . . and then I began to yell at the top of my lungs at the people sitting around us on the beach,

"WE NEED A SIX-PACK! PLEASE HELP US! THIS MAN IS DYING! PLEASE! IT'S A MATTER OF LIFE AND DEATH! WE NEED BEER! WE MUST HAVE A SIX-PACK TO SAVE HIS LIFE! . . . COLD HEINEKEN IF YOU HAVE IT! IMPORTED STUFF IS GOOD, BUT BUD WILL DO . . . HELP!!!"

Steve started laughing and we knew then that he was going to make it.

Father and Son Moment

The world is a different place than it was when I grew up . . . unfortunately.

Picture this: A father is concerned that his little boy is staying inside too much and playing videogames all day, and he wants to get him out in the fresh air, so he takes his son for a walk along the beach . . .

They are strolling along in the sand near the shoreline when the small child points at a man emerging from the water and exclaims, "Look dad, look! It's a skin-diver!"

His dad shakes his head and says. "No son, look closer. That man's not wearing a black wetsuit, he was just swimming in an oil-slick."

"Oh."

A few minutes later, the little boy points at something lying on the beach and yells excitedly, "Look dad, look! It's a jellyfish! It's a jellyfish!"

His father looks down and says sadly, "No son, I hate to disappoint you, but that's not a jellyfish, it's just a plastic bag that washed up on the shore."

"Oh."

A little further down the beach, the kid again points at something in the sand and shouts, "Look dad! It's an eel!"

His father checks it out and says, "No son, I'm sorry to say that's not an eel, that's a used prophylactic."

"What's that, dad?"

"Never mind. That's for another day."

Further down the beach, the little boy jumps up and down and screams, "Look dad, there's some shells on the beach! Am I right this time? Are those really shells on the beach?"

His father says, "Yes, you are correct this time, son, those *are* shells on the beach. That one's a shotgun shell . . . there's a .22 over there . . . and this one is from a .38. Let's go home and play with the computer."

<u>Casper's Revenge</u>

Do you believe in ghosts?

I didn't . . . that is, I didn't until I went out with a girl who *lived* in a haunted house.

She moved into an old house in historic Salem, Massachusetts that was built in the early 1750s. The girl I was seeing didn't know the old house was haunted when she bought it, but weird things stated to happen soon after she moved in.

Latched doors would open on their own . . . Objects would be moved around . . . Several workers saw people who weren't there . . . so she contacted the previous owner of the house who told her that the house was, in fact, haunted. My girlfriend started to ask around and learned that the house's reputation as a center of paranormal activity was well-known to local ghost-hunters.

I was psyched.

"I think that is sooo cool! You live in a real haunted house! Awesome!"

She said, "You might think it's exciting, but you get to leave here whenever you want. I have to live here with that . . . that . . . *thing* . . . that spirit . . . and I never know when the damn thing is watching me. I'm always looking over my shoulder."

"What do you mean? Are you trying to tell me that you can't get any privacy because the house is supposedly haunted?"

"Well, yeah! That's how I feel. It can be uncomfortable at times."

"It's not uncomfortable, it's *crazy* to think that."

"No it's not! Think about it, Paul. Put yourself in my place for once. When I'm all alone and I'm taking off all my clothes . . . or when I'm wet and naked, stepping out of the shower . . . or when I'm putting cream on my legs or undressing for bed, sometimes I feel a little weird . . . like that ghost might be watching me . . . and, and I feel like I need to cover up. It gives me the creeps."

It gave her the creeps but, to tell you the truth, it was actually kind of turning me on . . . the idea that some voyeur ghost was watching my girlfriend when she was naked around the house.

Boo!

After that, whenever we fooled around, I used to imagine that the ghost was watching us doing it. And I always tried to do a good job and impress the ghost, just in case the specter was judging me against a couple centuries of exhibitionism.

"Check out this move, Casper."

I have to admit, it was kind of exciting

Well, that was until my girlfriend did a little more research and found out that the house was allegedly haunted by the spirit of a thirteen year old boy who died in 1805 from something they called "Brain Fever" at the time.

Thirteen years old?

All of a sudden, it wasn't a turn-on anymore.

"Awww, that's no good."

Everything is so politically correct now, especially in the Far-Left state of Massachusetts, I was afraid that the morality police might show-up with an arrest warrant some day and slap a set of handcuffs on me.

"What's this all about, officer? What am I being charged with? What have I done?"

"We have reports that you exposed yourself to an underage ghost."

"Underage? No way! This is a mistake! . . . That kid died in 1800, he's over 200 years old now! . . . and besides that, *he's a fucking ghost! Has everyone lost their minds?*"

"Read the new statute that those Poltergeists' Rights protest groups got passed . . . The kid was only 13 when he died and he stays that same age forever. It's right there in section GG, subsection B, paragraph 23, around line 47."

"Ohhh. That's just not right!"

"I don't make the laws, buddy, I just enforce them. Let's go, you paranormal pervert."

And, even if that never happened to me, I didn't want this pubescent ghost watching us having sex anymore. I couldn't perform in front of him. Why? Because *I know what I was like* when I was thirteen years old!

All I could think of, when we were in bed together having sex, was this awkward, goofy, zit-faced, teenage ghost standing in the corner, gawking at us and doing the five-knuckle shuffle . . . buffing his banana . . . cuffing his carrot . . . jerkin' his gherkin . . . take your pick . . . *burping the worm*.

"Ahhhh! I've been slimed!"

We broke up shortly after that.

Musk Ox

I love watching those nature shows about wild animals on the Discovery Channel or *Animal Planet* and I'll often retain some otherwise useless information because it is so fascinating I couldn't possibly forget it if I tried.

Here's one example . . .

Do you know what a Musk Ox is?

Well, it's like a giant water buffalo that lives in Arctic North America, has long, mangy, matted Bob Marley dreadlock Rasta hair all over its body and smells terrible. (I can only assume.)

So listen to this remarkable tidbit the narrator provided:

He said that the male Musk Ox only urinates one time a year . . . for three and a half hours at a time.

Let me repeat that . . . only ONE time *A YEAR* . . . for 3

½ hours!

My first thought was, "I think I was behind that guy in the men's room at Fenway Park once!"

(Looking at my watch.) "Come on, pal! It's been over an hour! Are you gonna be here all day?"

"Just about . . . Mooooooo."

I can only imagine some poor Musk Ox, leaning against a tree, two hours into his annual piss, thinking, "Whewwww . . . I sure picked a bad day to eat asparagus."

Or a Musk Ox's aggravated wife going, "Let's move it, we're going to be late for the theater!"

And the Musk Ox husband saying, "Look honey, I can't just cut it off in mid-stream after an hour and a half . . . I'll have to meet you there. I'm not going anywhere for a while."

"You knew we had these tickets! You had to start today? You couldn't go yesterday when we had nothing to do but graze?"

"I'm sorry, but I didn't *have* to go yesterday."

And just who is the videographer who followed a Musk Ox around for an entire year just to make sure he didn't take a leak?

You don't think the other Musk Oxen in the herd messed with his head?

I picture one Musk Ox dancing around, obviously uncomfortable, and saying under his breath to his Musk Ox friend, "Forget this stupid practical joke, Lenny, I gotta go *real* bad! Is that guy with the camera ever gonna fall asleep?"

"No, not yet. You've got to hold it a little longer, Eddie. Hang in there, he's getting drowsy. Think about something else."

"I can't do it! I don't think I can make it"

"He's starting to close his eyes, Eddie . . . Just hold on another minute."

"I'm gonna piss myself, Lenny!"

"You've had this guy fooled for eight months, don't blow it now. You wanna be on *Animal Planet*, don't you? . . . Wait a second . . . OK, he's out. Go for it."

"Thank God!

"Ahhhhhhhhhhhhhhhhhhhhhhhhhhhhhhhhhhhhhhhhhhhhhh hhhhhhhhhhhhhhhhhhhhhhhhhhhhhhhhhhhhhhhhhhhhhhhhhh hhhhhhhhhhhhhhhhhhhhhhhhhhhhhhhhhhhhhhhhhhhhhhhhhh hhhhhhhhhhhhhhhhhhhhhhhhhhhhhhhhhhhhhhhhhhhhhhhhhh hhhhhhhhhhhhhhhhhhhhhhhhhhhhhhhhhhhhhhhhhhhhhhhhhh hhhhhhhhhhhhhhhhhhhhhhhhhhhhhhhhhhhhhhhhhhhhhhhhhh hhhhhhhhhhhhhhhhhhhhhhhhhhhhhhhhhhhhhhhhhhhhhhhhhh hhhhhhhhhhhhhhhhhhhhhhhhhhhhhhhhhhhhhhhhhhhhhhhhhh hhhhhhhhhhhhhhhhhhhhhhhhhhhhhhhhhhhhhhhhhhhhhhhhhh hhhhhhhh . . ."

with Dane Cook

At Stevie D's Comedy Tonight in 1987

CHAPTER 5:
ALMOST HALF WAY

Wedding Rehearsal (*an excerpt from L.A. Misérables*)
Day 798 - May 17, 1998:

The following story is true . . . I wish it wasn't.

I had two shows tonight and the first show was an experience I will not soon forget. Mike Clarke asked me if I wanted to make a couple extra bucks before my scheduled show at Giggles Comedy Club and I told him, "Of course, I'm broke. I need the money."

He sent me to perform at a private party, a wedding rehearsal dinner, in a very traditional, old-Italian section of East Boston.

I walked into a little Italian restaurant that was owned by the groom's parents and it looked like a scene straight out of *The Godfather*, no lie. The very Italian mother, dressed entirely in black because someone died twenty-five years ago, approached me.

"Hi, I'm Paul, the comedian."

"Nice-a to meet-a you. Do you want-a some pasta? Come on, I feed-a you."

"No . . . no thanks, really, I just ate."

"Come on! You gotta eat! *Mangia*! Let me make-a you a nice plate o' pasta."

"No, I really can't, thank you. I'd love to, but I need to be out of here by 8:30 because I have another show."

"OK, OK . . . There's-a my son, Kenny, the groom, and his-a girlfriend Paula, sitting over there. You do whatever you have-a to do. You give-a them a hard time or bust-a their balls or whatever you have-a to do . . . You sure you don't want-a any pasta?"

"I'm sure, thank you."

I was on stage . . . well, not actually onstage . . . There was no stage or microphone. I was standing among the tables in the dining room while the families finished up their meal. In the middle of my act, which was being very well received by the guests, I was ribbing the bride and groom about the wedding night when, suddenly, the bride-to-be's muscle-bound, steroid-freak, totally drunk and absolutely crazy brother bolted up from his seat in a 'roid-rage, yelled, "THAT'S MY SISTER YOU'RE TALKING ABOUT!" and whipped . . . and I mean whipped . . . a kitchen knife as hard as he could at me from across the dining room.

I seemed to watch in slow motion as the knife hurtled end-over-end at me from across the room . . . *whoosh* . . . *whoosh* . . . *whoosh* . . . *whoosh* . . . *whoosh* . . .

I always wondered how I would react in a crisis situation. I'd read about a car jumping a guardrail and hitting another car traveling in the opposite direction on the other side of the divided highway and I'd think that, in that same situation, I certainly would have swerved the wheel, made some brilliant maneuver and pulled out of it with the split-second reflexes of a fighter pilot.

Evidently, not true.

I watched the knife heading at me and, instead of utilizing my lightning-fast instincts to swiftly dodge the approaching projectile, the only action I could accomplish was to concentrate all my efforts into generating the lifesaving gesture of forming the word "FUCK!" on my lips.

I simply didn't have any time to react, it happened so fast. The knife was a blur . . . it just missed me . . . not by very much . . . less than an inch . . . whizzing by my abdomen and close enough that it actually grazed my shirt, as I stood there stunned and speechless.

The out-of-control brother was grabbed by several guys around him, there was a melee and he was hustled out of the room and tossed out into the street, where the altercation continued. I stood there, along with everyone else who remained in the restaurant, craning our necks and listening to the angry confrontation that was taking place on the sidewalk. Everyone's attention was directed at the chaotic scene outside, their heads turned away from me as I stood there, frozen in shock.

Eventually, the people that remained in the dining room began sitting down or turning around in their chairs, yelling out apologies to me from their seats.

"We're so sorry . . . He's-a nuts! He does-a this all-a da time!"

"He's a piece o' shit. Don't-a let him wreck-a the day."

"Go on . . . Go on . . . tell-a you jokes . . . He's-a fucking crazy man. Go on-a with-a the show! . . . " (Clap-clap . . . trying to get everyone going again.)

Now the mother says. "Come on! (clap-clap) He's gonna tell us-a the jokes . . . Go ahead . . . you tell-a you funny stories and we laugh . . . OK? . . ." (Clap-clap.)

"Sure . . . no problemo . . . nooooooo problem whatsoever . . . more jokes? You want to hear more jokes? . . . Let's just skip right over that little incident like nothin' ever happened . . . ha, ha . . . OK? Listen, not for nothing, you know, I don't want to be a bad sport about this or anything, I'm a real trooper . . . everything's cool . . . I'm totally cool with this . . . but, if it's not asking too much, if it's not too much to ask, would you mind if

I took a minute . . . just give me a minute, please . . . to hit the men's room and change my underwear, because I'm pretty sure I just shit my pants? . . . Would that be asking too much? . . . To allow me to at least empty this warm load of poop out of my soiled underwear? Just let me know. Is that an unreasonable request under the circumstances?"

And guess what? I finished the show. That's right. I finished the damn show because I needed the money. Hey, times are tough and, if need be, I planned on going on until I got the whole, matching place-setting thrown at me.

When I left I was afraid that the nut might be outside, waiting to beat the shit out of me. I worried that he had keyed my father's car, or had planted a bomb in it, or had gone home to get piano wire and some brass knuckles. I got in the car in a hurry, high-tailed it out of there faster than you can say "hit man," and drove to my other show at Giggles Comedy Club in Saugus. My adrenaline was flowing, my nerves were shot, my hands were shaking, and the ride seemed like a dream to me.

When I got to Giggles I was met by comedian Johnny Pizzi, who was hosting the show.

"Am I late, Johnny?"

"No, you have a few minutes." He looked at me, all frazzled and fidgety. "Something wrong? You look like you just saw a ghost."

"I did that private party for Mike and the bride's crazy brother threw a knife at me during the show."

"WHAT?"

"You heard me. I was teasing the bride and groom about the wedding night and he got pissed-off and threw a fucking kitchen knife at me with all his might. It missed me by an inch."

"Holy shit! . . . Was it a steak knife or a butter knife?"

"How the hell do I know? Does it matter? But, listen, Johnny. Mike doesn't need to know about this, OK? Promise

116

me, he just doesn't need to hear this. This is between just you and me, *capisce*?"

"No sweat, Paulie . . . I promise you. Wow, I can't believe that."

I should have known better than to tell Johnny. If I ever want to make sure that a story gets out to as many people as possible, in as short a time as possible, I just tell it to my friend Johnny and make sure that I adamantly stress to him, "Johnny, you have to promise me *on your life* that you won't tell anyone. Nobody else whatsoever, understand? This is only between you and me, right? Johnny, swear to me on the Bible that this will never get out . . . " And, guaranteed, the whole world will know about it in ten minutes.

Want to get a story out there? There's telephone . . . television . . . telemarketing . . . and tell-a-Pizzi. Never fails.

If you think that's the end of it, keep reading.

Day 804 - May 23, 1998 (*One week later.*)

I swear to God, the following text is the complete and accurate transcription of a recorded message that I listened to on my answering machine when I got home late tonight . . . and if you don't believe me, I saved the cassette.

The two voices were those of Johnny Pizzi, who saw me immediately after the incident, and Mike Clarke of Five Star Comedy, the agent who books Nick's Comedy Stop in Boston and Giggles Comedy Club on the North Shore, as well as some private shows . . . for instance, like the ill-fated wedding rehearsal dinner I performed at one week ago.

By the way, Mike is the guy I was referring to when I begged Johnny, "Mike doesn't need to know about this. Please don't tell him."

Remember?

COMEDIAN JOHNNY PIZZI:
(anxiously, with some urgency)
Paul, it's Johnny Pizzi . . . Pick up . . .
(short pause)
Are you home, Paul?
(theatrically emphasized)
I got neeeewwwws for you!
(laughter under his breath)
You know that party you did last Sunday? . . . The wedding is
OFF . . . How's that? . . .
And it's all because of what happened during the show . . .
(clears throat)
. . . 'cuz they called Mike up today . . . Can you imagine that?
The wedding is OFF . . . and it was all because of what happened . . .
(beat)
. . . so she was explaining to Mike what happened or something, but . . .
*(Turning his head away from the receiver so his voice
trails off momentarily.)*
(continuing)
Mike just walked in . . . But, anyways, I thought that was a riot.
(beat; amazed)
. . . So . . . No wedding, Paul . . . Noooooo wedding . . .

MIKE CLARKE, AGENT:
(voice heard in background, from a distance)
Is that Paul?

JOHNNY PIZZI:
(yelling; voice directed away from phone)
I'm leaving a message for him . . . Here, Mike . . . talk to him.

MIKE CLARKE:
(from a closer proximity)
Give me the phone . . . let me talk to him . . .
*(Taking the phone from JOHNNY . . . continuing; loudly
into the receiver)*
This is a first!
(enthusiastically, sarcastic)
Sooo . . . You start a knife fight and now, the wedding is off!
(chuckle)
The woman called me today . . . She can't believe it . . . She's
actually happy . . . so, you know . . . But you're the start of the
whole thing . . .
(chuckle)
The wedding is off . . . There's a big feud in the family!
(beat)
Give me a call . . . Talk to you later.
(Sound of the telephone hanging up.)

Uh-oh. Something tells me that this might be a good time
for me to leave Boston and return to Los Angeles.

The Corleones and the Gambinos are at war and they both
probably have a contract out to bust up my kneecaps. At this
point, I'm afraid it's a race. The major issue for them isn't
whether or not they're going to do something to me . . . but
who gets to me first.

Suddenly, three thousand miles doesn't seem far enough
away.

Suicidal Pilot

I recently read a story about a Jet Blue pilot who threatened to crash the commercial airplane he was flying if his estranged girlfriend didn't go back with him.

That's not the first time something like this has happened.

A few years ago, I read a newspaper story about Moroccan airline pilot who was terribly despondent because his girlfriend broke-up with him, so he took the plane he was flying into a suicide dive, right into the side of a mountain, killing all 43 passengers aboard.

And it was all because of a woman.

All because some selfish pilot was bummed out over a break-up.

Can you imagine that?

What about those poor, helpless passengers whose fate was in his hands?

Tragic . . .

What most people don't know is that, after they retrieved the black box and played the cockpit tapes, you can hear the frantic passengers in the background, yelling . . .

"SHE WAS NO GOOD FOR YOU!!! YOU CAN DO BETTER!"

"DON'T DO IT! I HAVE A COUSIN WITH BIG TITS, I'LL FIX YOU UP!!!"

"I'LL MASSAGE YOUR NECK WHILE MY FIANCÉ BLOWS YOU!"

Out of the Mouths of Babes

One of the things that sucked about being a criminal defense attorney was trying to get some of my dirtbag clients to pay for my legal services.

Sometimes it was my fault. I was too trusting.

"You know me, Paulie . . . I'm good for it. I'm a friend of your brother, Jay."

That fact alone should have raised my suspicions.

When the case was still hanging over the defendant's head; when these guys had their backs against the wall and were looking at jail time, at least I had some leverage to collect my fee. However, once the case was over, getting money out of them was like pulling teeth.

There was one disgustingly fat slime ball that owed me five hundred bucks for representing him on an assault and battery charge that I got dismissed.

Now that he was off the hook, he was doing everything he could to avoid paying me.

I kept calling and calling him, and he kept making excuses and putting me off until it got to the point that this asshole wouldn't even answer the phone anymore.

In fact, he was such a loathsome coward that he began using his cute little four-year-old son to screen his phone calls.

One time I called his house and the kid answered.

"Hello."

I said, "Hello. Is your father there?"

"Just a moment, please."

There was the pitter-patter of little feet running away, I heard faint whispering in the background, and then the sound of tiny feet running back again to pick up the receiver.

"Who's calling?"

I said sternly, "This is his lawyer. Tell him this is his attorney calling."

"Just a moment, please."

Once again the little boy put down the phone, I heard the pitter-patter of his little feet, whispering, and the sound of him running back again.

"My father is un-unavailabable."

"What did you say?"

"I said, my father is unabailabab-ble."

I was getting pissed off.

"You're four years old! You don't know what the word 'unavailable' means! . . . Who's there? Who told you to say that? Tell me, who told you to say 'unavailable?'"

The kid hesitated. " . . . N-n-nobody."

"Are you sure your father's not there?"

"Uhhhh . . . um, yeah."

I thought for a moment.

"Well, that's too bad . . . I was going to come over your house with my good friend, Barney the Dinosaur."

I heard the kid scream . . .

"DADDY, BARNEY'S COMING OVER!!! HE SAID BARNEY'S GONNA COME TO SEE ME, DADDY, BAR-NEY'S COMING OVER!!!"

Ah hah! I *knew* it, you little bastard!

Well, I outsmarted the four year old, but not his father . . . he still owes me the money.

The Good, the Bad and the Stupid

Before I took my annual physical, I had to give blood samples so the lab could test it. At my appointment, I asked my doctor what the results were.

He said, "I have good news and bad news"

I said, "Good news and bad news? What do you mean?"

He told me, "Well, your bad cholesterol is good, but your good cholesterol is bad."

I asked, "Is that good or bad?"

"It's good *and* bad."

I remarked, "You know, doc, to tell you the truth, I didn't

even know there was such a thing as good and bad cholesterol."

The doctor said, "Then I bet you didn't know that there are
both good fats and bad fats as well."

I said, "No, that's not true, doc. I certainly *DO* know that
there is both good fat and bad fat."

"You do?"

"Yes, I do. Bad fat is when you look in the mirror and realize how chubby and unattractive you've become . . .

"Good fat is when you run into your ex who broke your
heart and dumped you for somebody else . . . and realize how
chubby and unattractive *they've* become."

My doctor was happy to report that the only thing that is
sick about me was my mind.

Good and bad.

Bad and good.

I once recall telling someone, "Did you hear about so-and-
so? They were in a car accident."

Their reply?

"Was it a bad accident?"

Huh? Seriously now, what accident *isn't* bad?

(Well, besides, "Hey, you got chocolate in my peanut butter!" "You got peanut butter in my chocolate!")

What answer did they expect to hear from me?

"Funny you should ask. Actually, it was very *good* accident.

"Thanks to the initial violent jolt and the subsequent flipping and rolling motion of the car, the car's CD player is working again . . .

"Aaaand, luckily for our friend, the guy who caused the accident happened to be a big movie producer who just happened
to be looking for someone to play the part of a bleeding para-
plegic in his next film!

"Talk about hitting the jackpot!"

Dating Service *(excerpt from L.A. Misérables)*
Day 551 -September 14, 1997

Remember that stupid questionnaire that I filled out and mailed in for the video dating service?

Big mistake.

A representative called me and said, "Paul, this is whoever from so-and-so dating service and I'm looking at the personal profile that you sent us . . . Are you interested in meeting intelligent, professional women in your area? We have over 7,000 members in the greater Los Angeles area alone, half of which are beautiful, successful women who are dying to meet someone like you . . . blah blah blah blah blah . . . "

I said, "Listen, before you waste your breath and go any farther, how much is this going to cost me?"

"The cost is a small price to pay to meet dozens of rich, horny, professional women who crave a man and live within five miles of your home . . . "

"How much is it going to cost me?"

"Our fees are competitive within the industry and much less in the long-run than, say, the price of hiring a comparable call-girl or jerking off on a 1-900 sex line, so let me go on . . . "

"Please, I would like to know how much is this all going to cost?"

"All this will cost you to join is an initial $200 deposit . . . that's all. Just $200 down to have access to hundreds of pillow-chested, sex-starved, moist, virgin, kinky, co-ed sluts who are looking for a man just like . . . "

"Whoa! Hold on! Why can't you tell me how much it's going to cost?

"As I said, if you put just $200 down . . . "

"Are you a car salesman? I put $200 down, then what? How much after that?

"Are there monthly payments? Is it a one-time fee? Can't you tell me?

"Is there a price list? . . . Do you charge by the pound? . . . Is it like a taxi? Do you keep a meter running while I'm out on the date? . . .

"Do you offer a flat-rate, like a long-distance service, 10 cents a minute? No charge if she's busy?

"Is it like renting a car? Can I get a girl with unlimited mileage? Is 'ugly insurance' available for an additional fee? Is there a weekend rate? If I want, can I upgrade to a better model?

"Do you give rebates if the girl has a bad-hair night or gained weight since she recorded her video? . . . Do you auction the women off? Do we bid? Is that how you determine the cost? . . . Do you have specials on women that aren't being asked out very often? . . . Do you have a warranty like Federal Express, 'She's absolutely guaranteed to be there overnight?'

"How about discounts on defective girls? You know, do you take a few bucks off if the woman you choose has a drug problem or has hang-ups because her perverted uncle Lester used to whip out 'Mr. Happy' when he babysat?

"Do you have irregular merchandise? Women who have one arm longer than the other or ladies who lean to the left a little?

"Do you work on commission? Do you only get paid a percentage of my cost for dinner if I get lucky? . . . Do you have sales, like, 'this week, all office workers and clerical staff 25% off" or 'From 5 to 6 o'clock redheads are 2 for 1 during Happy Hour!' Do you do that? . . . Why can't you tell me how much it's going to cost? Do you thieves make the price up as you go along?"

"Sir, if you insist on being difficult . . . "

"Being difficult? You're being evasive! I asked you a simple question! I don't trust anyone who can't give me a straight answer when I ask how much this is going to cost me!"

"Sir, I understand you're tense . . . it's obviously been a long time since you got laid or else you wouldn't have contacted us in the first place. If you could just calm down long enough to understand that cost is unimportant when we have literally thousands of uninhibited, cock-hungry, clean-shaved, sperm-swallowing, bisexual nymphomaniacs who love it in the ass and have been asking for you by name . . . "

(Click.)

Day 552 - September 15, 1997
(The next day)

Early this morning . . . just as I feared . . .

(Ringgggg.)

"Hello . . . "

"Hi, this is someone else from so-and-so dating service and I heard that you had a little problem with one of our representatives."

"I don't have a problem . . . You have a problem, because you're so deceptive about discussing your fees that I can't trust you people. So, if it's not top-secret, classified information, why don't you tell me . . . just how much does it cost?"

"Let's put it this way, sir . . . If you consider the typical price you pay, going into clubs looking for a date, only to be continually disappointed in the quality of women that you're meeting, relatively speaking, our costs are comparative to, say . . ."

(Click.)

(Ringgggg.)

" . . . for an insignificant preliminary deposit of only two hun . . . "

(Click.)

(Ringgggg.)

". . . PUSSY! LISTEN, WE HAVE PUSSY! DON'T HANG UP! ADMIT IT, YOU'RE A LONELY LOSER AND WE'RE YOUR ONLY HOPE!! HOW MUCH WOULD A WASHOUT LIKE YOU BE WILLING TO PAY FOR WILLING, HOT, YOUN . . . "

(Click.)

Hearty Ha Ha

My health insurance sucks.

I have $100,000 deductible and they will only cover me for illnesses contracted on the third Wednesday of an even week in an odd numbered month in a year divisible by seven when the moon is in Pisces within three years of the Chicago Cubs winning a World Series.

They didn't want to pay for my colonoscopy.

To get an exam I had to go down to Boston's Logan Airport, get in line at the security checkpoint, wrap my jacket around my head and yell, "ALLAH AKBAR!"

Believe me, they looked *everywhere*.

Now I'm worried. What if I need a major operation? Do you think those cheapskates are gonna cover me? No way!

This is my greatest fear . . . Someday, I'll need a heart transplant to keep me alive. My family will be waiting frantically outside the operating room at the hospital when the doctor comes out of surgery.

As the surgeon removes his rubber gloves, my worried mother says, "Doctor, is my son, Paul, all right?"

"Well, as you know ma'am, your son has shitty health insurance and, even though he desperately needed a heart transplant,

127

they absolutely refused to cover the costs of the operation, so my team of surgeons and I had to get creative in order to save his life.

"As a result, we have just performed the world's very first artichoke heart transplant."

(Stunned.) "Did I hear you correctly? You gave my son *an artichoke heart?*"

"Yes, we did, ma'am."

"I can't believe you gave my son *an artichoke heart!* . . . That's the most ridiculous thing I've ever heard. An artichoke heart . . . Was it a success?"

"Well . . . ummm . . . yes . . . and, uh, no."

(Concerned.) "Yes *and no?*"

"Correct, ma'am. The good news is, your son is alive . . ."

"And the bad news?"

"He's a vegetable."

Tattoos

Tattoos used to be cool, I guess, but now everyone has one so it's not like they make you unique anymore.

If you're an adult and you decide to get a tattoo, at least you can appreciate the permanence of them, but I don't think that some kids get it.

I saw a really skinny fifteen or sixteen year old girl walk by with a half-shirt that showed her bare midriff and she had a mural on her lower back of some dolphins frolicking in the waves.

I wanted to go over and shake her and say, "Hey honey, your tattoo looks great now, but I have news for you . . . a lot of people are skinny when they're sixteen.

"You better stay skinny.

"You better diet, and exercise, and lay off the fried foods, and turn down the desserts, and not eat late at night, and give up ice cream, and not snack and hit the gym on a regular basis for the rest of your life or those sleek dolphins who are playing in the surf are going to look like dimpled, old walruses beached on a cellulite-sandbar.

"EEEEEiiiiiiiiiii . . . EEEEEiiiiiiii . . ."

"What's that, Flipper?"

"EEEEEiiiiiiiiiiii . . . EEEEEiiiiiiii . . ."

"You say you're trapped inside a giant pair of high-waisted, cotton granny-panties? . . . I'll save you, little buddy! I'll save you!!!"

"EEEEEiiiiiiiiiiiii . . . EEEEEiiiiiiii . . ."

Chinese Zodiac

Know how sometimes they have those placemats in Chinese restaurants that have signs of the Chinese zodiac on them?

It tells you if you were born in the year of the lion, or the pig, or the dog, the rooster, the buffalo, the horse, the tiger, the goat, the snake, the dragon, the rat or the monkey.

And the placemat will give you information such as "Roosters are generous, hard-workers, born leaders, quick tempered and patient," etcetera.

It will also tell you which mates you are most compatible with, like for instance . . .

"The pig gets along best with the dog."

Or . . . "Stay away from the buffalo!" and "Avoid the horse!"

I met this girl once and we started to go out, but I couldn't tell if we were right for each other so, one night, I came home drunk and called a Chinese restaurant to ask if they could look at the place-mat to see if this girl and I were a good match.

The conversation went something like this.

(Chinese guy) "Herro . . . China Jade Palace. Prace you' o'der."

"Hi, I don't want to order food, I just need you to look on your place-mat and tell me if the rat is compatible with the monkey."

"No rat, no monkey . . . jus' cheecken, beef, pooork, shimp, and veg'able."

"No, you don't understand. I need to know if the rat gets along with the monkey."

"All out rat, no mo' monkey . . . just cheecken, beef, pooork, shimp, & veg'able. You o'der now."

"Just forget it."

"Anyting else?"

"As long as I have you on the phone . . . do you deliver?"

World's Worst Magician

One time, many years ago, somewhere in Manchester, New Hampshire, I was doing a show and had to follow a magician.

The young magician was doing his act and I was standing in the back with the owner of the club.

The magician was absolutely horrible . . . I mean *terrible.*

He was very unprofessional and every trick was a disaster.

Then he almost set the drapes on fire during his grand finale.

As I watched him frantically snuff out the flaming curtain, I said to the owner, "This moron has to be the worst fucking magician I have ever seen in my life."

The owner said, "That's my son."

I said, "Really? . . . He has potential."

Lei'd

I recently went to the island of Tahiti in the South Pacific when I was working on a cruise ship and, I think most of you know this, but when you arrive by airplane or by ship at some tropical islands, such as Hawaii or Tahiti, it is often a tradition to be greeted by one or more native women who welcome you by placing a string of fresh flowers around your neck.

These flowers are called a "lei."

Now, this is when most novice, wannabe hack amateur comedians would use this opportunity to get a cheap laugh by saying that tired, old, worn-out joke that you've heard a million times about how they got "lei'd" on the island.

"Yeah, I got 'lei'd' on Tahiti!"

It's so stupid . . . So obvious . . . So juvenile.

I want you people to know that I am *NOT* one of those hacks who would make a stupid joke about getting "lei'd" on the island.

Not because I'm a good comedian.

No, because, when it was my turn to get my lei, the woman with the flowers looked at me and said, "You know, I'm sorry but I just can't do this . . . I have a splitting headache, I'm crampy and, besides, I have to get-up really early for work to-morrow morning."

Then she skipped me and went to the next person in line.

So I couldn't even get "lei'd" on Tahiti.

What If?

Want to piss-off a comedian . . . guaranteed?

Do this.

When you are introduced to a professional comic, make

sure you open-up the dialogue by challenging him with, "So, you're a comedian? . . . Say something funny."

And, for a lawyer, there isn't a more annoying infringement on your precious leisure time than to be relentlessly hounded for your gratuitous legal opinion.

Every summer for many years, my childhood friend Tony has a big bocce tournament at his home in my neighborhood, "The Gulch," and hundreds of people attend, most of whom I know personally . . . for better or worse. Every year I would show up, but I would never stay long because I would inevitably get inundated with an endless barrage of legal questions from inebriated locals who were looking for free advice. And, every year, I would eventually get fed up and surreptitiously slip out the back, unnoticed.

Here's a typical conversation, (multiplied times ten)

One of my brother's friends would come up to me, all fidgety and jumpy, and constantly sniffling and fiddling with his nose.

"Hey Paul, what's up? Mind if I ask you a legal question?"

"What is it?"

"OK, let me give you a hypothetical situation . . . you know, just like a 'what if?' kinda situation that's like totally make-believe, you know what I mean?"

"Yeah, go ahead."

"All right, so say this guy . . . not me, just some guy . . . say this made-up guy was driving his car . . . let's say, for the sake of argument, on maybe Farm Street, you know right near the high school just before Nahant Street . . . you know, hypothetically speaking.

"Now let's imagine that this make-believe guy gets pulled over by the cops, for instance, because, let's say, his registration was expired, even though this totally imaginary dude never got notified by the registry even though he had been living at the same place on the West Side for over ten years, but that's another story."

"Go on."

"Anyway, so then what if, hypothetically, the cops ask to see this made-up guy's papers and the guy . . . not me but the fictitious guy in the story . . . goes to get his paperwork out of the glove compartment and a bag of cocaine falls out onto the floor mat . . . Am I fucked or what?"

I said, "No, *you're* not in any trouble at all . . . but that poor bastard in the story? He is *definitely* fucked . . . big time . . . OK, gotta go. I have an early show. Good luck with your case. Bye-bye!"

Babysitting Service

I have never been married and I have no children, so I know absolutely *nothing* about kids and my lack of experience with children can lead to some embarrassing situations.

One time I was out in public with a bunch of people when I had to cover my eyes and look away.

They said, "What is it? What's wrong Paul? Is something the matter?"

I continued to shield my eyes.

"I'm sorry, but can't even look. I hate to see that. That is just so sad."

"What's so sad, Paul?"

"Over there . . . the little kid in the wheelchair. His parents have to push him around because he can't walk on his useless little legs. It breaks my heart to see it."

They said, "You idiot, Paul, that's not a wheelchair . . . it's a baby stroller."

"It doesn't matter what you want to call it, it's still tragic."

As you can probably imagine, I have little patience with children.

I once visited some friends who had a little baby boy. The kid was sitting in his high-chair when they asked if I would watch him while they went out jogging.

I have news for you . . . anyone who leaves their kid with me should be immediately investigated by social services because I have no clue when it comes to caring for babies.

"We'll be back in less than a half hour, Paul. He shouldn't give you any problem."

I said, "Are you sure you want to do this? I don't know how to take care of a kid . . . and I have never changed a diaper in my entire *life!*"

The wife said, "You have *never* changed a diaper, Paul?"

"No, I haven't, and I don't plan on doing so any time soon . . . in fact, I don't even like to wipe my *own* ass."

"Don't worry, Paul. I just changed his diaper and if he starts to cry, just feed him some baby food . . . Here are some strained carrots you can give him."

Of course, as soon as they walked out the door the kid went ballistic.

"WHAAAAAAAAAAAAAAAAAAAAAAAAAAAAAAAA!!!!!! . . . . . . WHAAAAAAAAAAAAAAAAAAAA!!!!!"

I remembered what they told me and got the baby food out but, when I tried to feed it to him, the kid clamped his mouth shut and folded his little arms defiantly.

Even though I was inexperienced with babies, I did know what to do when a kid won't eat because I have seen other parents do this with their children. "OK, let's try this . . . Here comes the choo-choo train . . . choo-choo-choo . . . it's going in the tunnel . . . choo-choo . . . Here it comes, open up!"

But nothing. The kid refused to open his mouth . . .

"Come on, kid. The choo-choo can't get through the tunnel

unless you open it up . . . choo-choo . . . Here comes the choo-choo train . . . choo-choo, choo-choo . . ."

No way. He continued to defy me and I was losing patience really fast.

"Let's go, you little brat . . . You're making Uncle Paul very upset . . . so open up the stupid tunnel now! . . . Choo-choo, choo-choo . . ."

Nothing. He wouldn't cooperate. And, to make things worse, he was giving me a bratty little smirk, to let me know he was winning.

Finally, after five frustrating minutes, the kid was done playing his little game and opened his mouth expecting to eat but, by that time, I was so pissed-off that I missed his little mouth and smeared the strained carrots all over his face.

"Sorry kid . . . *Amtrak!*"

'Perfect 10'

It's funny how your standards change as you get older.

For example, dating . . .

When I was a young man, if you had asked me, "Paul, what makes a girl a 'perfect 10?' "

I would have answered, "A 'perfect 10?' That's easy . . . A 'perfect 10' is a really pretty girl with a great body."

Simple. Right?

But, as you get older, things get more complicated because, after you've been in a few relationships, your priorities change and it's not only about just looks anymore. You start to take other factors into consideration.

I went on a blind date recently and was out to dinner at a restaurant with a woman that I was meeting for the first time. She was telling me all about herself, going on and on, "Blah

135

blah blah . . ." but, the whole time, in my head, I was thinking, "Ehh, this girl's not very pretty. On a scale of 1 to 10 she's, uhh, maaaybe a 4 on a good day. Sorry, but I'm really not that interested in her."

But she kept talking, "Blah blah blah . . ." until I heard, ". . . and I've been so tired because I've been working two full-time jobs . . ."

Suddenly, I reconsidered and thought to myself, "Oooh! . . . Wait a second! Did this girl just say that she has two incomes? I wonder what it would be like to go out with a woman who isn't whining to me every month, going, 'Paul, I just bounced another check! They're gonna shut my phone off if I don't pay, but I don't have it right now. Don't worry, I'll pay you back, Paul, I promise . . . along with the other money I owe you. I didn't forget.'

"That sure would be a nice change. You know, maybe this girl is not quite as bad as I thought she was. She seemed like only a 4 at first but, if you add those two incomes, she's really more like a 6."

And she kept talking, "Blah blah blah . . ." until she said, "You didn't know I have a twin sister? Oh yeah, we're identical twins, but we're nothing alike . . . My sister can be a little *wild and crazy*. I really have to watch her around my boyfriends because she's been known to . . . well . . . oh, never mind."

And I thought, "Oooh, that's worth 2 points, right there!. . . This girl is getting better looking before my eyes! She might be a 6 but, if you add the identical twins, she's actually looking more like an 8 now. I am impressed!"

And she continued, "Blah blah blah . . ." until she mentioned, ". . . and I have these two Siamese cats that can be mean and they scratch a lot and totally destroy the house, but they're my baaaabies and they sleep with me every single night."

And I thought, "Oh, great. That's all I need . . . sharing a

136

bed with her and those two frisky felines while my privates are dangling out there like a tantalizing little mouse toy from Petco. What could possibly go wrong there? . . . Scratch off a point for each one of those two psycho cats and this chick's back to a 6 again. This just isn't going to work."

And she went on, "Blah blah blah . . ." until I heard her say, ". . . and my parents just sold their business for a lotttttt of money and now they're looking to buy a really big house on the ocean . . ."

And I considered, "Whoa! What's that? . . . She's got two rich parents? You know, this girl's not that attractive, but I bet she'd look a hell of a lot prettier with ocean waves crashing in the background. This girl had been a 6 but, if you add those two wealthy parents, she's back up to an 8 again. I think I'm really starting to like her."

Until . . .

". . . and I'm so busy, I just can't find the time to work out or exercise anymore and I can see the difference. I'm *so* disgusted . . ."

I looked her over.

"Hold on a second. Is that a double-chin? This girl's really letting herself go. I guess I was wrong about her. She's certainly no 8 . . . If you subtract those two chins, she's maybe a 6 at best. That's it, I'm outta here. One and done, baby."

That was, until . . .

"You're a Patriots fan, Paul? No kidding! Me too! I have two season tickets, right on the 50-yard line! They're amazing seats! You'll have to come to a game with me."

And I thought to myself, "Are you serious? . . . two seats on the 50? Oooh, that just improved my eyesight considerably! Now that I get a better look at her, this girl's actually a lot prettier than I thought. She might be a 6, but if you add on those two tickets, she's gotta be at least an 8."

And . . .

" . . . and there was a time when I thought about trying out for the cheerleaders because I'm double-jointed . . . I'm still pretty flexible. I can still get my leg and put it behind my head."

That got my attention.

"Did I hear that right? . . . She's double-jointed? Wait a second . . . If this girl is an 8 and you add her double-joints . . . (Counting on my fingers) . . . Oh my God, this girl is a perfect 10!!! I have found my dream girl! It's true love . . . I hear wedding bells! Start printing up the invitations! I have found my soul mate."

And everything was good, until . . .

"Blah blah blah . . . and I don't care what anyone says, I think President Obama is doing a *fantastic* job."

OK, that's minus 10, right there.

Game over.

"Waiter! . . . Oh, waiter! Over here. Check please!"

Hugh Hefner *(an excerpt from L.A. Misérables)*
Day 184 - September 12, 1996

Playboy magazine was a part of my life growing-up.

I was watching A&E channel's *Biography* tonight and the subject was Hugh Hefner who built the Playboy Empire.

Some people admire him. Some people resent him. Some people are jealous of him. But the truth is that many would consider him to be the luckiest man alive.

Hugh is getting along in age and, from time to time, the thought must go through his mind that there is no possibility that the Kingdom of Heaven can be any better than his life on earth.

There's no way that Hugh Hefner will enter the pearly gates

and some saint will direct him to a mansion where hundreds of the most beautiful, and sexual liberated, large-breasted women in the entire world walk around half-naked in lingerie and string bikinis, and are at his disposal twenty-four hours a day.

And he doesn't even have to wear a necktie to work. He can just lounge around in his silk pajamas, throw parties, fondle women and sip cocktails.

Heaven has *got* to be a letdown for him.

If there is any equity in life, what kind of horrific past lives do you have to endure to get Hef's gig on this earth?

What kind of suffering would he have to experience to be blessed with every man's fantasy life?

I can picture God going over an unborn child's past-life chart with St. Peter.

"Let's see . . . oh, my my . . . this poor guy really got a raw deal."

"Why do you say that, Lord?"

"Well, it says here that he made his debut as early man and met a horrific death when he was eaten alive by a giant Tyrannosaurus Rex."

"Terrible . . . terrible."

"But that's just the beginning. In his next life he worked as a slave on the pyramids of Egypt. Hard labor, eighteen hours a day in 110 degree heat for thirty years until his death by whipping."

"Tragic."

"Just wait . . . it gets worse. Upon reincarnation as a Roman, he lost his home and family in the volcano at Pompeii, then he was a galley slave, rowing a ship until he was eaten by a lion in the Coliseum."

"So unfortunate."

"But there's more. In his subsequent lives he got the Bubonic Plague, was beheaded during the French Revolution, then was burned as a witch in Salem, took a musket ball in the groin during the Civil War, spent one of his lives as the Elephant Man, went down on the *Titanic*, was imprisoned in Auschwitz, . . . and, whoa, look at this! The poor guy! . . . He's scheduled to become the fifth Beatle!"

"He's going to be Pete Best? Oooooooh . . . now *that*'s a rough one."

"Whew! Talk about getting the shaft! How did this poor bastard slip through the cracks? He really got a bum deal."

"What do you think Peter? Let's give him that big mansion, silk pajamas and beautiful naked women thing we've been saving? I'd say he deserves it!"

"Wait, wait . . . one last touch to really put it over the top, as an added bonus, right around the time when he's getting too old to do it . . . we'll let them invent Viagra!"

"Brilliant!"

The show informed us that Hef personally chooses the centerfold each month.

I guess that's not a job you retire from so that you can play more golf.

CHAPTER 6:
SOME MORE FUNNY STUFF

Clay

One late afternoon I was covering for Freddie Cronin at the District Court Session in Peabody District Court (I was the supervisor of the jury session) and had to handle the arraignments and bail hearings for a group of prisoners the police had just transported from lock-up.

The "dock" where they kept the prisoners was in the right-hand corner, way in the back of the courtroom and, as I sat at the prosecutor's desk, I couldn't help myself from continually turning completely around to stare at the beautiful blonde girl they had in custody. She was absolutely stunning, looked just like Marilyn Monroe, had a killer body, and I couldn't keep my eyes off of her.

There were a bunch of police officers from the city of Lynn standing around next to my desk and I could hear them chuckling.

"You like her, Paul?"

I turned back around. "Are you shitting me? Of course I do, she's gorgeous!"

They all laughed.

"That's Clay."

"Huh?"

"That's Clay. It's a guy."

"Huh?"

"She's a he."

I said, "No fuckin' way! Not in a million years! That's one of the prettiest girls I've ever seen, I don't believe you. It can't be a guy. Impossible! No way!"

They giggled.

"If that's a girl, Paul, then why is she handcuffed to all the other men?"

"Shit, you're right! Wow! OK, I believe you, but I have to say, he . . . she . . . *whatever* is gorgeous!"

One of the cops said, "You want to hear a funny Clay story, Paul?"

"I'm all ears."

"All the guys on the vice squad know Clay because we've arrested him a bunch of times for soliciting and we picked him up again last night. Clay just got breast implants and he was very proud of them so, while he was under arrest in the back of the cruiser, he kept lifting up his shirt and going, 'Hey boys, do you like my new breasts?'

"Yes Clay, they're very nice, now please put your shirt down.

"When we got to the station, the sergeant was booking him and he did it again. 'Sarge, how do you like my new breasts? I just got them. Aren't they nice?'

"Yes Clay, now keep your clothes on.

"And he did it to anyone walking by . . . 'Hey guys, check these out!'

"While this was going on I went into one of the adjacent offices and Rick Donnelly was doing some paperwork. He said, 'Hey, what's all the commotion about out there?'

"I told him, 'There's a pretty girl who's showing everyone her boobs.'

142

"Rick said, 'No way! Are you serious?'

"I said, 'Yeah. All you have to do is say *Show me your tits* and she'll lift her shirt up for you.'

"Rick got all excited and said, 'Wow! I'll go out there as soon as I get finished typing up this report.'

"Anyway, while Rick was busy typing the police report, they finished the booking process and brought he/she downstairs to the holding cell for his/her court appearance in the morning. Right after Clay was taken away, another woman walked into the station to report a sexual assault and she was told to wait on the bench for the detective.

"While she was sitting on the bench, sobbing and wiping away tears with a Kleenex, Rick poked his head in the door with a big smile on his face and saw her sitting there.

"Before we could stop him, he yelled out, 'HEY BABY, SHOW ME YOUR TITS!'

"The poor woman burst into tears and we spent the rest of the night apologizing to her."

In life, as in comedy, timing is everything.

The Coconut

I can remember being a little kid and going grocery shopping with my dad. We were in the produce aisle and my younger brother Jay and I were pleading over and over again, "Dad, will buy us a coconut? . . . We want a coconut! . . . Please buy us a coconut . . . We want you to get us a coconut . . . Please dad, will buy a coconut? . . . We never had a coconut . . . Can we get a coconut? . . . Pleeeeeeease?"

I guess he was tired of listening to our relentless whining, so our dad bought us a coconut.

"Yeah! Dad bought us a coconut! . . . He's our hero! . . . We have the best dad! He got us a coconut!" And we started singing, *"Dad got us a coconut, dad got us a coconut, dad got us a coconut!"* and *"2-4-6-8- who do we appreciate? . . . Dad! Yeah!"*

Forty-five minutes after we got home, my brother Jay and I were moping around in the garage, dejected, moaning, "Daaaaad, when are you going to open up the coconut?"

Meanwhile my father (who had already unsuccessfully tried using a screwdriver, a ball-peen hammer and a wood-chisel) now had the coconut locked in a vise while he was smacking it with his nine-iron and yelling . . .

"BE QUIET OR I'LL GIVE YOU KIDS A DAMN CO-CONUT . . . RIGHT OFF THE FRIGGIN' HEAD!"

Decisions, Decisions

I think women are trying to slowly and systematically drive men crazy over time because, if they make us lose our collective minds, then women can control us.

It sounds farfetched but it's the only explanation I can think of for their otherwise illogical behavior.

Case in point:

Has this ever happened to you?

(Man): "Let's go out to eat. My treat."

(Wife or girlfriend): "OK."

"What do you feel like? Where do you want to go?"

"I don't care."

"No, honey, please pick a place to eat."

"It doesn't matter to me. I don't really care where we eat."

"I know what you're like. Just tell me, what kind of food do you want?"

"I told you, I really don't care. We can go anywhere you want to go. I'm not even that hungry . . . You pick a place.

Whatever you decide is fine."

"Are you sure?"

"Positive."

"Positive? . . . OK then, let's get Chinese food."

"No."

"What's wrong with Chinese? I thought you just said that you didn't care where we eat."

"Just not Chinese. *Anything* else but Chinese."

"OK, we'll go to an Italian restaurant."

"I don't really feel like Italian tonight."

"But you said . . ."

"Just pick something else."

"Alright, let's go to a seafood restaurant."

"No, not seafood, I had fish for lunch."

"How am I supposed to know that? I'm not a mind reader . . . Wanna go to the Mexican place?"

"I don't like Mexican food!"

"Sushi?"

"Ugh! You know I don't eat sushi!"

"Fast food?"

"Fattening. It's not good for you."

"Thai?"

"Be serious."

"Barbeque?"

"I'd rather starve."

"Pizza?"

"Ehhh . . . I'm sick of pizza."

"OK, we're getting nowhere. Can't you just pick someplace?"

"See . . . this is exactly what I keep telling you. You never listen to me . . . How many times did I tell you, I don't CARE where we go? Why is it so difficult for you to make a decision? I like a man who can take charge of a situation."

"All right, that's enough. You want me to make a decision? OK, here's my decision . . . Forget the Chinese food.

"Why don't you get into your car, drive to the supermarket, grab a shopping cart, walk up and down all the aisles picking out groceries, wait in the long line at the checkout, pay for the groceries *with your own money*, load the bags into the car, drive home, carry all the groceries inside, set the table, whip up a salad, prepare the meal, throw something on the stove, put some other stuff in the oven, serve the meal, take a couple minutes to eat before you clear the table, top it off with some nice desert and pot of coffee, then clear the table again, wash all the dirty dishes, clean the kitchen and put everything away when you're done?

"What do you think about that?"

"Hmmmmmmm . . . I think I'll get the Crab Rangoon, Pork Fried Rice and Chicken Chow Mein."

"I thought so."

Bummed Bum

No matter how bad you think you have it, remember . . . there is always someone worse off than you.

Have you ever been sitting at a traffic light and have a homeless person approach your car begging for money?

I was in traffic once and there was a poor guy begging on the side of the road who was totally disgusting.

He was filthy and gross and dressed in rags. He stunk to high heaven, his hair was all matted, there were flies buzzing around him and he was wearing a sign that said,

HOMELESS

LOST JOB

LOST FAMILY

SICK WITH NO HEALTH INSURANCE
BROKE AND HUNGRY
HAVEN'T EATEN IN DAYS
PLEASE HELP

The bum approached my car and I felt really bad for the poor guy, so I took out my wallet, hoping I had some singles, and handed him a dollar bill.

He said thank you and I waited to go, but traffic was all backed-up and, when the light changed, nobody could move, so I was stuck there with this homeless guy standing in the street next to my open car window.

I kept looking straight ahead with my hands on the steering wheel, muttering to myself, "OK, this is getting uncomfortable now, let's go! . . . Get me outta here now!"

It was an awkward situation.

Once I realized that neither the homeless guy nor I was going anywhere fast, I wanted to be nice, so I made a decision to try and make conversation with him.

Without thinking, *this* is the best I could come up with . . .

"So, how are things going?"

As soon as I said it I cringed, realizing what a stupid thing that was for me to say.

How did I expect him to answer?

"How am I doing? So nice of you to ask.

"Let's see, I only have one tooth left . . . and it's loose.

"I'm infested with the crab lice so bad I walk sideways.

"It smells like I'm raising a family of skunks in my pants.

"I have sucked down so much car exhaust on the side of the road that I'm coughing up charcoal briquettes.

"My feet are rotting like three-week-old bananas.

"And I'm using my shorts as a Port-O-Potty as we speak."

"But . . . thanks to the *BUCK* you generously gave me, Mr. Trump, happy days are here again and my future is looking rosy!"

Thankfully, all he did was grunt something incomprehensible and the light finally changed.

Whew!

Modern Sports Heroes

Sports heroes aren't what they used to be.

Not all of the athletes are exactly what you would call great role models for the kids.

Professional sports used to be a great escape from the pressures of everyday life but, lately, following sports is becoming a little too much like the reality we're trying to escape. So many professional athletes are being arrested for heinous crimes, getting busted for drugs, beating their wives, choking their coaches, complaining about their multi-million dollar salaries and generally acting like spoiled assholes, that reading the sports page is getting as depressing as reading the headlines.

I saw that a Major League Baseball player just set the world record for the most hits in one day with an incredible total of 22 hits.

It's true. Here's the breakdown . . .

The player got 3 singles in his baseball game . . . that's 3 hits.

After the game, he and his entourage hit 3 nightclubs . . . that would be 6 hits.

In the limo, between clubs, he took 4 hits off of a joint . . . that equals 10 hits.

Then the ballplayer hit on 5 different women . . . now he's up to 15 hits.

This wasn't a big hit with one of the girl's boyfriend . . .

So the player ended up hitting the jealous boyfriend . . . that's 16 hits.

And then got hit himself, by 2 bouncers . . . we're talking 18 hits.

He got hit with charges of assault and battery and disorderly conduct . . . up to 20 hits.

Then the league hit him with both a 2 game suspension and a $10,000 fine . . . for a grand total of 22 hits.

About the only thing that *didn't* take a hit was his popularity, because we expect so little from our heroes these days.

I predict the record won't last long.

Terrorist's Computer

I read in the newspaper that the CIA arrested a group of suspected terrorists that were part of an Al Qaeda "sleeper cell" here in the United States.

The article also mentioned that the federal agents seized the terrorists' computer, which could yield important information about their terrorist activities.

So, I was wondering . . . just what does a terrorist's computer look like?

Are there icons on his desk-top that look like this?

NUKES   HIT-LIST   FLIGHT SCHOOLS   PORN

TARGETS   SECRET HIDEOUTS   SUICIDE SCHEDULE   DIRTY BOMBS

Will they find porn that has been downloaded on his computer?

And what does Taliban porn look like? Are there photos of women wearing burkas, seductively pulling down their eye-hole to show some nose-cleavage?

Do terrorists use Quicken Finance or Turbo-Tax software? What would their balance sheet look like?

EXPENSES

Razorblades:	$0.00
Shoes:	$0.00
Deodorant:	$0.00
Toothpaste:	$0.00
Dental Floss:	$0.00
Timer:	$50.00
Detonator:	$120.00
Weapons-Grade Plutonium:	$3,000,000,000.00

I'm sure the CIA will intercept many e-mail messages. If so, do terrorists have screen-names like FanaticOne@Earthlink.net or Madman666@aol.com?

I'd like to see their Buddy List . . .

- Osama bin Laden
- Mahmoud Ahmadinejad
- Hugo Chavez
- Muammar Gaddafi
- Sean Penn

Maybe they'll find a personal ad for an online dating service . . .

SINGLE MALE TERRORIST:

Father of 47; swarthy, hirsute terrorist with uni-brow, permanent 5 o'clock shadow and shifty eyes; my friends describe me as having a lust for life (as well as a lust for the death of many others) I'm into plotting, scheming, torturing, bombing and mini-golf. Seeking a subservient woman who can take an occasional beating for an extremely short-term relationship. Face and body type not important, but must have nice eyes. Must like to travel, often on very short-notice. Helps if you are suicidal and can fly an airplane. (No freaks or weirdos.)

* * *

Sleaze, Please

Just to put things into perspective, do you realize that lawyers are the only profession of which someone could say . . .

"What do you think of attorney so-and-so?"

"Him? He's a low-down, rotten, lying, sneaky, shifty, deceitful, underhanded, devious, crooked, corrupt, back-stabbing, ruthless, arrogant, relentless, hard-headed, stubborn, insensitive, conceited, egotistical, contemptuous, condescending, little prick."

"Would you hire him for yourself?"

"For myself? Absolutely . . . In a second."

Life in the Fast Lane

Did this ever occur to you?

If we have now been blessed with so many, so-called "time-saving" devices, why is it that no one ever seems to have any free time anymore?

Do you ever wonder where the time goes?

You'll run into an old friend and exclaim, "Hey! How have you been? I haven't seen you for months!"

And he replies, "Months? What are you talking about? It's been at least two or three years since the last time we got together!"

"Two or three years? No way! Are you serious? Has it really been that long? Wow, where the hell does the time go?"

I'll tell where the time goes . . . The pace of our lives has become so hectic and fast-paced that it's very easy for people to lose track of time.

Everyone is always in such a big hurry.

The following account could be a typical, frenzied, 24-hour day for any working person in this day and age.

The night before a work day you set your alarm clock early enough to give yourself plenty of time to take a long, leisurely shower, make yourself a nice, healthy breakfast and take your time getting to work without having to rush.

But . . . BZZZZZZZZZZZZZ . . . when the alarm goes off, you are so exhausted from the day before . . . and the day before that . . . and before that . . . that you sleepily say to yourself, "What's another five minutes?" and hit the snooze button.

Five-minutes later . . . BZZZZZZZZZZZZZ . . . the alarm goes off again and you think to yourself, "It really doesn't have to be a long, leisurely shower, I can make it a quick one" and press the snooze button again.

When the alarm goes off again, five minutes later . . . BZZZZZZZZZZZZZ . . . you convince yourself, "You know, screw it, I don't really need a big breakfast . . . " and you whack 'snooze' again.

Five-minutes later . . . BZZZZZZZZZZZZZ . . . the alarm goes off yet again and you reason with yourself, "If I drive really fast and take a short-cut to work, I think I can still make it on time" and hit the snooze button one more time . . .

Until . . . BZZZZZZZZZZZZZ . . . five-minutes later when the alarm goes off and you scream, "OH SHIT! I'M RE-ALLY LATE NOW!" . . . and jump out of bed in a flash.

You run into bathroom and think, "I don't have time to

take a shower, so I'll use this Speed-Stick on my underarms and put Rapid Shave on my face."

You quickly pick-up the Mach III razor from Gillette . . . but three times the speed of sound is just not going to be fast enough this morning, so you grab the new Mach IV *Turbo* . . . *Faster than a speeding bullet!* . . . zip!! zip! zip! . . . and, suddenly, you're ready . . .

. . . to run downstairs and surmise, "I'm running late . . . but I can use the instant hot water to make instant oatmeal and instant coffee and wash it all down with a Carnation Instant Breakfast . . . and then I'll need to take a big instant *crrrrap* because all that instant stuff is gonna go instantly through me . . .

. . . and you eventually bolt out of the bathroom, jump in your car and fly out of the driveway . . . only to get stuck in bumper-to-bumper traffic . . . which will cause you to be quick-tempered, because you're wondering why you spent an extra $15,000 for a turbocharged car that does 140 miles per hour and accelerates 0 to 60 in less than 5 seconds . . . just so you can get stuck in traffic, every single day, that never goes more than 15 miles per hour or 20 feet at a time.

HONNNNNNNK!!!

"LET'S GO PEOPLE! I'M LATE FOR WORK!"

You wish you could use the carpool lane so you could go faster, but you just don't have time to pick anyone up in the morning.

"WHAT'S THE PROBLEM PEOPLE!!! . . . LET'S MOVE IT!!!"

Then you finally arrive at your job, dart in, and immediately go to work on a brand-new computer that was only purchased six months ago . . . and is already obsolete.

"This computer is like molasses! It took me over 15-seconds to download this four-hundred page document from Hong Kong, translate it into English, and print it out . . . I can't work with this . . . this . . . *DINOSAUR!*"

Then, before you know it, it's lunchtime.

You have to hustle during lunch because you only have an hour to run all the errands that you don't have time to do the rest of the day, which includes dropping your clothes off at a 1-hour dry-cleaners and bringing your photos to Walgreens for 1-hour photo printing . . .

"When will those pictures be ready?"

"In one hour."

"That's right, I should have known that!"

You scurry out of the store and need to grab a quick bite to eat, so you go through the drive-through at a fast-food restaurant, order the express lunch, and gulp it down in a hurry because, before you have to rush back to work, you need to stop at the drive-thru express-banking window to make a Quick-Cash withdrawal.

Taking a brief moment to glance at the receipt, you say to the teller, "Hey, there's no money in my account!"

And, through the speaker, she informs you, "We knew you were in a big hurry, so we spent it for you."

"Great, thanks . . . That sure saves me a lot of time! This really *is* a full-service bank."

Then you burn rubber out of the bank because you're running late to get back to work and, after you sprint inside the building, your boss is there to inquire, "Where the hell have you been?"

"I'm sorry boss. I got tied-up near the Jiffy Lube and Speedy Muffler."

"OK, but I just wrote this important letter and I need you to get it to our big client as soon as possible."

"OK boss, I'll mail it right away. It will be there in three days."

"No, that's too slow."

"OK boss, I'll send it Priority Mail. It will be there in two days."

"Not fast enough."

"OK boss, I'll overnight it. It will be there in the morning."

"Still not fast enough."

"No problem, I'll fax it . . . but, remember, we have a slow paper feed."

"You're right, you better e-mail them instead."

"You know what, boss? I'm one step ahead of you . . . I just hired a full-time psychic in secretarial. You know that letter you just wrote? . . . They got it *yesterday*. They're waiting to hear from you."

"Good thinking! You're on the fast-track in this company!"

The day races by and the next thing you know, it's quitting time . . .

"Oooh, 5 o'clock already!? . . . I gotta fly out of there because I have a date with my girlfriend who I met when I was speed-dating."

So you rush out of the building . . . rush out to your car in a big rush . . . but get stuck in rush-hour traffic listening to Rush Limbaugh on the radio . . . or the band Rush . . . or some people talking about Russia . . .

"Wow! What a rush!"

But now you have to get gas . . . so you use your Mobil Speed-Pass and then run into the Quik-Mart to play the lottery.

"I'll have a Quick-Pick . . . When's the drawing?"

"Wednesday."

"Wednesday? Not soon enough. I can't wait until then, I need money right now . . . Give me a scratch ticket and hurry-up, I'm running late!"

As you're sprinting back to your car, you're approached by a guy who's trying to make a fast buck . . .

"Hey man, you wanna buy some speed?"

"What are you, nuts?! Get outta my way! I don't have time to do speed! . . . Can't you see I'm in a hurry? Back off!"

You fly home, make a mad dash for your house . . . and realize that you haven't had any free time to work out lately, so you go through your collection of workout videos . . .

"Let's see . . . What do I have? OK . . . '3-Minute Abs,' . . . hmmm . . . '7-Minute Biceps,' . . . I don't know . . . or '10-Minute Aerobics,' . . . hmmm.

"Ahhh, screw it . . . Let's see, 3 + 7 + 10 equals . . . I'll just take a 20-minute nap.

21 minutes later . . .

"Oh shit! I overslept by a minute! Now I'm behind schedule!

"I have to make dinner . . . Let's see what I have in the fridge . . . Minute Rice aaaaand minute steaks . . . Damn, I slept late. I don't have a whole minute. I'll just put them in the microwave and they'll be ready in 30 seconds."

DING!

"I can wash it down with some Nestlé's Quick but, starting next week, Slim Fast!"

Then, all of a sudden, you start to hyperventilate and feel dizzy, and that's when you realize, "Oh my God. I have been rushing around so much, I think I'm having an anxiety attack."

You're still anxious, but then you look at your watch and say to yourself, "You know, I really don't have time to have an anxiety attack right now. I just can't fit it into my busy schedule!"

Then you suddenly remember, "Oh shit, I was supposed to call my girlfriend!" . . . so you speed-dial her and hurriedly explain, "Yeah, honey, I'm hurrying, I'm sorry I got held up. I'm doing the best I can . . . OK, OK, I'll come right over and we can watch a movie."

So you jump back in your car and race to her house as fast

as you can, only to hear, "Where the hell have you been?"

"I'm sorry, but I got here as fast as I could."

"You're late!"

"I'm sorry, but I had to go the speed limit because there were two speed traps, five speed bumps and an accident in the high-speed-lane.

"Come one, we'll watch a movie . . . Look, they have that old Keanu Reeves movie, *Speed,* on demand. It's really exciting . . . If the bus goes under 50-miles per hour, it will blow-up!"

But she reminds you, "I have to get up early for work tomorrow. If we watch that movie, we won't have time to fool around."

"That's OK, honey, we'll watch the whole movie on fast-forward! . . . Look, the movie is even more exciting when you watch it this way! Now the bus is going twice as fast and Keanu only has 1/2 the time to save all the people on it!"

As soon as the movie's over, you immediately ask your girl-friend, "We got through that film pretty fast, do we have time to fool around?"

"You know I need to get up early. If we do it, it will have to be a quickie."

And you reply, "This is your lucky day! I suffer from premature ejaculation! . . . I finished while we were undressing!"

"Good, it's late. Now let's go to sleep. I set the alarm a little earlier so we don't have to rush in the morning."

Then you finally close your eyes and fall asleep, totally exhausted . . .

. . . and the next sound you hear is . . .

BZZZZZZZZZZZZZZ . . .

. . . and you start all over again.

And *THAT'S* where the time goes.

Shovel Ready Job

For five summers, when I was home on break from college, I worked at the Wakefield Public Works with the Water and Sewer Department basically digging ditches, mostly installing water mains and services, as well as sewer connections, to local homes.

State and city workers have a universal reputation for being lazy. A rep like that is usually based in fact and our town workers were no different. The temporary summer help did a great deal of the physical labor but none of us really minded because we were young, strong and in good shape, so using a pick and shovel and jack hammering were just another way of working out. Even so, I was constantly looking for any opportunity to goof off.

One day we were working at a job site, laying down a new water service line from the water main under the street into a house on Montrose Avenue, not far from my parents' home. The crew needed someone to make a coffee run for our morning break and I was anxious to volunteer . . . not only because it was an excuse to screw off, but it was also a chance to practice driving the challenging, manual stick-shift transmission in the old, beat-up, town pick-up truck, which was really tough to master.

I got the coffee list from the guys, hopped in the cab, turned the key and put the truck in gear, but I had mistakenly jammed the transmission into reverse instead of drive and the pick-up bolted backward, running over all of the shovels and rakes that were lying directly behind it. I jumped out of the truck and saw that the handles on most of the tools were splintered. The guys were laughing their asses off, but I was horrified.

"What are we going to do now?"

The foreman said, "You're going to have to get on the radio and tell the barn what you did."

"But they're going to think I'm an asshole for breaking all the shovels!"

"That's because you are, Paul."

Oh great. I reluctantly got on the truck's radio and, just my luck, I was answered by the director of the whole public works department, Dick Boutiette.

Sheepishly, I said, "Hi, this is Paul down at the job site. I had a little problem. I'm learning to drive the stick shift in the pick-up and, by accident, I backed over all the shovels and broke the handles. What should we do?"

Without missing a beat, he answered, "You'll have to lean on each other until the new shovels get there."

Hilarious.

Movie Review *(an excerpt from L.A. Misérables)*
Day 114 - July 2, 1996

Since I moved to Hollywood I have tried to digest everything I can about the film industry and its mechanizations. One of the things I'm learning is that newly released movies put a big premium on critic's reviews and display excerpts from the reviews prominently in the full-page ads that appear in the Calendar section daily. I also suspect that any portion of a quote from a review can be manipulated like a resume. You don't have to lie, but through creative editing and modifying the context, you can make the best of a bad situation.

For example, if Paul D'Angelo, arts and entertainment critic for the *LA Newz,* or some newspaper, wrote:

> *"When the director of this stink-bomb excuse for a movie makes up next year's schedule, his #1 priority should*

be to go back to film school to learn how to make a hit movie. Between the incompetent director and the unqualified producer, the two must have had their thumbs up their asses during the entire production. It's amazing that, in the age of the computer, the special effects were so phony looking and unbelievable. Poorly edited, with a sub-standard plot, this was a poor excuse for an action movie. If my name were on the credits, I'd have my bags packed before I was run out of town."

A snip-snip here, and a snip-snip there, and *voilà!* next to the ad appears:

"The . . . year's . . . #1 . . . hit!" "Two . . . thumbs up!" "Amazing . . . special effects!" "Unbelievable! . . ." "Action . . . packed!" says Paul D'Angelo of the *LA Newz.*

See what I mean?

Viva Las Vegas

Las Vegas is so extravagant. Every casino tries to outdo each other with spectacular entertainment. It's really out of control now.

Here's a typical conversation between a bunch of businessmen in Las Vegas for a convention . . .

"Where do you guys want to go tonight?"

"I have just the place. I heard about a casino that has a show with fifty beautiful showgirls wearing skimpy outfits!"

"OK . . . I'm in."

"No, no, no! That is sooo lame. I can beat that. There's another casino that features a hundred *gorgeous* showgirls who are topless, dancing in a cage with white tigers!"

"Sounds good to us!"

"Relax, fellas, I got you both beat . . . I heard about a casino that has two-hundred *stunning* showgirls that are totally naked, *having sex with* white tigers on an exploding pirate ship that you watch from a rollercoaster that circles an erupting volcano in downtown Paris!"

"Wow! Let's go!"

"Wait guys, I have an even better idea . . . let's gamble and drink for free until the sun comes up!"

"Yeah! *Now* you're talking!"

Lobster

Wherever you go out to eat at any restaurant, what is always the most expensive item on the menu?

Right . . . lobster.

On most menus they don't even list a price. The menu will say 'MARKET PRICE,' which basically means that the restaurant can make-up whatever price they want and people will still buy it.

"Waiter, could you please tell me, how much is the lobster tonight?"

"The lobster? Uhhh . . . I don't know . . . Let's see . . . How about, uhhh . . . $45?"

"OK."

Why is lobster so expensive?

Let's imagine that you are from another country and you don't know what a lobster is. You've never heard of lobster . . . You have never seen a lobster . . . You have absolutely no idea what a lobster even looks like.

Now, here you are, sitting down at a nice restaurant and you ask the waiter,

"Waiter, I am curious, what is this food called lobster? And why is it the most expensive thing on the menu?"

"Lobster is delicious."

"Really, what does this lobster look like?"

"Well, let me think . . . Have you ever seen a cockroach?"

"Yes, I know what a cockroach looks like. We have large cockroaches where I come from."

"Well, it looks like that, but about a thousand times bigger."

"Mmmm, sounds good so far . . . please tell me more!"

"Well, it's covered with a hard shell and has eight legs."

"Like a spider?"

"Yes, just like a spider."

"Oooooh, my mouth is watering."

"But that's not all . . . it also has two huge claws, two eyes located on the end of stalks and long, whip-like antennas sticking out of the top of its head."

"Yum yum . . . and to think, I was gonna order steak!"

"And you'll *love* the tail."

"You can *EAT* the tail?"

"Yes you can, it's the best part . . . and sometimes it has all this gooey, green stuff that looks like the cook blew his nose in it."

"Sounds DE-licious! M-m-m-m-m . . . My tummy is doing cartwheels! Tell me, what do these lobsters eat?"

"Oh, they eat dead and decomposing things off the bottom of the ocean. Stuff like raw sewerage, rotting fish and decomposing corpses."

"They eat corpses?"

"Are you kidding? Lobsters *love* corpse."

"Mmmmmm. Start melting up the butter!"

"Wait . . . I haven't even told you the best part yet! You're gonna love this. We're keeping your lobster alive in the back room and we're going to kill it just for you!"

"How? . . . Firing squad? . . . Electric chair? . . . Gas chamber?"

"No, we throw it in boiling water and it dies a painful death for your dining pleasure."

"No way! Name your price!"

Holy Moley!

I got into trouble one time . . . well, not one time, a lot of times, but this one time . . .

A few years ago I was shopping with a girlfriend when she ran into an old friend of hers she'd grown up with but hadn't seen in years. This woman, who was named Molly, had apparently relocated out of state but had recently moved back. Molly was running late for an appointment and couldn't talk for more than a few seconds, but I had my camera with me so the girls asked me to take their picture, which I did.

A couple days later, my girlfriend called me and said, "I got an e-mail from my friend, Molly, and she asked me if I would get her a copy of that photo you took of us. Will you please e-mail the picture to me so I can forward it to her?"

I said, "No problem. I'm really busy now but, as soon as I get a minute, I'll clean the photo up and crop it in Photoshop and make it look real nice before I send it to you, OK?"

"Yeah, great. Thank you, Paul, I really appreciate it."

I was in the middle of a bunch of projects the next day when I remembered my promise to pass that photo on to my girlfriend, so I took a few minutes to hurriedly work on the picture, quickly attached it to an e-mail and went back to whatever it was I was doing.

A little while later, the phone rang and I had a feeling that my girlfriend was very angry because the phone glowed red and the caller ID said "666."

She screamed, "Paul! What the hell did you do?!"

"Huh?"

"What did you do to that picture?!"

I said, "Nothing. I just cleaned it up a little in Photoshop. . . you know, I cropped it and played with the contrast a bit, fixed a few things. Why? What's the problem?"

"What's the problem, you ask? What's the problem? . . . Did you remove Molly's mole?"

"What?"

"Did you remove the mole on my friend's lip?"

"Huh?"

"My friend Molly had a big, black mole on her lip that everyone used to make fun of and it's not there now! Did you remove it in Photoshop?"

"I-I might of . . . I did a bunch of things. I was kind of in a rush, but if it was gross looking I probably did remove it, I really don't recall . . ."

She was livid.

"How in the world could you do that, Paul? I don't care how disgusting you think it was, you can't just remove a mole that someone's had on her face all of her life! What's wrong with you? If I sent that photo to Molly without noticing I would have been incredibly embarrassed! I can't believe you! I just thank God I checked the picture before I sent it to her."

I asked, "What do you want me to do about it?"

"Molly's waiting for the picture. Just send me the original image the way it looked before you touched it up."

"Uh, I'm sorry but I don't have the original picture anymore. I made all the changes and then I just saved it. That version is all I have."

"You gotta be kidding me, Paul! . . . Damn it! . . . Well, then you're just going to have to add it back in."

"Add what?"

"Molly's mole."

"How am I going to do that? I didn't save Molly's deleted mole in one of my files. Where am I going to get a mole?"

"You figure it out, Paul, but hurry-up because I told Molly I was sending her the picture and she's waiting for it."

(Click.)

Shit.

I went back into Photoshop and opened up the picture.

Hmmm . . . How am I going to pull this one off? . . . Hmmmm . . . then, suddenly, "Eureka! I got it!" . . . and I simply typed a period onto the woman's lip . . . but the dot was too small, so I increased the font size and looked at it again . . . but the period still didn't show up too well, so I clicked BOLD and contemplated my masterpiece . . .

 "Beautiful. That looks like a mole now. She'll never know the difference."

 . . . then I attached the photo to an e-mail and sent it to my girlfriend.

It seemed like the phone rang almost simultaneously . . . which can't be good.

"Are you serious, Paul?"

"Huh?"

"It looks like there's a big, black bowling ball stuck to my friend's lip!"

I defended myself.

"It's not my fault! How am I supposed to remember what your friend's stupid mole looks like? You told me it was big and black."

"Well it's not nearly that big and not nearly that black. You better fix it . . . *NOW!!!*"

(Click.)

Shit.

So I went on the Internet, did a Google search for 'mole'

and sifted through some pretty disgusting pictures of moles, freckles, skin-tags and birthmarks in an attempt to find a mole matching this woman's skin tone. I finally found a mole that was somewhat similar and proceeded to cut and paste it onto her friend's lip.

I admired my work . . . "*Voila!* That should do it. Molly's mole has been restored. My girlfriend will be mollified!" (mol-li-fy *vb* **-ied** 1: to soothe in temper: APPEASE.)

I e-mailed my girlfriend the photo and then called her up to see what she thought.

"How's that?"

"It's not perfect, but I guess that mole's pretty close to how I remember it. I don't think she'll be able to tell. It's just a good thing we caught it, Paul. I just didn't want to be humiliated and hurt poor Molly's feelings. We put her through enough shit when we were kids."

"You did?"

"Not me, but yeah," she said. "Kids can be so mean and cruel sometimes. They would tease Molly and call her 'Moley.' I really felt bad for her."

I said, "Well you're a good person and I know you'd never do anything to hurt Molly's feelings. She's lucky to have a friend like you."

"Thanks, Paul. I'll send Molly the picture right away."

Well, about a week later, I was out to dinner with my girlfriend and she bumped into another woman that she also grew up with.

My girlfriend exclaimed excitedly, "You'll never guess who I saw who just moved back to town."

And her friend said, "I know! I know! I saw Molly too! I haven't seen her for years and years."

"Me too," my girlfriend said, "and she really looks great. In fact, I e-mailed Molly a nice picture of the two of us about a week ago, but I never heard back from her, which is a little strange. I thought she'd get back to me by now, for sure. I hope everything is all right."

Her friend said, "Yeah, Molly looked great . . . but, you know, I was looking at her and there was something different about her appearance, and I couldn't figure out what the hell it was . . .

"It was really bugging the shit out of me! Was it her hair color? Did she have a facelift? Did she lose weight? . . . I tell you, it was driving me crazy!

"Then, after I'd been talking to her for almost ten minutes it finally dawned on me . . . She had that hideous black mole removed from her lip!"

And two people looked at each other in horror and screamed at exactly the same time:

"Noooooooooooooooo!"

"Noooooooooooooooo!"

Restless Spirits

Have you ever had your life flash before your eyes?

A moment when you thought you might not make it? A time when you feared imminent death?

I did and, to be honest, I am ashamed of the way I reacted.

It happened when I was on an airplane. We hit some terrible turbulence and the plane dropped hundreds of feet in a matter of seconds. It felt like the end was near.

Now, what would most normal people think of in their final moments? Possibly their last minutes on earth? People with families . . . a career . . . a life . . .

A normal person might think . . .

"If this is it, will my family be all right? Did I provide for them? Was I a good husband and father? . . . How will people remember me? What kind of legacy will I leave behind? . . . There were a lot of things I never got to do, but I have so many good memories . . . I better start praying for my soul . . ."

Not me.

You know what I was thinking of?

I'm ashamed to say that I was busy making a mental list in my head of all the embarrassing shit in my apartment that my family and friends are going to find when they start to go through my stuff.

When we hit that turbulence some people around me were screaming.

Others were praying.

Some were on their cell phones, making calls to their families and talking to their wives.

"If we don't make it, I want you to know that I love you . . . and tell the kids I love them too . . ."

Other people were on the phone with their girlfriends.

"I never told you I love you but if . . . i-if we ever get out of this alive, I'm gonna marry you!"

I was on the phone with my brother, screaming at him with urgency . . .

"YOU GOTTA GO TO MY APARTMENT *RIGHT NOW!* . . . BEFORE ANYONE ELSE GETS THERE!

"THERE'S A KEY UNDER THE DOORMAT. GO IN-TO MY BEDROOM IN MY BACK CLOSET ON THE VERY, VERY TOP SHELF, WAY OVER TO THE FAR LEFT CORNER UNDERNEATH A PILE OF SWEAT-SHIRTS, INSIDE AN OLD SHOE-BOX WITH ELASTIC BANDS AROUND IT . . .

"JUST SHUT UP AND LISTEN TO ME!!! THIS IS VERY IMPORTANT!!!"

Hey, don't judge me . . . as they say on those commercials,

"What's in your wallet?"

See, the worst thing is that, if you're dead, you don't have the opportunity to explain yourself.

Everyone has something funky in their home that, say, if you were cleaning the house with a friend and they pointed and said, "What the hell is that?" . . . you'd laugh out loud and say, "Oh, *that*? Ha ha ha! *That* thing? . . . Ha ha ha, wait till I tell you the story! Ha ha ha! . . ."

YOU'RE NOT THERE TO EXPLAIN!!!

For example . . .

Just imagine that there is a really nice guy.

He has been a good, decent person for his entire life. He never did a bad thing. He is honest and hardworking. He attends church. He gives to charity. This kind man doesn't drink, smoke or even swear. He is just a respectable person . . . an honorable human being.

And this nice guy attends, maybe, one bachelor party in his whole, entire life.

And *he* is the designated driver, because this wonderful guy is the only one of his friends who doesn't drink and act like an idiot.

The next morning, after the bachelor party, the nice man goes out to his car to clean-out all the empty beer bottles that his out of control, drunken buddies left in the car and, while he's picking up the pile of trash in the back seat, among the junk he finds an adult, novelty sex-toy that his friends bought as a practical joke for the bachelor party . . . like mischievous friends often tend to do at bachelor parties.

The nice man jumps back and exclaims, "Oh my!"

He's embarrassed . . . horrified . . . He has no idea what 'it' is, but he knows that 'it' is something dirty . . . something indecent, and he doesn't even want to touch 'it', but he has to get rid of 'it,' and brings 'it,' this sex toy, into the house to throw 'it' away.

But, just as he is about to throw it in the trash . . . DING-DONG . . . the doorbell rings.

He doesn't know who could be at the door . . . DING-DONG . . . What if it's his mother or his sister coming to visit?

He hesitates before tossing this sex toy into the trash because he doesn't want to take the chance that whoever is at the door will throw something away and see 'it' in the trash . . . and how on Earth would he explain this . . . this . . . this *thing* to them?

So . . . DING DONG . . . "I'M COMING! JUST A MO-MENT!" . . . the kindly gentleman runs into his bedroom and hides that disgraceful thing in the back of his sock drawer, intending to chuck it out with the trash after his guest leaves.

But then the nice man answers the door, gets caught up in conversation with whomever it happens to be, one thing leads to another, and he totally forgets about that strange object in his sock drawer.

Three weeks later . . . POW! . . . The nice man is crossing the street and gets hit by a bus.

Now this lovely man goes to heaven . . . of course . . . and he's looking down from a billowy cloud as his elderly parents are cleaning out his belongings from his apartment.

He feels terrible for his mother and father and wonders how they are taking the tragedy, so he listens in to see what his parents are saying as they are going through his stuff.

His sobbing mother says, "I still can't believe our Paul got hit by a bus. He was such a good boy . . . a perfect son. So sweet. He was an angel, I tell you! A saint! Never gave us any problems . . . and now he's gone . . . sob, sob . . ."

She takes a deep breath and struggles to continue . . . "Here are his pictures . . . and his favorite books . . . and what are we going to do with all of his clothes? Look at this sock drawer,

Jack. It's so full, I can hardly close it . . . AHHHHHHHH!"

The sweet, modest man sees his aged mother jump back with a horrified look on her face and wonders what in the world could make an old woman scream like that.

The nice man's terrified mother whimpers and points a shaking finger, "Jack, wh-wh-what's that . . . that, that big, rubber thing in Paul's sock drawer?"

And, looking down from heaven, the demure, pleasant man screams out, at the top of his lungs, hoping that his desperate cries can somehow be heard from the hereafter . . .

"NOOOOOOOOOO!!! . . . NOT THE SOCK DRAWER! I FORGOT ABOUT THAT THING! THIS CAN'T BE HAPPENING! PLEEEEASE, NO!"

His concerned father says, "Well, what does it say Frances? . . . Read the package."

His mother, holding the mysterious object with trembling hands, hesitantly reads . . .

"It says, 'New and improved . . . Jumbo Butt Plug . . . with Ultra Probe . . . Multi-speed vibration system for maximum pleasure . . . ' What would our son use this for?"

And, up in heaven, the really nice man begins hyperventilating, panics and cups his hands around his mouth as he shouts with all his might, "OH MY GOD! NO! . . . IT WAS A JOKE! IT'S NOT EVEN MINE! I SWEAR! IT BELONGS TO MY FRIENDS! CAN YOU HEAR ME? LOOK UP HERE!!! UP HERE!!!"

The kind, likeable man's poor old mother snivels, "B-but, b-but, I don't, I don't understand."

His father takes charge and says, "Well, we'll just have to take it with us and show it to all of Paul's friends. Maybe they'll know what he uses it for."

And the quiet, sweet, gentle soul who never, ever raised his voice or cursed shrieks, "FUCKKKKKKKK!!! . . .

171

PLEEEEEASE! . . . GET THE OUIJI BOARD, I CAN EX-PLAIN EVERYTHING! GET THE FUCKING OUIJI BOARD!

"CROSS OVER, GOD DAMMIT!!! CROSS OVER!!!

"BEETLEJUICE, BEETLEJUICE, BEETLEJUICE!!!

You know, this is how you get those "restless spirits" that they talk about on those paranormal and ghost shows on TV.

You don't think that, for the next year or so, various objects won't be flying around the house?

You don't think dishes won't be rattling? . . . The lights won't be flickering? . . . The TV won't go haywire? . . . Things won't go "bump in the night" in that cursed home?

The occupants will eventually have to call the Ghostbusters who will come in with all their paranormal-detecting equipment: "Oh yeah. You've got yourself a poltergeist all right."

And they'll set up microphones and sensitive recording equipment around the home and hold a séance to try and contact the enraged spirits.

They'll turn the lights down low and hold hands around the table as the psychic closes her eyes and swoons . . .

"Oh, Restless spirit that inhabits this home . . . Please send us a message from the other side . . . Speak to us from beyond the grave and tell us why you're so angry . . . Why is your soul so tortured? . . . What it is that torments you so? . . . Why can't you find peace and move on?"

"Wait! We're picking-up something on the recorders!"

"That's great. Play it back!"

But, when they hit 'play,' there is nothing but a jumbled, unintelligible message on the tape.

"It doesn't make sense."

One of the ghost hunters gets a brainstorm . . . "Maybe it's like a Beatles album . . . you know, with those hidden messages. Try playing the tape in reverse."

"OK, here goes . . ."

And an eerie, haunting, anguished voice cries out from the tape . . .

"IT'S NOT MY BUTT PLUG . . . NOT MY BUTT PLUG!"

"Huh? . . . I don't get it."

**The filming of Paul's *Court Jester* DVD
Tupelo Music Hall - Londonderry, New Hampshire**

Giggles Comedy Club - Saugus, Massachusetts

with Dennis Miller

CHAPTER 7:
STILL GOING, NOT DONE YET

The Astrologist

One year when I was really down and out, frustrated and depressed about the way my comedy career was going, I got a Christmas card from some old friends. The husband was a top-notch defense attorney when I was a prosecutor in the Essex County District Attorney's office and, over the years, I got to know his family very well but hadn't heard from them in quite a while.

The lawyer's wife was apparently a psychic or astrologer who did card readings. She sent me a lovely card with a very exciting message handwritten inside the cover.

The note read:

> Paul –
>   This is YOUR YEAR!
>   The "stars" and "planets" are all in the right places for HUGE success!
>   Take chances and grab any and all op-portunities that WILL be coming your way!
>   When you make it big, invite us to visit you in your big mansion in Hollywood!
>   You won't have another year like this one for quite a while, so GO FOR IT!
>   Love, Dick and Adele

What amazing news!

This was just what I needed to hear!

Maybe, finally, after more than twenty years of hard work and frustration, I would finally get the big break I'd been waiting for!

I had to call her right away because I wanted to hear more.

"Hi, Adele, this is Paul."

"Ohhh, Paul . . . I am SOOOO excited for you!"

I could hear the enthusiasm in her voice. My heart was racing with exhilaration.

"Then it's true? You really think this is going to be my year?"

"Oh yes! Without a doubt, Paul! I did your astrological chart. It's incredible. Every single sign points to the amazing success you have been patiently waiting for all these years."

"Are you sure?"

"Of course I'm sure. At first I couldn't believe it, so I checked it twice so there would be no doubt. I've never been so sure. Do you understand what this means for your career? This is the opportunity of a lifetime! A chance like this won't come around again for at least another thousand years!"

"Could you see the house I'm gonna be living in? Is it nice?"

"Oh, don't worry, you'll be able to afford the home of your dreams, Paul. Money will be no object."

"Oh, that is such good news. I was beginning to feel like I should give up. I never seem to catch a break, but you've given me new hope. Thank you so very much, you've really inspired me. This is great."

"Well, you truly deserve it, Paul."

I was giddy.

"You have made me so happy . . . I don't really know what to say."

"Paul, just don't forget us little people when you're a big star in Hollywood."

I was effusive. "Oh, I won't. Believe me . . . Thank you . . . thank you again. This is such good news. I'm so excited. My luck is finally going to turn. I can't thank you enough."

There was a momentary pause, "Paul, you *are* a Scorpio . . . right?"

"*Scorpio?* . . . Me? . . . Uhhh . . . no . . . um, actually, uh, actually I'm, I'm an Aries."

(Long, awkward silence.)

"Ohhhh . . . ummmm . . . I am *really* sorry."

(Click.)

Some things never change.

I may have been born an Aries but, right now, my moon is most definitely in Feces.

Progress?

I read that plastic surgeons and dermatologists are using a new process of recycling fat by "harvesting" excess body fat from people's dimpled buttocks and re-injecting it into their aging, wrinkled faces to restore youthful fullness.

This is progress?

Essentially, what this means, is that it is now physically possible to actually sit on your own face.

The only upside I can see to this procedure is that, when you visit your family on holidays and they give you a smack on the cheek, you can smile to yourself knowing that, for once, they are kissing *your* ass.

Outed

Did you ever have a conversation with a complete stranger where everything you say just comes out wrong? You're completely misunderstood?

It happened to me.

One of my best pals from Los Angeles came to stay with me in Boston and you know what they say about houseguests. They're like fish. After three days they start to stink. Well this guy stayed with me for almost a month!

He's a nice guy and a good pal but I couldn't get rid of him! It was a nightmare!

I only have a small place and I had no privacy. He slept really late every day so I had to be quiet in my own house and he was really starting to get on my nerves.

The final straw was that he was eating me out of house and home. I mentioned that I was tired of feeding him and he promised to help me out with the grocery shopping the next day.

The following day came, but I couldn't wake him up . . . and it was 1:30 in the afternoon!

After unsuccessfully trying to get him out of bed for forty-five minutes I finally gave up and had to go shopping alone. And, believe me, I was bullshit!

I went to the supermarket fuming and in a foul mood. Then, to make things worse, I went to the deli section and there was a really long wait, so I had to take a number.

While I was waiting for them to call my number, the man standing next to me says, "This is really frustrating."

In response, I started venting, going on and on about my lazy houseguest.

"You think *this* is frustrating? Well let me tell you . . . my friend from Los Angeles has been living with me and, even though we've been together for a long time, he is really starting to make me very upset.

"I mean, I really love this guy, but he's driving me *crazy!* I've had it with him!

"Aaaaand, to top it off, he's still lying in bed while I have to do all the shopping! Needless to say, I am *furious!*"

The man took a step back and looked at me funny . . .

And I thought to myself, "Oh my god, this guy thinks I'm gay!"

And from that point on, everything I said to the stranger came out wrong.

"Uh, uh . . . I mean I *assume* he's in bed . . . he has his own room . . . and there's a lock on his door . . . but I just couldn't get him up.

"Uh . . . Oh no, that's not a good choice of words . . . uh. . . I didn't mean 'get him up' like that. I meant to say that he's really starting to rub me the wrong wa— . . .

"Uhh, that's not good. I don't mean that either . . . I-I-I mean my buddy is getting to be a real pain in my ass . . . uh, not good . . . um . . . "

That's when the man in the apron behind the counter yelled out, "Number 69!"

"Oh . . . What a coincidence. That's me."

I took out my shopping list and it had to be the worst list of all time for the situation I was in.

"Yes, hi. Can I have a half-dozen hot dogs . . . a pepperoni . . . and, you know, one of those big pickles."

I glanced at the guy I had been talking to . . . and he *smiled!*

Oh no, this is not good. Not good.

From behind the counter, "Yeah, pal . . . What else you need?"

"OK, great . . . I also need three sub sandwiches."

"Subs? What kind?"

"Oh boy, this isn't gonna come out right . . . uh, OK, I'm gonna need a large sausage and two small meatballs."

I was afraid to look . . . but I had to . . . and the guy next to me *winked.*

I suddenly felt really uncomfortable, panicked and blurted out, "Oh, God, no! Those aren't for me! . . . No! They're for my friend.

"And me? For ME? . . . Of course, I'll have some breast. Chicken breast . . . turkey breast . . . ham breast . . . cougar . . . yum, cougar, it really doesn't matter, any kind of breast would be good at this point . . . I just *LOOOVE* breast . . . Can't get enough of 'em . . . Crazy about the breasts . . .

" . . . aaaaaand, how about giving me a pound of your best vagina . . . *Virginia!* I meant to say 'Virginia!' Virginia Ham . . . that's it . . . Virginia . . . (♫) *you say Virginia, I say vagi . . .* and how 'bout those Patriots?"

(Grunt; snort; flex shoulders.)

Dumb Criminal

When I was an assistant district attorney, I came across some dumb criminals.

My personal nominee for dumbest criminal?

I prosecuted a criminal case that that arose from a long, bitter custody battle between two divorced parents.

One night, while the estranged wife was sleeping, a burglar wearing a dark ski mask to carefully conceal his identity, broke into her home and yelled out:

"I WANT TO SEE MY SON!"

Now who the hell do you suppose that mystery man could be?

Buy American

For years I drove Japanese cars and Japanese motorcycles and had great luck with them until about twenty years ago.

I had both a Toyota and a Nissan car . . . never had a problem with them. I don't even think I changed the oil. They were very reliable and dependable and virtually maintenance free.

I rode Kawasaki and Yamaha motorcycles that were every bit as trustworthy. You could leave them outside in the snow all winter and, come spring, they would start right up and off you'd go.

That was until my friends got on my back.

"What are you doing with the Japanese cars and motorcycles, Paul? Don't you know that when you buy Japanese products you put Americans out of work?"

"Really?"

"Yeah, you have to buy American made vehicles because, when you buy American cars and motorcycles you create jobs for Americans. You put Americans to work."

I was convinced.

"OK, you're right. I want to do my part for my country. I want to put Americans to work."

So I sold the Nissan 300ZX and I sold the Yamaha motorcycle and I bought myself a Corvette and a Harley Davidson. . . made in the ol' U.S. of A.

And my friends were right, I *did* put Americans to work . . . because it seemed like I had ten guys fixing the damn things every week!

I put tow truck operators to work . . . I put mechanics to work . . . I put my insurance company to work . . . I put cab drivers to work . . . I put people in the parts department to work . . . I put the car rental people to work . . . and I kept the people in customer service very busy as well.

Family Tree

This country is really screwed up and getting worse and I think that one of the biggest reasons is the erosion of the traditional family unit.

It used to be that a family consisted of a father and mother, brothers and sisters, aunts and uncles, grandparents and cousins.

Not anymore.

How would you like to be a kid growing up in 2014?

Your mother is on her third or fourth marriage.

Your father is on his fifth or sixth marriage.

So you're Irish-Italian, but you have two brothers named Ying-Tao and Tsing-Chow.

"Who the hell are these people in my family?"

Or your father remarried a girl who was only a freshman in high school when you were a senior.

"Paul, can you give your mother a ride uptown, she only has her learner's permit?"

"Dad, you know I'm gonna need therapy someday for this, don't you?"

Or maybe your Uncle Leo had an operation and, when you pick him up at the hospital, he's now your Aunt Sheila.

"Hi kids!"

So you lost an uncle, but you gained an aunt, and your cousins no longer have a father but they *do* have two mothers now.

"Holy shit! What happened to my family?"

Or maybe your aunt Gladys and her butch, softball-playing "companion" with the wiffle haircut get married in a ceremony that is not officially recognized in your state, so you aren't really sure if these women are your two aunts, your two wannabe uncles, or just your aunt and her friend.

Together, they adopted an orphaned Eskimo child who is now your cousin . . . you think . . . and are now trying to conceive a baby with a strap-on turkey baster and naming Frank Purdue as the father.

"What?"

Or perhaps your brother did a lot of drugs growing up and his wife gives birth to a hermaphrodite, so he gave out cigars that say, "IT'S A BOY! . . . *AND* IT'S A GIRL!" and you aren't sure if you have a little niece, a little nephew or maybe even a little of both.

And maybe your real mother's best friend couldn't have children, so she asked your mom to carry her baby through in vitro fertilization but, after your mother gave birth to the child, she got attached to it and refused to hand the baby over . . . so now you have to wait for a court decision to learn if the infant is your little sister or a total stranger to you.

"I am so confused."

Or it's possible that your father got divorced from your first step-mother and remarried for a second time to a woman who wants to have a family, but your father didn't want any more kids and had a vasectomy, which required your second step-mom to be artificially inseminated by an anonymous sperm donor . . . so your mulatto half-brother isn't really even related to you because your real dad had no input whatsoever into his being.

"Huh?"

And when you plug in all this crazy information to trace your ancestry, by some convoluted formula you are informed that you have become your own brother and you can't even masturbate because it is considered an incestuous relationship.

I'm just saying . . . it's hard to be normal when your family tree is a tumbleweed.

Mr. D'Angelo

When I was living in Los Angeles, times were tough, relatively speaking. I was having trouble getting paid work, there was absolutely no hope on the horizon and the bills were piling up fast. I was desperate for someone to give me a break . . . an opportunity . . . a chance . . . anything at all.

Then, one day, just when I had seemed to hit bottom, I finally got the phone call I had been patiently waiting for.

"Hello."

"Yes, hello, is this Mr. D'Angelo?"

"Yes, it is."

"Good, good. I have been trying to reach you for some time. I'm glad I am finally able to get you on the phone. This is so-and-so from wherever and we are very interested in hiring you to perform at our theater."

I said, "That's great. I'm all ears. Tell me about the venue."

"It's a beautiful theater that seats 5,000 people and I'm sure we can sell out the show."

"Fantastic. Sounds good. Do you mind if I ask how much you're planning on paying me for this show?"

"Well, of course, the amount is open to negotiation, but I am willing to make an initial offer of $20,000."

I was so stunned I couldn't reply, and the caller must have taken my silence as a show of displeasure with his offer, because he was quick to add, "But if that's not enough, we can certainly discuss the price."

I snapped out of it and tried not to sound as blown away as I truly was.

I said, "No . . . no . . . that's good, that's good," but inside, I was thinking, "Holy shit! That's a lot of fucking money!"

I couldn't believe it! This was the opportunity I had been begging for, and it had come just in time because I was flat broke and getting extremely discouraged by my lack of success. My prayers had been answered.

I talked to the guy for a little while longer, discussing the logistics of the show and making arrangements for my flight and accommodations, when he abruptly interrupted our conversation and asked, almost apologetically, "Excuse me, this is really embarrassing b-b-but can I ask you a . . . a question?"

I sensed a problem. "Sure, go ahead."

He seemed to hesitate, then finally got up the courage to say, "I'm sorry. I-I don't mean to insult you or anything b-but, uh, this is so awkward, how do I say this? . . . Uhhh, are you black?"

Am I black? What the hell kind of a question is that?

That's when it suddenly occurred to me that, all along, this guy thought he was talking to a popular rhythm and blues singer named 'D'Angelo,' not Paul D'Angelo, the comedian from Boston.

Oh no! *SHIT!* I'm going to lose my dream gig! What will I do?

That's when I morphed into Stepin' Fetchit on the phone.

"Oh yeah, I be black . . . Yessir, you right . . . I as black as night, black as coal, dat's me. Havin' m'self some fried chicken and watermelon as we speak, home-slice . . .

"Nobody knows, the trouble I've seen . . . "

"Oh, Mr. D'Angelo, I am sooo sorry."

"Brother, you ain't half as sorry as I is!"

(Click.)

Fuck!

Slinging Mud

Wow, politics has become really nasty lately.

I don't know why anyone in their right mind would want to

run for public office these days. Politicians have people in their campaign whose job it is to dig into a candidate's personal and professional background in an attempt to uncover and discover every little mistake, misstep, indiscretion, gaffe, error in judgment . . . every single example of misbehavior, overindulgence, insensitivity . . . that their adversary has ever made in their entire life.

How would you like *your* whole life to be subject to that kind of scrutiny?

How bad is it?

Did you know that, leading up to the 2012 presidential election, the Democrats actually accused Republican candidate Mitt Romney of bullying another student . . . *when he was in prep school.*

The man was sixty-five years old when they brought it up! Even if it happened, even if it's true, it happened *over fifty years ago!*

Give us a break! Where will it end? What are the limits? How low can you go? How far back are political parties willing to go to smear an opposing candidate in our upcoming elections?

I can just imagine a Senate hearing in the not-too-distant future . . .

"So, are you denying these shocking allegations, Senator?"

"Well, no, I'm not denying them . . . *technically* . . . but please allow me to explain . . ."

"So, you don't refute these lurid accusations, Senator? Is that your answer?"

"Well, yes . . . but no . . . I can explain if you'll just give me one minute to defend myself . . ."

"So, Senator, as I understand it, you are basically admitting to this committee that you were once caught in public without your pants on . . . *totally naked from the waist down!* . . . shamelessly lying on your back, with your two legs up in the air . . . in the restroom of a busy restaurant, accompanied by a much older woman? Are those essentially the facts, Senator?"

"I have been trying to tell you if you would just *listen* to me . . . Yes, yes, that's all true, but I was only six months old at the time! My mother was changing my dirty diap . . ."

"Senator, that calls for a simple 'yes' or 'no' response. Just answer the question!"

Modern Christmas Carol

It's funny how you forget things. I suppose there is only so much room on the cranial hard drive and, at some point, every time you download a new piece of information, you need to delete a file to make room.

Then again, sometimes our memory seems to be subconsciously, or even purposefully, selective of the past. We only remember what we want to remember. As often happens when you break up with someone and, as time goes by, you may remember only the good things or only the bad things about that relationship, depending on how it ended.

It always seems that we were happier in another time. How many times do you hear, "Those were the good ol' days."

I remember, when I was a young man, I would look at myself in the mirror and say, "I hate the way I look . . . I hate my body . . . I hate my hair . . . I wish I looked different."

Then, you look at old pictures of yourself in a photo album, years later, and think, "What the hell was I complaining about? I would *KILL* to look like that again! . . . I had no idea I was going to get this ugly!"

You think that things were much better in the old days, but they weren't always better, we just think so.

I do it myself sometimes. I'll be reminiscing with old

friends and say, "Yeah, those were the best days. I wish I was back in high school again. I was so happy. I had no worries . . . no problems . . . no pressure . . . none of the bullshit I have to put up with now. I wish I had it to do all over again. Young and happy. Life was great."

Guess what . . . Hindsight is always 20/20. As I've said many times, my basic philosophy is that everything's relative and I think most people would be surprised if they were able to get inside their head and know what they were thinking back then . . . back then, when things were so good and they were so happy.

Maybe, like in Charles Dickens' classic *A Christmas Carol* . . . maybe if I could be visited by ghosts who could show me my past, present and future . . . then I'd know better. Maybe then . . . maybe then . . . maybe . . .

. . . th-zzzzzzzzzzzzzzzzzzzzzzzzzzzzzzzzzzzzzzz . . .

"I must have dozed off . . . What time is it? Oooh, I feel a draft . . . Who are you? How'd you get in here? The door was locked."

"I am The Ghost of Your Lifetime Past, Paul. Come, come with me . . ."

"Are you crazy? Get away from the open window . . ."

"Come, touch my robe and fly with me."

"Why are we stopping here, spirit?"

"Do you recognize this building?"

"Why yes . . . Yes I do! That's my old high school. But who's that gangly, skinny geek? What kind of a doofus wears flood-length, striped bell bottomed jeans with multi-colored platform shoes and a tie-dyed T-shirt? And what's with the stupid haircut, the long sideburns and the piece of rawhide tied around his neck? Do they have mirrors in this loser's house or what?"

"Look closer, Paul."

"The zits! My God, all the zits! The poor son of a bitch has a face like the bottom of a Nestlé's Crunch bar. And that wispy excuse for a moustache that looks like a football game . . . eleven on each side. Sorry to say, but this total dweeb doesn't have much of a future."

"Don't you recognize the stupid expression on his face?"

"Yes, I do . . . Wait a second . . . It's me, isn't it, spirit? That pimply geek is a young Paul, isn't he?"

"Sssssshhh. Quiet. Let's listen to the conversation he's having with his friends."

"Man, I am hating life right now! I hate high school! It sucks!"

"Yeah Paul. I can't wait till we graduate."

"I wish I was older. Then I'll be happy. I can't wait till I'm working and I have a job. That will be so cool. I won't have to use my parents' car all the time. Then I can buy my own car . . . and make my own payments, and pay for my own gas, and my own insurance, and be responsible for my own repairs . . . instead of using their stupid car every night. That would be awesome.

"When I work I can have my own place. That's freedom, man. No one tells you what to do. I'll be paying my own rent, and my own health insurance, and buying my own groceries, and cooking for myself, and washing my own clothes. I'm tired of my mother having a hot dinner waiting for me every night and washing and ironing and folding all my clothes when I don't even ask her. They're making me so miserable. I can't wait to be on my own."

I yelled, "PAUL! YOU STUPID SHIT! YOU HAVE IT MADE! YOU DON'T KNOW HOW GOOD YOU HAVE IT! STOP COMPLAINING! ENJOY YOURSELF! BE HAPPY WHILE YOU CAN!

"GROWING UP SUCKS! YOU HAVE NO PROBLEMS

189

NOW! YOU DON'T HAVE ANY IDEA WHAT PROB-
LEMS ARE! YOU'RE SO LUCKY! HAVE FUN WHILE
YOU'RE YOUNG! . . . LISTEN TO ME, DAMMIT!! WHY
WON'T YOU LISTEN TO ME?!?!"

"Ha ha ha . . . Don't bother, Paul. No matter how loud you
yell, he cannot hear you. These are but shadows of things that
have been . . . they are not conscious of us."

"Oh spirit, why are you showing me this? . . . Spirit? . . .
Spirit? . . . Hey, who the hell are you? Where'd the other spirit
go?"

"He has left. I am The Ghost of Your Lifetime Present.
Touch my hand and come with me."

"Not again."

"Does this location look familiar, Paul?"

"Yes, it's one of the nightclubs that I go to with my friends
in Los Angeles, circa 1998 . . . whatever the hell that means.
And there I am with my friends. They seem frustrated with me
for some reason . . ."

"Life sucks. I'm never gonna meet any women."

"What are you talking about, Paul. That chick across the bar
has been checking you out all night."

"No way, guys."

"Really. I swear. She keeps looking over here . . . there, she
did it again. I'm telling you, she wants you. Go talk to her."

"Are you kidding? I can't."

"Why not? What do you have to lose?"

"C'mon. What girl would want me? It's Hollywood, I don't
have any money and I don't *look* like I have any money. She
can't be looking at *me*. Maybe she has astigmatism. I'm not
gonna walk up and make a fool of myself."

"Paul, you're gonna blow it. She looks like she's getting
ready to leave."

"Hey, what can you do?"

"PAUL! GO FOR IT! HAVE SOME BALLS! I'M ASHAMED OF YOU! YOU ARE *SUCH* A LOSER!

"NO WONDER YOU CAN'T GET LAID! LIFE IS SHORT, TALK TO HER OR YOU'LL NEVER KNOW! . . . WHY WON'T YOU DO WHAT I TELL YOU, YOU WIMP? WHAT'S WRONG WITH YOU?!?!"

"Ha ha ha . . . You're wasting your breath, Paul. He . . ."

"I know, I know, I know . . . He can't hear me, but wh . . . Hey! Now where the hell did *he* go? Ahhh!! Who are you? . . . No, no . . . Let me guess. You are The Ghost of My Lifetime Future, right? . . . What, you're not answering me? Fine, let's go . . . I know the drill.

"Oh, no . . . A nursing home. Why are we here? Who is that grouchy, elderly man wearing the Depends undergarments? Shit, let me guess . . . Hey, someone's coming . . ."

"Mr. D'Angelo . . . Mr. D'Angelo . . ."

"Huh?"

"Mr. D'Angelo, there's a man here to see you. He says it's something about a student loan."

"Huh? What was that again, sonny?"

"I said there's a man here who wants you to pay your student loan."

"Phone? Phone, you say? Then answer it, dammit! What the hell are you asking me for? It might be an agent calling me back! Maybe *The Tonight Show.* Answer it, damn you!"

"No, Mr. D'Angelo . . . not phone, LOAN . . . I SAID 'LOAN' . . . LOAN!"

(Whispering) "I heard you, numb-nuts . . . Just go with it, will you . . . I'm trying to get rid of this guy. If you haven't noticed, I'm still waiting for my big break in show business . . . work with me or I'll leave a present for you in my bedpan tonight, understand?

"WHAT, YOUNG MAN? . . . HUH? . . . I CAN'T HEAR

191

YOU! SPEAK UP! SAY, DO YOU WANT TO HEAR A JOKE? I GOT A MILLION OF 'EM! I'M GONNA BE HUGE SOMEDAY! I'LL NEVER GIVE UP . . ."

"Oh, spirit of my lifetime yet to come, show me no more. I cannot bear it any longer . . . Are these the shadows of things that *will* be . . . or are they shadows of things that *might* be? Please, spirit . . . Show me a sign that I may be saved from this horrible fate that awaits me . . ."

And then I actually saw *a sign* . . . coming into focus . . . into focus . . . into focus . . .

. . . and it said, "ENTERING HOLLYWOOD, DIM YOUR HOPES."

I woke in a cold sweat . . . "I'm alive! The spirits have done it all in one night! I didn't miss my set at the Improv!" Then I realized I had no set at the Improv . . . or anywhere else for that matter, as usual, and went right back to sleep, learning absolutely nothing.

Sloppy Seconds

Apparently I made quite an impression when I worked as an Assistant District Attorney because there are an awful lot of policemen, judges, attorneys and court personnel who fondly recall my tenure as a prosecutor. I guess it was because I was not only very good at my job, and serious when I had to be, but I always kept things entertaining.

I recall one time when I was involved in a pretrial conference with a defense attorney who, years later, became a district court judge. We were in a discussion with several detectives from the Lynn (Massachusetts) vice squad in the upstairs lobby of the Peabody District Court because the attorney was representing a young woman who had been arrested by those officers and charged with prostitution.

I'd been dealing with this defense attorney for many years, but had never seen him so adamant and passionate in professing the innocence of his client.

"Guys, I swear, this is a big mistake! Believe me, this woman is no prostitute or anything of the sort. You know me, I never felt so strongly about a case. I really, truly trust her when she tells me that she was just in the wrong place at the wrong time. She's actually a sweet, virtuous person who is just the victim of a big misunderstanding and I'm *begging* you to dismiss this case."

From time to time, as the lawyer argued on and on, sincerely pleading with me and the detectives to drop the charges, I would glance over at the cops to get their reaction.

I saw them intermittently rolling their eyes, snickering to themselves and shaking their heads because they obviously knew from experience that the hoodwinked attorney's claims were far from the truth.

They told him, "Counselor, we know this girl is very convincing . . . she obviously has you fooled . . . but your client is not as innocent and wonderful as you believe her to be. We don't necessarily want her to do any prison time, but we do insist on a guilty plea to some reasonable term of probation."

But the lawyer persisted.

"I'm telling you guys, I genuinely believe her when she tells me she's innocent. This girl is not a streetwalker and I'm so absolutely sure of it . . . so totally confident, I will accept nothing less than a full dismissal of all charges against her."

This is when I intervened.

I asked the detectives, "Would you gentlemen mind if I make a recommendation and try to resolve this?"

Skeptical, but intrigued, they answered, "No, go ahead Paul."

I drew the cops and lawyer into a tight circle and pointed at the defendant, sitting on a bench across the lobby.

"Here's the deal, counselor. If you are truly convinced of this girl's innocence . . . If you are absolutely, positively certain that she's not a hooker . . . If you have no doubt whatsoever that she's telling you the truth, I'll tell you what . . . I'm willing to dismiss the case and make it all go away on one condition. . . I need you to walk over to her and give your client a long, deep, sloppy tongue kiss in front of all of us."

The lawyer turned and looked at his client, contemplating my offer.

"She'll take probation."

"I thought so."

One in a Million

No one stays together anymore. Marriages don't last anymore, not like they used to. The truth is that it is really hard to meet the right person.

But we all know people who have been married for 30 . . . 40 . . . 50 . . . even 60 years!

Where do they find someone like that?

If you notice, they all say the same thing, "I'm lucky. He (or she) is ONE IN A MILLION."

Do you know where they get that phrase, "One in a million?"

Well those are the approximate odds of finding the right person to spend the rest of your life with and actually be happy.

You don't believe me?

Well, I can prove it . . . because I did the math.

OK . . . Let's do this together.

To find that "One in a Million," you have to start off with a pool of how many people?

(Pause.)

A million! . . . Come on! The answer was right there in the question! Let's go people, work with me!

OK, so we'll take a random sample of one million people of the opposite sex who live in your immediate area.

First of all, unless you happen to reside in a very densely populated area such as, say, Manhattan . . . these million people you are going to choose from are going to be spread out all over the place.

As a result, some of them will be "geographically undesirable."

In case you're not familiar with that term, this basically means, "I don't care how good looking they are, I'm not driving that far every night. Forget it!"

And you also have to find someone in your age range so, no matter how old you are, there are going to be a lot of people in this group who are either way too old for you or way too young for you to go out with.

So now, even though you started with a million possible candidates for true love, you're already down to 500,000, and we haven't really even started.

Now, look around you . . . You're not attracted to everyone you see. Right?

Realistically, you're probably only going to be physically attracted to about 10% of the people around you . . . so you've gone from 500,000 down to 50,000 possible life mates.

And believe it or not, out of that 10% of the group that you're attracted to, only about 10% of *them* are going to look back at *you* and say, "Ooooh, I gotta have that! He/She is for me!"

That means that you've reduced the number from 50,000 to 5,000.

But don't get too excited, because your parents are going to hate half of them right off the bat.

This leaves you with only 2,500 people that you could possibly spend your life with in wedded bliss.

Now you'll need to eliminate anyone that doesn't speak English; they're from another country; you don't understand them . . . and you're down to 1,500 . . . and, these days, I think I'm being *very generous* with that number.

So you're saying, "Paul, that leaves only 1,500 eligible candidates to be my soul mate out of the original group of one million?"

No, not so fast, because of those 1500 people left, 2/3 of them aren't available because they are already married to someone else OR they are currently involved in a relationship, so they're off the market.

The result is that you are only left with 500 people.

But that number is really not 500 because . . . out of that 500, about 100 of the people who *are* eligible either just got out of a bad relationship and they aren't ready to start dating other people yet . . .

OR . . . they have a crazy ex that's stalking them who is "NOT READY FOR THEM TO START DATING AGAIN!!!" either . . . so that leaves you with only 400 potential spouses who will fit just right in your life.

Then there's the whole smoking controversy . . .

"I hate you because you smoke!"

Or . . .

"I hate you because you won't let me smoke in the house!"

And this reduces the number down to 350.

Now you have all the other conflicts that necessarily put a strain on any relationship.

"Our schedules conflict . . . this is never going to work."

"I want to have kids."

"I don't want children."

"I'm a morning person."

"I'm a night person."

"I'm neat."

"I'm messy!"

"I'm a conservative."

"I'm a liberal."

"Go Red Sox!"

"Go Yankees!"

And dozens of other reasons why this thing just isn't gonna work out for the two of you.

So now you're down to only 200 possible true loves.

Now, of those 200 people left, what are the odds of you having the right chemistry with them? You know . . . that certain magic that's absolutely essential for a successful relationship if it is going to last?

Right, maybe 1 out of 10, *IF YOU'RE LUCKY!*

So now the number is reduced to only 20 people out of the original number of one million.

And no matter how nice these remaining 20 people are, you don't want to marry someone who . . .

1) has a drug addiction or drinking problem

2) is a degenerate gambler

3) has a significant criminal record

And you most likely won't consider marrying someone who happens to have a Siamese twin attached to the side of their head.

"Hi, you wanna double-date?"

"Hi, you wanna double-date?"

"No . . . and no! I don't want to go out with either one of you!"

So now you're left with only 16 people that are perfect for you.

You wouldn't want to get stuck for the rest of your life with someone who's . . .

1) a computer geek
2) a couch potato
3) a psycho
4) or a pervert

It's down to 12.

And you'll never last fifty years or more with someone who laughs like a pig in heat.

"Snort . . . snort . . . snort . . . That's funny! . . . snort . . . snort."

And there will be at least one person you really like who has a pet that you're allergic to . . .

"AHH-CHOO! . . . I'm sorry, but this isn't gonna work out."

So now there are only 10 prospective partners left who happen to be your perfect match.

But you don't want to marry anyone without a job, do you? Money problems often lead to tension, then fights, then divorce. The unemployment rate is around 10%, which eliminates 1 and leaves 9 people to choose from.

And they say 3 out of every 10 people are either gay or lesbian. Subtract them and now you're down to only 6 people.

Of those 6 people remaining, you'll eventually find out that 5 of them were lying about one thing or another and that's the only reason they got this far . . .

. . . and this leaves you with that . . .

(Sing along with me!)

"*. . . my one in a million . . . !*"

CHAPTER 8
GETTING NEAR THE END

<u>The Bail Argument</u> *(an excerpt from L.A. Misérables)*
Day 427 - May 13, 1997

I represented one of my brother Jay's friends on a seemingly unwinnable case in which he was charged of breaking into and robbing a pharmacy, receiving stolen property, and numerous other serious crimes. Believe it or not, we went through a series of trials and motions to suppress evidence in several different courts and appellate forums, and I eventually got "not guilty" findings and dismissals on every one of the complaints against him, not that I felt good about it.

It wasn't easy. The defendant was arraigned on the breaking and entering charges a number of years after the actual incident because he originally fled the jurisdiction when he learned that the cops were looking to arrest him. He left town to raise a family and start a new life in Florida, remaining a fugitive from justice until he returned to Massachusetts and was arrested on the old default warrant.

At the arraignment and bail hearing, the police prosecutor was reading an incident report to the judge that referred to my client's alleged crime and his eventual flight. While the defendant sat next to me at counsel table, things were looking bleak as we listened to the prosecutor paraphrasing the investigating officer's summary of the incident.

> *"We got information that this defendant had robbed the pharmacy and stolen a variety of drugs during the heist. An informant provided us with a tip that the perpetrator had wrapped up the stolen narcotics in a box with Christmas wrapping paper and a ribbon and dropped the package off at a friend's home, asking his friend's mother to hold the gift so his wife would not discover it before Christmas.*
>
> *"After we searched the box and recovered the stolen items listed in the inventory attached hereto, the informant notified us that the defendant knew we intended to apprehend him and fled town by initially stealing a red Mazda pickup truck from 128 Mazda Olds in Wakefield.*
>
> *"From the informant, we also learned that the defendant was heading for Florida and received periodic communications from various police departments indicating that he was suspected of stealing a green Toyota in Connecticut, then hotwiring a brown Oldsmobile in New Jersey.*
>
> *"After abandoning that motor vehicle, he was then a prime suspect in the larceny of a white Chevy van in Virginia.*
>
> *"Our final tip suggested that the defendant dumped that vehicle in Georgia and stole a black truck from a restaurant parking lot . . ."*

As the assistant district attorney continued reading, my client nudged my elbow, leaned over and angrily whispered in my ear, "This is bullshit man! This is all a lie! The cops are liars! This is all bullshit!"

I was encouraged.

"Really? . . . Good. You mean you didn't do it?"

"No, that truck wasn't black. It was more like a dark blue."

And you wonder why I'm a comedian now?

"The Killer"

I had the honor and privilege to open up for over 60 inter-national recording acts at various 1,500-5,000 seat theaters around the Northeast United States. To be honest, I didn't even get to meet most of those acts and, in an era before cell phones with cameras, I rarely thought to have my picture taken with them. Besides, stars need their privacy and I didn't want to be a pain in the ass.

Still, even on the occasions when I did get to meet some of these musical and comedic legends, it is rare that any one of them would live up to their grandiose reputations.

Rock n' Roll icon Jerry Lee Lewis was the exception.

I was scheduled to open up for Jerry Lee at the South Shore Music Circus in Cohasset, Massachusetts, which is a 2,300-seat tent theatre-in-the-round.

One of the first inductees of the Rock and Roll Hall of Fame, Jerry Lee Lewis was nicknamed "The Killer" because of his violent style of piano playing and is regarded by many as rock n' roll's "first great wild man." He became infamous when people learned that, at age 22, his third wife happened to also be his first cousin, once removed, and . . . if that wasn't enough . . . she was only 13 years old.

"What? . . . You gotta problem wit' that?"

Anyway, I got to the sold-out tent with my then girlfriend, Kelly, and the entire staff was running around backstage in a panic.

I asked the stage manager, "What's going on?"

"Man! Jerry Lee landed at Worcester Airport over an hour ago, got picked up by his limo driver and we haven't heard from them since. He should have been here a long time ago, so listen up . . . I want you to do 20-25 minutes, but if I give you the stretch sign, just keep going. That means we're running late and I'll need you to kill some time."

"No problem," I said, relishing the possibility of getting extra stage time and surmising that this was not the first time "The Killer" had been missing in action over his long career.

You have to consider that this was in 1994, which was still years before a time when each and every one of the 2,300 audience members, from ages 8 to 80, would have a cell phone in their pocket, so there was no way to communicate with the limousine.

When I took the stage twenty minutes later, there was still no sign of Jerry Lee.

I was having a great set when I got the stretch sign from the frazzled looking stage manager and went on with my act.

During the "bonus" addition to my act an incredibly intense thunderstorm began raging outside, complete with deafening thunder and cracks of lightning so intense it actually drove a family of skunks into the packed theatre, briefly causing a mini-panic in the back row.

That night, Jerry Lee was accompanied by Elvis Presley's old back-up band and, coincidently, Elvis' daughter, Lisa Marie, had recently shocked the world by marrying pop star/child-enthusiast Michael Jackson, of all people.

When the lightning caused all the lights in the tent to flicker on and off, I took the opportunity to hold a séance on stage, in an attempt to contact Elvis in heaven and see how he felt about the wedding.

As the thunder claps boomed and the lights blinked on and

off, I held my hands over one of the amplifiers, summonsed the spirit of "The King," asked him what he thought of his new son-in-law, shook my hips, curled my lip and answered, in my best Elvis impersonation, "I DON'T WANT THAT FRUIT-CAKE GOIN' NEAR MY LITTLE GIRL!!! . . . IF THAT MOONWALKIN' SCARECROW TOUCHES MY DARLIN' DAUGHTER I'LL PUNCH HIM RIGHT IN WHATEVER'S LEFT OF HIS NOSE!!!"

Paul's original scratchboard drawing of 'The King'

The crowd howled in laughter but the stage manager was now giving me the cut sign, conveyed by drawing his index finger across his neck as if he was slashing his own throat . . . Never a good sign.

I immediately said goodnight, got off the stage and went directly up to the stage manager.

"Did I do something wrong? I was doing good, why'd you cut me off so abruptly? Did I offend somebody?"

"No, noooo, your act was great, but you were gonna get electrocuted, you nut! Lightning bolts were striking the tent and you were standing on stage holding a metal microphone plugged into a 10,000 watt amplifier . . . not a good combo."

"OK, as long as I didn't screw up . . . By the way, did Jerry Lee ever show up?"

"No . . . and we have no idea what happened to him."

While Kelly and I waited backstage near the dressing rooms, the venue drew the intermission out as long as they could before the crowd started to get restless and began yelling for Jerry Lee. When he still didn't appear, they sent the back-up band on stage without him to kill some more time. That kept the crowd content for a couple songs but, when they got to the fourth or fifth number, the impatient crowd understandably began to get edgy again.

Things were starting to get ugly . . .

And that's when "The Killer" finally sauntered in, in no big hurry whatsoever . . . like he was an hour early, rather than an hour late.

I later learned, from the limo driver, that they got hopelessly lost looking to buy a bottle of whiskey. (Remember, besides being pre-cell phone, there were also no GPS devices in 1994 either. How did we ever survive?) I guess Jerry Lee wanted Wild Turkey or Jim Beam or something like that, but Cohasset was a dry town and they had to drive all over hell to find a liquor store.

As he nonchalantly strolled past us, "The Killer" glanced at Kelly, stopped dead in his tracks, pointed right at her and said, "If you were any prettier, we'd have to kill them all!" and then walked into his dressing room.

I exclaimed, "Wow! Did you hear that? That was sooo cool! 'The Killer' said, 'If you were any prettier, we'd have to kill them all.' I'll never forget that! Whoa!"

Kelly asked, "What exactly does that mean?"

I answered, "I have absolutely no idea whatsoever . . . but it just sounded so damn cool!"

Jerry Lee finally took the stage to a delirious crowd and launched into one of his big hits, "Great Balls of Fire" or "Whole Lotta Shakin' Goin' On," banging wildly on the piano, sometimes with his right foot.

Then, right in the middle of the song, he stopped, the band stopped, and Jerry Lee said confidently, in his smooth Southern drawl, "I'm sorry I was late but, hey . . . *that's rock and roll!*" before assaulting the keyboard again.

The crowd went wild.

A couple weeks later I read in *Rolling Stone* magazine that Jerry Lee owed the IRS oodles in back taxes so, in an effort to raise funds, he opened his home up as a museum. Only problem was, he was still living in it and was known to come downstairs in his bathrobe and yell at his adoring fans.

"WHAT'RE YOU PEOPLE DOING IN HERE?! . . . GET THE HELL OUTTA MY HOUSE!"

Classic.

Comedian at Law

It was inevitable that there were a number of times when my two simultaneous careers of public prosecutor and stand-up comedian crossed paths.

One such occasion was recalled by a lawyer who was sitting in the Peabody (Massachusetts) District Court Jury Session in the late 1980s, waiting for his case to be heard. He told the story to me and a group of his friends following one of my comedy shows. I had no recollection of the incident until he brought it up after twenty some odd years.

The occasion was the sentencing of a drunk driver after a plea of guilty to Driving While Intoxicated. There was a new procedural rule in Massachusetts that required a judge, upon a conviction or admission to operating under the influence of alcohol, to ask the defendant to reveal the name of the establishment where he was served his last drink in an effort to crack down on bars that continued to serve inebriated customers.

The presiding judge addressed the offender and said, "Sir, by law I must inquire as to where you had your last drink on the evening that you were arrested."

According to my friend, the defendant answered, "Your honor, it was at Stevie D's Comedy Tonight in Middleton . . ." and then he turned and pointed at me ". . . and *THAT GUY* was the headliner!"

And, like any insecure comic constantly seeking validation, he told the group that I immediately pivoted, walked over to the defendant and asked, "Despite everything that happened afterwards, did you enjoy the show?"

My Golf Game

I suck at golf.

How can I explain it in a way that you don't need to have played golf, or know anything about golf, to understand how bad I am?

Let me use this example . . .

I used to fly from Boston to Los Angeles all the time.

If you flew from Boston to Los Angeles the way I played golf, your flight would go something like this:

You would take off from Boston's Logan Airport, hoping for a nice, direct flight with a minimum of stops but, during the takeoff, even though he has been told a thousand times not to do it, the dumb pilot forgets to keep his head down and the airplane immediately veers off course heading waaaay off to the right and lands in the middle of the woods somewhere near Buffalo, New York.

"#$%&*@%!"

At this point you would spend the next fifteen minutes looking for your airplane.

"Where's my airplane? . . . Did you see where my airplane went? . . . What gate did it land at? . . . I know it's here somewhere. DAMMIT!"

Once you find it, the airplane would have to take off from deep in the woods.

It starts heading towards Los Angeles, but the airplane would hit a branch shortly after takeoff that makes it change direction and it ends up crash-landing right in the middle of Lake Michigan.

"SON OF A . . . !"

Now you'd have to take off in a brand new airplane out of Chicago.

You'd take off, heading west towards LA . . . towards LA . . . towards LA . . . until, at the last second, a sudden gust of wind blows the plane off course and it ends up landing on a beach in San Diego.

"SHIT!"

Now the plane is buried deep in the sand.

Trying to launch the airplane out of the deep sand, the pilot gives the engines too much power and the plane blasts off out of the sand sooo hard that you end up flying waaaaay past Los Angeles and land all the way up near San Francisco.

"AGGGGGGGHHHHHH!!!"

When the airplane takes off from San Francisco, the stupid pilot doesn't concentrate because he is still upset over his last, lousy take off and lifts his head up again so, this time, the airplane never leaves the ground and rolls right through the middle of Los Angeles all the way back to San Diego.

"YOU HAVE GOT TO BE SHITTING ME!!!"

You would then take-off from San Diego once again and finally land within the Los Angeles city limits . . . But it's not over yet because then you'd have to take three different cabs to get to the airport . . . the second cab stopping two inches short of the fucking terminal!

"&$#@!*&%$@&*%$#%$#*@$%!!!"

And, on the scorecard you'd give yourself a . . . um . . . six, no, five. Yeah, a five.

Mink Coat

People don't think.

It was a frigid winter evening in Boston and I was out with a bunch of people. Everyone was freezing their ass off except for one lucky woman who was wearing a beautiful, warm mink coat.

But someone had to ruin it for her.

An angry woman approached her and snarled, "I can't believe you're wearing a mink coat! You should be ashamed of yourself, making a coat out of a poor mink. We shouldn't be making minks into coats. It's just not right."

The woman wearing the coat felt bad, but I looked at the

lady who was yelling at her and she was wearing leather shoes, a leather belt and was holding a big leather handbag.

I said, "Hey, sweetheart, do you think that the cow signed an organ-donor card for you?

"Do you think the cow was in ICU with a lawyer sitting next to the bed moaning, 'Moooo . . . Cough, cough . . . I'm fading fast . . . wheeze . . . I'd like to make my last will and testament . . . Cough, cough . . . I would like to bequeath my hide to Gucci . . . Gasp . . . I'd like to donate some steaks to Morton's . . . and Burger King can have my ass . . .' I DON'T THINK SO, LADY!"

Tell me, what else are minks good for?

Minks won't fetch a ball or catch a Frisbee.

Minks don't taste good. I've never seen mink burgers on a menu.

Minks make a lousy team mascot.

And you don't go down to the track to see the minks run.

Let's be honest, when a mink grows up, he wants to be a sleeve . . . or earmuffs . . . or a collar . . . or the trim on a hood . . . or the lining in a jacket . . . because that's what minks do!

The Raviolis

One Saturday night, several years back, I was headlining two shows at one of my "home" venues, Giggles Comedy Club at the Prince Restaurant in Saugus, Massachusetts.

Between shows the host for the evening, Johnny Pizzi, and I decided to eat dinner together. Johnny ordered a ravioli dinner and I thought it sounded good, so I got the same thing.

I said, "All I've had is the pizza here, and it's great, but I never tried the raviolis, Johnny."

"Aww, they make good raviolis. You'll like them, Paulie."

I did, and we finished up just in time to start the second show. Johnny opened the show, brought on the feature act, and then introduced me to close the show with a 45-minute set. When I was done, Johnny would be there to take me off stage, then wrap things up and say good night.

Everything was going great until I got about forty minutes into my act, when I felt a low rumbling, deep within my belly.

Forty-one minutes into my act, my tummy began making some very disturbing, gurgling sounds that had me concerned, but I continued to do my time.

Forty-two minutes into my act, my stomach was moving around like two rabid ferrets were fighting over a lamb chop inside my abdomen.

Forty-three minutes in, my insides suddenly turned into molten lava and I was pinching my butt cheeks together like it was my first night in prison.

In the forty-fourth minute, I cut my set short and quickly said, "Good night! Now here's your host, Johnny Pizzi" and literally bounded off the stage, ran backstage, through the restaurant's kitchen, almost knocking over several workers, flew up a flight of stairs taking two steps at a time, sprinted into the owner's office and rushed into his private bathroom with about 1.2 seconds to spare before Mount Vesuvius erupted in a violent explosion.

"Oh, the humanity!"

Funny thing was, the bathroom was located right over the stage and I could hear Johnny on the microphone hurriedly announce, "Ladies and gentlemen, Paul D'Angelo! Thank you and good night!" and abruptly close the show.

The next thing I heard was the sound of frantic footsteps bolting up the stairs and racing across the office straight to the bathroom, then the sound of the locked door's doorknob turning desperately without success.

"SHIT! SHIT! SHIT!"

I yelled out from the toilet, "JOHNNY, IT'S ME IN HERE! . . . IT MUST BE THE RAVIOLIS!"

Thinning the Herd

I bought a can of antiperspirant that advertised, "20% MORE FREE!"

I don't think that the antiperspirant company was necessarily being generous. I think they just needed to add some extra length to the can so they could fit all the stupid warnings on it:

USE ONLY AS DIRECTED
KEEP OUT OF REACH OF CHILDREN
AVOID CONTACT WITH EYES
DO NOT PUNCTURE OR INCINERATE

It seems that a company has to post some of these warnings based on the lowest standard of the most ignorant, literate imbecile that could possibly use their product . . .

For example . . .

DO NOT SPRAY NEAR OPEN FLAME

What moron would yell, "THE STOVE'S ON FIRE! QUICK! GET ME THE RIGHT GUARD! . . . NO, NO, THE SPRAY, NOT THE ROLL-ON, YOU IDIOT!"

Or . . .

HARMFUL OR FATAL IF SWALLOWED

It's antiperspirant.

If you're too young to read the warning . . . or if you're not intelligent enough to be able to read . . . then a written warning on a can will do you no good anyway.

Therefore the warnings on the can only be intended for

211

people who are intelligent enough to READ the warning . . . but who are *crazy enough* to look at an aerosol can of antiperspirant and say, "You know, I seem to be spitting and drooling an awful lot lately. Maybe this Arid Extra-Dry will help . . ."

Please, do not save these people from themselves!

Let 'em do it!

In fact . . . *encourage* them to experiment.

It's not cruel . . . It's called evolution; survival of the fittest; natural selection; thinning of the herd . . . or what I like to refer to as "suicide by stupendous stupidity."

Why?

For starters, if we let these people have kids, the next time you're watching an arrest for some gruesome crime on the evening news or *Jerry Springer* or some live police chase or some ridiculous reality show or *Celebrity Rehab* or rioting crowds or Congress and wonder, "Where the hell do these fucking whackos come from?" . . . you'll know where.

Do you want to take the chance that someone that stupid might someday be driving a cab with you in it?

Do you want this genius to do the electrical wiring throughout your house?

Want to take the risk that a nut like that might do a brake job on your kid's school bus?

How'd you feel if you found out shit-for-brains was running a day care center?

I thought so.

Thinking With the Big Head

Everyone is all excited about this amazing new miracle drug, Viagra. People think that Viagra is the greatest thing.

"Viagra has changed my life!"

212

"It's a wonder drug!"

"I can still have sex in my eighties!"

To tell you the truth, I'm disappointed that they discovered this drug because I was *DYING* for the day that I would lose my sex drive.

It would make my life sooo much easier.

If you take the possibility of having sex out of the picture you can finally be honest with yourself and others.

That's why old guys dress bad . . . they just don't care anymore.

Why do you think some old men wear plaid, polyester pants with a checkered shirt and a baseball hat that doesn't fit? If you can't get it up, why would you care about your appearance?

If you see a seventy year old guy who still works out, has a tan and colors his hair, I guarantee he's still in the game. If not, why wouldn't you let yourself go?

No more exercise . . . No more dieting . . . You don't have to shave every day . . . You don't have to comb your hair. And who cares if you wear a sweat suit everywhere? Valentine's Day becomes just another day.

None of your guy friends will ever say to you, "I can't believe you're wearing that. Go back and change your outfit!" Why would they give a shit? The only time a guy cares what his friends look like is when his pal looks so ridiculous that it's gonna keep *him* from getting laid.

That is why I believe that men should masturbate before they make any major decision.

It takes sex out of the equation and allows men to clear their head and make sound judgments without sex to influence their choice.

Think about it.

For generations, parents have told their teenage sons not to touch themselves because it will make them go blind.

This is bad advice.

The truth is, when these boys grow up, if they learned to touch themselves right after a bar announces, "LAST CALL!" they would discover that their eyesight would suddenly improve considerably.

"Ewwww! That was a close call. What was I thinking?"

For example:

Have you ever been in a new-car showroom, sitting behind the wheel of a little, red sports car . . . daydreaming of driving down the street on a warm sunny day and gunning the engine with the top down as women look at you, dying for a ride, while the car salesman goes, "This baby has 400 horsepower. It will do 150 miles per hour and go 0 to 60 in less than 5 seconds."

"Great! I love to drive fast."

"Of course, you realize it's a two-seater and there's no trunk room because the convertible top folds down into where trunk should be."

"Ahhh, that's not really important. How many times do I use the backseat anyway? Almost never. I'll let other people drive for a change. No biggie.

"And who needs a trunk? I can live without that. I always wanted a convertible. I can drive with the sun in my face and the wind in my hair. That shouldn't be a problem."

"But you understand that this car is very expensive, it costs a fortune to maintain and gets terrible gas mileage?"

"That's OK. I really can't afford it but, if I cut out some unnecessary luxuries like cable TV, electricity and my health insurance, while I take on a second job, I think I just might be able to swing it."

At that point, do yourself a favor and ask the salesman, "Can I please use your bathroom?" and take care of business.

When you eventually leave the dealership, you won't be driving the impractical, little red sports car. You'll be in a six-cylinder mini-van that you really needed in the first place, saying to yourself, "This is so much more practical.

"I mean, how fast can you really go? There are speed traps everywhere and the surcharges for speeding are ridiculous! Plus, with the traffic backed-up all the time and the price of gas these days it just makes so much more sense.

"Besides, it's probably lousy in the snow and you gotta have room in the trunk, you know, for groceries and Christmas presents, and a backseat comes in handy now and then and really . . . how many days can you put the top down? It just messes up your hair and you could get sunburned.

"I really can't afford it anyway. I should really be saving to have the roof replaced on the house. This mini-van makes sense . . . I think I'll drive it home, put on my velour sweat suit, eat a box of donuts, watch *Wheel of Fortune* and just give up living."

Beauty Tips

Right next to the check-out counters of every grocery store are racks of women's magazines on display as impulse items and each and every one of them seems to feature an article that promises to reveal the beauty tips of some gorgeous Hollywood starlet who is featured on the cover.

So women of all types and shapes and sizes will spend millions and millions of dollars a year to buy these magazines so that they can learn the secret of how to look just like these attractive celebrities.

And then the hopeful women who read these articles will spend many more millions to purchase the same moisturizing treatment that Jennifer Aniston uses . . . and buy the same special makeup that Beyoncé recommended . . . and they'll go on the same diet that Cindy Crawford is on . . . and do the exact same workout as Cameron Diaz . . . and use the very same beauty hints that Angelina Jolie revealed . . . and take the same supplements that Jennifer Lopez takes, so they can look as good as the starlets on the magazine covers . . . yet, most of these women will ultimately end up feeling disappointed with the results.

Why?

Because the big problem is that the magazines conveniently forget to mention the #1, most important beauty secret *of them all* . . . and that is, before you try any of these things, you need to start out with someone *who is beautiful*.

Ouch! Bummer.

There's always a catch.

Charity

People say that you should save your money for a rainy day.

I'd like to save my money for a rainy day but it seems like, right near the end of every month, my financial forecast is "partly insolvent with a 40% chance of overdrawn accounts and a bounced-check advisory in effect."

I get so many calls from people asking for money, pleading with me to "Save the Whales! . . ." "Save the Rainforests! . . ." "Save the Children! . . ." "Save the Planet! . . ." "Save the Environment!"

I have a new charity . . . It's called "Save Your Breath."

I give to some good, legitimate charities such as the Make-A-Wish Foundation, Jimmy Fund, the American Heart Association, the American Cancer Society, and more.

But, I swear, if you give to one of them, they must put you on some kind of master list . . . Or maybe they get the other charities on the phone to say, "Hey, this guy gave us some money, you should try too! Give him a call."

Now I'm getting phone calls and junk mail from organizations like the Excessive Earwax Foundation . . . the Coalition for Constipation . . . the Toenail Fungus Treatment Center . . . the Jock-Itch Institute . . . the American Flatulence Federation . . . the Acne Alliance . . . Parents Against Pinkeye.

Even the Lazy Eye Society . . .

"Who's Johnny looking at? You? . . . Or you, over there?"

(Reaching into your pocket.) "Here, take some money and fix his eye, fast, he's giving me the creeps!"

I was woken up out of a sound sleep at 8 a.m. on a Saturday morning by the sound of the phone ringing.

(Groggily.) "Hello."

"Hello, this is the Endangered Species Society. Did you know that there are less than 1,200 Great Spotted Owls left in Southwestern United States?"

"It's 8 o'clock in the morning. I'm sleeping . . ."

"How can you sleep knowing that there are only about 240 Long-Haired Siberian Yaks left in Northern Mongolia? These animals are endangered and may become extinct if you don't make a generous contribution to our cause."

"Listen, I'd like to help you out but times are tough. I have news for you. If I give everyone money who asks for it, my credit is going to be endangered and my savings are going to be extinct."

"But what about the poor yaks in Siberia?"

"I'm more concerned about my poor ass in suburbia. I'll tell you what . . . I feel terrible about your long-haired owls, or whatever the hell they are but, seriously, they don't really affect my life. If you want to get my attention, let me know when you're running low on something important, like maybe, I don't know . . . chickens . . . or cows.

"If you call up and say, 'Paul, guess what? We're almost out of pigs.'

"I'd say 'What! *NO PIGS?* . . . That means no more bacon! . . . No more ham! . . . No more pork chops! . . . Wait a second, they make footballs out of pigskin! Where's my Visa card?'

"Until then, please let me sleep!"

Then I added, "Wait! . . . Wait one second . . . Before you go, can I ask you a question?"

"Go ahead."

"Your group represents all of the endangered animals and birds whose numbers are dwindling, right?"

"Yes, we do."

"What is your organization doing about the 'Larry Bird?' "

"The 'Larry Bird?' What's the 'Larry Bird?' "

"The Larry Bird . . . You know. The American-born, Caucasian, NBA player. What are there, maybe 6 or 7 of those left in the entire world? . . . (Click.) HEY! DON'T HANG UP ON ME! . . . HELLO? . . . HELLO?"

Bedtime Story

I'm great with kids, even though I don't have any of my own.

Ironically, kids like me for the same reason women don't . . . I'm immature. That's why I can relate to them.

My friend has two young boys and they love it when I come over.

They will get all excited and yell, "Uncle Paul, will you read us a bedtime story!"

"Yeah Uncle Paul, you have the best bedtime stories! Please

read us one of your bedtime stories!"

So I'd sit next to their beds and read to them as they listened intently . . .

"I never thought the stories in your magazine were true until a couple of days ago. I'm an average looking guy and each summer I pay the bills working as an amateur photographer.

"One hot, August morning, I was shooting a portfolio for Sasha, a slender, young college senior from Finland who aspired to be a model. Sasha is tanned and 6 feet tall with firm, well-proportioned breasts and a perfect, tight, round ass.

"She was wearing a tiny, black lace thong that disappeared between her lovely ass-cheeks and a tight halter that left little to the imagination. Needless to say, it wasn't long before . . ."

"PAUL!"

"You better go to sleep now boys, before your Mommy gets mad."

"Goodnight, Uncle Paul!"

And visions of sugarplums danced in their heads . . .

Animal Planet

People wonder how terrorists can be so cruel . . . murdering innocent people, kidnapping children and cutting hostages' heads off.

They call these people animals, but that is an insult to animals.

Animals would never do what they do.

One day, my girlfriend was watching *Animal Planet* and yelled out, "The lion is going to eat the gazelle! Hurry up! Change the channel, quick! Hurry! Hurry!"

"Huh?"

She cried, "Hurry up and change the channel! Quick!"

I said, "Do you think that, if I change the channel in time, I'm gonna somehow save the gazelle?

"Do you think the lion will go, 'GRWWWL!' then look around, stop chasing the gazelle and say, 'Well, if no one's watching, why bother?' . . . then walk away? . . . NO!"

She said, "Why doesn't the cameraman help him?"

"Then what's the lion gonna eat? I'll tell you what he's gonna eat . . . he's gonna eat the cameraman . . . that's what he's gonna eat. But you don't care about him, do you, because he doesn't have fur."

"No, that lion is horrible. The poor gazelle is helpless."

"The lion's *not* horrible. That is the jungle! He has to eat to survive. He has to feed his family. If he doesn't kill the gazelle, his family will starve."

"He's still horrible."

"No, he's not. People are horrible . . . Not animals.

"The lion's not like us . . . The lion didn't kill the gazelle for the insurance money . . . the lion didn't randomly wipe out fourteen gazelles he doesn't even know because he had a bad day at the post office . . . and he's not acting up because his Uncle Mustafa touched him when he was a cub. He's just hungry!"

She apparently thinks that a lion can just pull up to a drive-thru window at dinnertime . . .

(Static from speaker.) "Welcome to McJungles, can I help you?"

"Yeah, can I have a medium zebra with cheese . . . an order of Antelope Nuggets with the Safari Sauce . . . a large pond water, hold the crocodiles . . . and two Monkey-Meals for the kids."

I don't think so.

The lion's not a serial killer or a suicide bomber or a hit man.

And the gazelle is not a victim.

He's fast food.

But, in this case, he just wasn't fast enough.

Twizzler Police

The world is upside down.

Our country's priorities are all screwed up.

Example:

I went to the theater recently and, about halfway through the show, the house lights went on and they announced that there would be a brief intermission.

I had a craving for something sweet, so I left my seat and went into the lobby to buy some candy.

I saw a sign behind the counter that indicated they were selling Twizzlers, so I was psyched but, when I got to the front of the long, slow line, I realized that they were only selling these five-pound Jumbo Family-Sized packages of Twizzlers that cost something like $8.50.

That's outrageous! Plus, I couldn't eat that many Twizzlers in a month!

It was a total rip off, but I had no choice. I figured, "Well, that's an awful lot of money for candy, but it's all right, I'll just share them with the people I'm sitting with and then bring the rest home with me."

Well, I ate maybe one and half Twizzlers when they started flashing the lights in the lobby to indicate that they were going to start the show.

I got in another long line to re-enter the theater when my attention was drawn to several serious looking, uniformed security guards standing at the entrance, waving their hands over their heads and yelling out, "No food or beverages are allowed in the theater! . . . There is a strict policy that all food and drink must be disposed of before entering the theater."

Then I noticed that the guards were taking away full boxes of people's Raisinets and Goobers and Junior Mints and Sour Patch Kids and throwing them into the trash.

I was indignant. "I just spent a fortune for this fucking candy. There is no way I'm letting the Candy Gestapo take away my Twizzlers!"

The next thing you know, I was locked in a stall in the men's room, duct-taping a couple pounds of Twizzlers to my torso like the drug smuggler in *Midnight Express* while I muttered angrily to myself, "This is America, the home of the free! They are not confiscating my fucking candy! I have my rights! Give me Twizzlers or give me death! . . . Don't tread on my treats! . . . Live sweet or die!"

I got back in line, but I was drenched in sweat, looking extremely nervous and incredibly guilty, as if I was a drug mule smuggling a kilo of uncut coke up my keister instead of a bag of twisted strawberry delights.

I could see the Candy Gestapo check-point up ahead and I wondered if the Sugar Police had Twizzler-sniffing guard dogs that might smell the candy on me, start barking and point at me like a bird-dog . . .

"He's got contraband . . . SEIZE HIM!"

I got near the front of the line and I heard them ask the elderly man in front of me for his ticket but, under the stressful circumstances, it came out sounding more like a German-accented, *"Show me your papers."*

What was I going to do when I got to the front of the line? Do they have x-ray equipment up there? Will they swab my hands to see if I have candy residue on my fingers? What if they pat me down?

"Sir, is that a Twizzler in your pocket?"

"No, I'm just happy to see you, fuck-face."

I knew one thing for sure. If I saw a guard putting on a rubber glove, I was going to immediately bolt for the parking lot.

I could picture myself confined to a little room in the basement of the theater, bent over a table with my pants down around my ankles, pleading, "Wait! What the hell are you people doing? . . . EVEN IF I HAD SOME CANDY, THAT'S THE ABSOLUTE *LAST* PLACE I WOULD EVER HIDE IT! . . . Stop it! . . . OWWWWWWWW!!!"

I noticed the old man in line ahead of me was wearing a medical alert bracelet and I thought about grabbing him in a headlock and threatening to force feed him one of the Twizzlers

"Back off or the diabetic gets it!"

But what would I do with the hostage? I didn't want to miss the rest of the show, which was starting soon.

So I panicked, stuck a Twizzler in the old man's jacket pocket, and yelled out, "This man is trying to sneak in candy!"

Everyone turned his or her attention to the poor, befuddled man and, in the commotion, I used the distraction to sneak into the theater.

Here's the bottom line: When it becomes much easier for an illegal alien and his entire family to sneak across our country's "secure" border than it is for a single, hardworking, taxpaying citizen to smuggle a package of strawberry licorice into a *Jersey Boys* matinee, it's the beginning of the end my friends . . . the beginning of the end.

with **Kevin Nealon**

At the legendary Friar's Club in New York City

CHAPTER 9:
NEXT TO LAST CHAPTER, ALMOST DONE

Humiliation

I was living in Los Angeles and so desperate for stage time that one time I actually agreed to perform in my friend Michael's mother's living room at her 70th birthday party . . . for free.

The experience wasn't nearly as bad as I expected it to be and someone who saw me perform wanted to hire me for his 65th birthday party in North Hollywood the following week.

Of course I said yes. If I could survive the 70th birthday party, how bad could this one possibly be? It was five years less.

When I arrived, the room was filled with people of all ages, from hordes of small children to the elderly. This mixture is standup hell to begin with, but I was confident that, after knocking them dead (not literally, but close to it) at Michael's mom's birthday party, I could make it work if I could just get the crowd to listen to me.

I never got the chance.

My friend Michael was at this event as well and I told him not to introduce me until he gathered everyone together, had them take their seats, and made sure he had their undivided attention. After five minutes of alternately pleading, yelling, begging and shouting at the unruly crowd, Michael just gave up, looked at me and shrugged his shoulders.

I said, "This is gonna suck. Let's just start this thing and get it over with."

The shitty Mr. Microphone he handed me had about a three foot chord, so I was forced to stand directly below dozens of annoying, white balloons clustered under the low hanging ceiling. With their long, curly ribbons hanging from each of the balloons, it looked like a bunch of giant sperm cells with their whip-like tails dangling around my head. Standing there, enveloped in the warmth and moisture of the overcrowded room and simmering in my own flop-sweat, I felt like an egg in an ovary that just had a close call.

As I began, I became painfully aware that it was like a busy playground in front of me.

At least eight little kids were doing cartwheels, running around and playing right in front of me and another little boy, about four or five years old, was trying to master a hula-hoop within kicking distance of my size 11's, which I was being more and more inclined to do as the three-ring circus continued on during my act.

There was also a tiny, little girl to my side who was afflicted with what can only be described as a rare and highly annoying strain of Tourette's syndrome in which she was compelled to yell out at the top of her lungs whenever I was approaching anything resembling a punch line.

The only distraction that could have possibly been more bothersome was if some kid was banging a drum set as he juggled flaming chainsaws, blindfolded, while choking and turning blue on one of those fucking balloons.

While all this was going on, there was a woman in a clown outfit who had been making balloon animals for the kids and thought it would be a great idea to walk right up to me as I addressed the crowd, shield me and my act from the people that I was attempting to entertain and struggling to win over . . . and crown my head with a multi-colored wreath of balloons.

I discreetly whispered to the clown, "What the hell are you doing to me? I was in the middle of telling a joke!"

She said, in a squeaky, happy clown voice, "Oh, be a good sport!" as all the little kids around us yelled, "Yeah, BE A GOOD SPORT, MISTER! BE A GOOD SPORT!"

From that point on in my act, the clown proceeded to walk up to me continuously and indiscriminately . . . every couple minutes or so . . . until she had managed to dress me in a multi-colored balloon belt to go with my inflatable hat . . . made a multi-colored balloon monkey for my shoulder . . . fashioned balloon wings to my back . . . and attached a multi-colored balloon tail to my ass . . . all of which was captured for all eternity by a guy holding a video-camera immediately in front of my face the entire time . . . probably seeing the opportunity as a winning lottery ticket if I should ever become a well-known celebrity.

He could sell it to *Before They Were Stars!* . . . or more likely, to a new show called *Just Before They Killed Themselves.*

The tail was the last and final blow of this humiliation gauntlet that I chose to put up with, so I abruptly turned to the guest of honor sitting behind me, shook his hand, said under my breath, "Happy birthday, mister . . . You can keep your fucking money, I'm outta here!" and stormed out the side door past a partly stunned, but mostly apathetic, audience.

Michael and his elderly mother followed me out to the parking lot yelling, "Paul, come back!"

I just covered both my ears and, like Pee-Wee Herman, loudly kept repeating "NA NA NA NA NA" in an attempt to drown out anything they were saying.

"Paul, wait!"

"Don't talk to me, I just want to go home! . . . NA NA NA NA NA NA . . ."

And I kept walking resolutely toward my car, breaking into a run at one point to escape them and the memory of their horrible party.

"I don't want to talk to anyone. I just want to get out of here as fast as possible, please!"

"But, Paul . . ."

"Bye, Michael."

I slammed the car door, started the engine and burnt a long strip of black rubber as I left the parking lot going 100 miles per hour.

I heard that, right after I left, Michael was bullshit at the disgraceful lack of respect and tore the clown another asshole in front of everyone, causing a disturbance, almost starting a donnybrook, and crowning his expletive-laden diatribe by flipping the clown the bird in front of all of the horrified little kids.

Michael called me when he got home that night.

"I'm so sorry you had to go through that, Paul. That was terrible . . . just terrible."

Dejectedly, I said, "Yeah man, I was disgraced."

Michael said, "You were disgraced? How do you think I felt? *I told all those people that you were funny!*"

Not Your Typical Scumbag
(an excerpt from L.A. Misérables)
Day 784 - May 3, 1998

My sister was at the late show tonight, along with one of her friends who was one of my best clients when I was a defense attorney. Why was he one of my best clients? Because he actually paid me.

Now he's in a bit deeper. I heard that he got real drunk at a party and stabbed some guy several times. Nice. Now I feel bad because I'm the one who saved his driver's license so he could get in his car and drive to the party where he ended up sticking his victim . . . a tenuous and remote causal connection, but guilt-provoking just the same.

The kicker is that this guy just got indicted for assault with intent to murder and he wants me to be a character reference and write a letter on his behalf to be used at the sentencing. I spoke to this guy's lawyer who tried to downplay the incident to me.

"Yeah, the DA wants to give this guy two years in the can. Can you believe it? For just two knife wounds? Big deal. One of the wounds was in the guy's chest, so that's not a big thing."

"Yeah, sure . . . I agree, there aren't any vital organs in the area of the chest. That's not serious. They shouldn't hold that against him."

"Exactly," said the attorney, disturbingly unaware of the sarcastic nature of my comment. "And it looks like there were two wounds in the guy's arm, but it's really just an entrance wound and an exit wound, not two separate wounds . . . the knife went right through the arm, so it's not fair to count them as two different wounds, if you know what I mean . . . On paper it looks worse than it really was . . . again, no big deal."

I said, "No, not unless it was your arm, I suppose."

Is it any wonder people hate lawyers? So the guy asks me to write a letter of recommendation for his client. Oh, sure. My pleasure . . .

> To whom it may concern,
>
> I am writing on behalf of the defendant in the above-titled case. I have acted as this fine young man's defense attorney in three different courts on a variety of heinous criminal complaints and found him to be an outstanding citizen

of the highest integrity. For example, on the occasion when this virtuous individual was driving his motorcycle 105mph in the breakdown lane, he possessed enough decency and righteousness to pull over for the police who had been chasing him for more than five miles and cooperated fully with the arresting officers shortly after being subdued with Mace and a Taser.

In addition, when he was arrested for whacking his girlfriend around, this kind, gentle soul had the presence of mind to use his bare hands rather than pick up a weapon, even though he was reportedly "wasted out of his mind," showing the deep respect he has for women, so the case before you is the exception, rather than the rule.

I would be remiss if I failed to mention that, during his trial, this gentleman's sense of integrity and profound respect for the judicial system was so compelling that he just barely . . . almost unnoticeably, in fact . . . lied on the witness stand while under solemn oath . . . hardly that much at all, really, for a guy who had his balls in a sling. His other case was nothing to brag about but, hey, nobody's perfect.

Furthermore, the word around town, from highly respectable sources, is that this meritorious young man is known for selling good-sized ounces of killer weed and never, ever rats out his suppliers.

In closing, let me say that this gentleman is one of the most outstanding pieces of shit that I have had the pleasure of being associated with and I would hope that you would take that fact into consideration when you are sending him to jail.

Yours truly,
(Anonymous)

Dad's Scotch

Years ago, someone gave my dad a very expensive bottle of Chivas Regal Scotch. It was the Royal Salute 21-Year-Old Blue, which goes for a couple hundred dollars a bottle but, unfortunately, I never got to drink it with my father.

Why?

It was because he was always "saving it for a special occasion."

That impressive bottle sat there, gathering dust as the showcase of his liquor cabinet, as I graduated high school, made the Dean's List at Boston College, earned my college degree, got accepted to law school, got my law degree, passed the bar exam, won big cases and comedy contests, and had two brothers and a sister get married . . . none of which was important enough to merit the opening of his precious prize.

"This is cause for celebration! How about we finally break out that good Scotch you have, dad?"

"No. I'm saving it for a special occasion."

I swore, if Frank Sinatra ever rose from the grave, walked to our home, rang the doorbell, and my father answered, the conversation would probably go something like this . . .

"Hi there pal, my name is Frank."

"Frank? . . . Frank *Sinatra?* Of course I know who you are. Are you kidding? I'm a big fan! B-b-but I-I thought you were dead?"

"Well yeah, I've been dead for quite some time, but I was given a short reprieve to emerge from the tomb and, as you can imagine, things can get pretty dusty down there (cough, cough), so I'm a little dry and I sure could use a drink."

"Of course Frank, come on in! Come in! My name is Jack, it's nice to meet you."

"I'm sorry, Jack, my shoes . . . you know, the dirt . . ."

231

"Oh, don't worry about that, Frank, my wife will clean the floor. Come on in. Now what can I get for you?"

Franks eyes light up as he points toward my dad's liquor cabinet and says, "Is that Royal Salute, Jack? Wow! It was my favorite. I used to go crazy for that booze. I'd love a belt of the stuff!"

"Oh no. I'm sorry, Frank. Not *that* bottle. I'm saving that for a *special* occasion."

Best Lawyer in New England

This is a true story . . . or, if you are someone who might get your panties in a bunch about the events as they happened, it might not be. I won't tell.

Anyway, I once represented a client who was basically a good kid, but he had been arrested for driving under the influence of marijuana by a local police department.

We took the case to trial and I managed to get him off, so he was on Cloud Nine when we left the courthouse. As we were walking down the big marble stairs in front of the court he was skipping down the stairs going, "You're the best, man! You did a great job. You're Number One, dude!"

I said, "As long as you're happy. Now just don't get into any more trouble."

When we reached the sidewalk, he thanked me again and started heading to his car but I said, "Hey, not so fast, I need to give you back the personal belongings that the cops confiscated from you that night."

I reached into the big manila envelope that the clerk handed me at the conclusion of the trial, pulled out his belongings, and handed them to him one by one.

I said, "OK, here's your wallet . . . and here are your car

keys . . . and here is the registration . . . and here is the . . . HOLY SHIT!" and I shoved whatever-the-hell-it-was back into the envelope.

My client said, "What? What is it? What's the problem, dude?"

I said, "Holy shit, the court gave you your pot back by mistake!"

He said, "Are you serious, man?"

"Yes, I am serious, there's an ounce of weed in the envelope."

The client said, "That's not my stuff, man."

"What do you mean, it's not your stuff?"

He said, "Remember, I only had a roach in the ashtray when they pulled me over, I didn't have an ounce on me, it was just that one little roach, dude, that's it."

"You're shitting me, right?"

"No . . . I'm positive, that definitely ain't mine, man . . . So whose pot is it?"

I said, "I dunno. The cops or the clerk or who the hell knows must have made a mistake and put the evidence from another disposed case with your belongings."

The client says, "What are you going to do?"

I said, "I'm gonna give it back, of course," then I looked up the marble staircase to the front door of the court where seven or eight police officers, state troopers and court officers were standing around, shooting the shit, handcuffs hanging on their belts and loaded guns in their holsters.

What a dilemma.

First of all, how the hell was I going to walk up the stairs, past all the law enforcement officials, put all my personal belongings in the plastic tub for the court officers to inspect, walk through the metal detector and explain the ounce of pot I was attempting to bring into the courthouse?

What could possibly go wrong there?

I didn't want to find out.

Besides, somebody obviously fucked up and, if I brought this to their attention, I was going to get someone I knew in the court system into big trouble.

I had to make a decision.

I closed up the envelope, handed it to my client and said, "Take this and get the hell out of here."

"Huh?"

"Just get the fuck out of here and tell everyone you have the best lawyer on the North Shore."

He was ecstatic.

"You are the best, man! You got me off and even got me a bonus too! You're the greatest!"

I said, "Stop dancing around like an idiot and get your ass out of here . . . *NOW!*"

As he walked away down the street, I could hear him yelling, "You're the best, dude! Nobody's better than you, man!"

Another satisfied client.

Might be true; might not be.

C's the Day

In my comedy career I've had the opportunity to perform at some very impressive venues, but none more prestigious than the luxurious Main Ballroom at New York City's legendary Waldorf Astoria Hotel. I was hired to perform as the opening act for recording star Michael Bolton at an annual black tie event sponsored by the 24 Karat Club of New York City, a prestigious organization of professionals representing the leading members of the diamond and jewelry industry.

I admitted to the audience of 1,200 people in attendance

that I had never been married, but explained that I almost bought a diamond ring once, many years ago.

I recalled that, when I was a young man right out of college, I got this bright idea that I was going to marry my current girl-friend *du jour* and went to a jewelry store to pick out an engagement ring.

Of course, at that age, I thought I knew everything and confidently proclaimed to the jeweler, "I know just about all there is to know about buying a diamond. It's easy. It's all about the 4 C's . . . (counting on my fingers) . . . Color, Cut, Clarity and Carat."

He said, "That is basically true, Mr. D'Angelo . . . but it's not quite everything. I am very impressed with your in-depth knowledge of our business but, unfortunately, I did a little background check on you and learned that there are actually four more C's that you have failed to take into consideration.

"You have no Cash . . . no Checking account . . . no Credit . . . and no Collateral.

"A diamond is not Cheap, so please allow me recommend yet another 'C' that might better fit your meager budget . . . and that 'C' is Cubic Zirconia."

I never did end up getting married because, soon after, I came to the realization that I had an inordinate fear of four other important C's that accompanied that sacred obligation: Commitment . . . Cohabitation . . . Children . . . and, eventually, Celibacy.

Working Stiff

Your girl broke up with you and you feel bad about it? Don't worry, it could be worse.

My friend is really into Internet pornography. In fact, he

was recently devastated when his computer crashed and he lost seven years of primo downloaded porn.

It was if he had a thousand girls break up with him on the same day.

Speaking of Internet porn, I saw a heading on a website that announced, "CLASSY AMATEUR HOUSEWIFE IN GANG BANG WITH FOUR BLACK DWARVES."

A couple questions come to mind.

How many black dwarves does a housewife need to have sex with at the same time on video before you lose your amateur status?

And . . .

Where does the word "classy" enter into the picture? Does she raise her pinky finger when she is blowing the midgets?

I often wondered about these "amateur housewives" and "girls next door" who pose for all these graphic pictures that are posted all over the world-wide web for millions and millions of people to see.

The "girl next door" has to live next door to *somebody*.

How do these people go into work the next day?

How do they face their co-workers?

All it takes is for one person who knows one person who works with her to see her pictures on the Internet and that link is going to be sent to every employee of the company she works for.

"Did you see the pictures of Lucy in accounting on the Internet?"

"Quiet Lucy? The shy girl with the glasses? . . . Let me see."

Accompanied by a growing look of astonishment they exclaim, "OH MY GOD! *That's* quiet little Lucy? You gotta be shitting me! . . . You need to forward that link to production!"

Can you imagine the comments and innuendos she'd have to endure at work? I would think that the guys in the office would be teasing poor little Lucy unmercifully.

"Hey Lucy. (Giggle.) Can you type this up for me, or are you going to be tied up all afternoon?" (Chuckle behind hand.)

"Hi Lucy, what are you working on, another *spread* sheet? (Stifled giggle.) No? Well I find that hard to swallow!" (Chuckle.)

"Hey Lucy (Giggle.) I'm going for coffee. How do you like yours? . . . Oh, I know . . . two blacks . . . one sweet and low . . . and lots of cream." (Snicker.)

"Hey Lucy, I know that you would bend over backwards to help me out and I don't want to rub you the wrong way, but you're getting too much behind . . . I mean, too far behind on your work and you don't want to blow it. (Stifled laughter.) Or maybe you do!" (Giggle.)

"We need to get a leg up on the competition (Snicker.) . . . or maybe two." (Ha-ha.)

"By the way, did you hear that they might have to lay Jack off?" (Killing himself.)

If I worked with a woman like, for example, the one that had sex with all the dwarves on film, I know I would get into so much trouble because there's no way I could ever hold back and keep my mouth shut.

I'd be at the office, standing in the hallway with some of the guys when . . . (Whispering.) "Pssst . . . Is that girl walking towards us the one with the dwarves?"

(Without moving his lips.) "Yeah, Paul, that's her."

(Softly.) "Pssst . . . What's her name?"

(Mimed.) "Mindy."

(Under my breath.) "Thanks . . .

"Ahhhh, Mindy, good morning! How are you doing today?"

"Oh, I'm good, thank you . . . How are you?"

"Me? Ohhhhh, I don't know . . . for some reason I seem to be feeling a little Sneezy . . . a bit Grumpy . . . kind of Bashful

. . . You know how that is . . . Well, gotta get back to my cubicle. *Hi-ho, hi-ho, it's off to work I go . . . "*

Doggie Bag

I took one girl to a lobster pound in southern Maine where you pick out your lobster from a number of large, saltwater fish tanks.

This girl couldn't have weighed more than 90 pounds, but she picked the biggest lobster in the restaurant. "I want *that* one."

I'm telling you, this lobster was *huge!* It was in a tank all by itself, apparently because it had *eaten* all the other lobsters in the tank. It didn't have elastic bands on the claws, it had chains . . . and tattoo on his arm that said "Rocky." That was one big lobster.

"Are you serious? That lobster is bigger than you are."

"Well, that's the one I want."

"You'll never be able to eat it."

She insisted, "Yes, I will."

I knew she really didn't *need* the big lobster, it was just a test of the Emergency Boyfriend System to see if I would buy it for her.

I finally gave in.

"I'll buy it for you, but that thing is going to be very expensive, so you better finish it," but of course she didn't.

She ate maybe one claw and went to throw the rest of the lobster in the trash.

I jumped up and grabbed her arm to stop her.

"What are you, crazy? You're tossing out the whole lobster! You can't waste lobster meat, there are starving yuppies in Kennebunkport! We'll get a doggie bag."

So we got a doggie bag filled with a couple pounds of lobster meat and started to drive home along the ocean road when she announced, "Stop the car, I want to take a walk on the beach."

I said, "A walk on the beach? What are we going to do with the lobster meat?"

She said, "Leave it in the car."

"It's got to be 88 degrees out and we have a glass sunroof! It's gonna be like a microwave in here."

But she wouldn't take no for an answer.

"We won't be that long. We'll just take a short walk. The lobster will be fine for a while."

It was supposed to be a short walk but, of course, we were gone much longer than expected and I forgot all about the lobster meat until we were walking back and I saw what seemed like hundreds of seagulls circling in the sky on the other side of a large sand dune where the car was parked.

She asked, "What's all the commotion over there?"

That's when I realized, "Shit! The lobster meat in the car!" and we broke into a run.

When I reached the top of the dune I saw dozens of seagulls wearing lobster bibs, standing on my car, while one of them worked a coathanger, trying to pop the lock on the door.

"Caw! Caw! . . . Start melting the butter, boys, I'm almost in! . . . Caw! Caw!"

Dance Recital

We, as adults, are shaped by events in our childhood.

That's why, as parents, you have to be careful of the things you do and say to your kids because they will carry the experience around with them all of their lives.

Things that happened to us years and years ago still control our lives.

For example, my sister is absolutely terrified of birds. She has no idea WHY she's scared of birds, she just is.

I said to her, "That's not normal. There has to be a reason. You must have been frightened by a bird when you were a little girl and you just don't remember it or something like that. It's the only explanation I can think of."

With that in mind, one time I was dragged to my friend's four-year-old niece's dance recital. We were supposed to go out for a drink but he had to attend this recital first, so I told him that I would meet him at the high school auditorium where it was being held.

To be perfectly honest, I was thinking that it was really going to really suck, but it was actually very entertaining.

Have you ever seen a dance recital with four year old girls? It is hilarious.

They've been practicing for months but you would never, ever know it. It's so funny to watch. They are supposed to be choreographed but they're bumping into each other . . . one turns this way . . . one turns the other way . . . one's crying . . . one is five seconds behind all the others . . . one's picking her nose . . . hysterical.

Then came the big finale.

All the little girls were lined up on one side of the stage. Then, one by one, each one walked to the center of the big stage in front of the packed auditorium of maybe two hundred people. Then each one bent over, put their head between their legs, grabbed their ankles and did a forward roll.

After the finished their summersault, each one of the cute little girls popped up in the "TA DA!" pose with their hands in the air and a huge smile on their face as everyone in attendance . . . parents and family and friends . . . clapped wildly in appreciation.

That is, every one of them except the last little girl.

She walked apprehensively to the center of the stage, looking out at all the people in the audience who were staring back at her, and it was obvious that she was scared to death . . . petrified . . . frightened . . . totally terrified.

Hesitatingly, she eventually made her way to the center of the stage . . . bent over . . . grabbed her ankles and then . . . nothing.

Nothing at all.

She couldn't do it.

The little girl was stuck there, paralyzed in fear with her head between her legs, as the crowd cheered her on, trying to encourage her.

But nothing happened . . . she couldn't do it and stayed frozen in that position for what seemed like an eternity until she eventually gave up and ran off the stage bawling her eyes out . . . humiliated in front of all those people.

Everyone in the auditorium felt bad and the entire crowd collectively went, "Awwwwww."

I heard the lady to my right said, "Aw, that's too bad."

I heard the man to my left said, "That was cute."

But not me . . .

I wasn't thinking about what happened then . . . at that moment in time.

No. I was looking twenty-five years into the future, when this traumatic incident comes back to haunt her.

I was picturing the little girl all grown up . . . a woman now . . . on her honeymoon night, sitting on the edge of a bed in a hotel room in Hawaii, sobbing uncontrollably while her frustrated husband paces the floor and pleads, "What the hell is going on?"

(sob) "I'm sorry." (sob)

"Every time we get in that position you just burst into tears? . . . I don't get it."

(sob) "I don't know why! (sob) For some reason, whenever I bend over like that, it makes me really, really sad. (sob) I can't help it! (sob) I'm sorry."

But *we* know why . . . don't we?

One Hit Wonder

Comedians always have to come up with new jokes.

Audiences can only hear the same jokes so many times, so you have to constantly write new material.

One the other hand, bands or singers can make a career out of one hit record or one popular song.

Examples?

Vanilla Ice, "Ice Ice Baby" . . . The Knack, "My Sharona" . . . Survivor, "Eye of the Tiger" . . . Soft Cell, "Tainted Love" . . . Billy Ray Cyrus, "Achy Breaky Heart" . . . 4 Non Blondes, "What's Up" . . . Devo, "Whip It" . . . Blind Melon, "No Rain" . . . Lipps, Inc., "Funkytown" . . .

One and done. Never heard from them again, yet I'm sure they still toured and played small venues, getting that request from the crowd, night after night after night.

Often overlooked is perhaps probably the most famous one-hit wonder in all of history, Francis Scott Key, who wrote our country's national anthem, "The Star Spangled Banner."

Can you tell me one other song he wrote? No. "Red Red Glare?" No. "Watchin' From the Ramparts?" No . . . Nothing! Blew his creative load and fizzled out.

Yet, he probably still made a career out of that one song. Francis could play Holiday Inns and lounges, and the whole show could suck out loud, but all he had to do was end the set with his one big hit and he'd be guaranteed to get a standing ovation every single time!

"You've been a great crowd. Drive safely. Now here's a little something I wrote at Fort McHenry. I think you'll like it . . . it's called "The Star Spangled Banner" and it goes something like this . . ."

"Ohhh say can you see, by the dawn's early light . . ."

And the entire crowd rises to their feet, stays standing throughout the song, listens respectfully and starts cheering wildly and whistling before the song even ends.

"I still got it, baby!"

Weight'a Go!

I have noticed that, as you get older, your body deteriorates so you learn to use your body less and your mind more to compensate for it.

For example . . .

Let's suppose that someone needed you to move something that weighs 200 pounds.

If you're in your twenties and someone asks you to move it, you'd respond by going . . .

"Move that? . . . No problem."

"You should get someone to help you with it."

"Are you kidding? This is no sweat. I'm only in my twenties. I can bench press that much weight ten times. This is like a workout for me. I don't need any help. Stay back, I got it. Piece of cake. "

When you reach your thirties, things begin to change.

You've been working regularly at a job for a while and you have learned how to get things done using a minimal amount of effort.

"Move that? No way. That thing is heavy. Why should I bust my ass for this idiot? I don't get paid enough. I'll use a dolly or rig up a pulley to move it . . .

"Oh look, it's my break time. I'll get to it later."

When you're in your forties, things start to catch up to you and it's more like . . .

"Move that? I could get hurt. I better get my friends to help me . . . Hey guys, can you give me a hand with this? I have a bad back."

"Well I have a bum knee."

"My shoulder is killing me."

"We'll all be careful . . . Let's not get injured. OK, everybody, all together now . . . and lift.

"Oww! My back!"

"Ahh! My knee!"

"Ohh! My shoulder!"

When you get to your fifties, you are more experienced.

"You want me to move that? . . . I'm not moving that. That's crazy. What the hell have I been working for all my life?

"Hey you . . . You there, in your twenties. You're young and strong. (Reaching into your pocket.) Here's some cash, move this thing for me. I'll supervise."

By the time you get into your sixties and they ask you to move it, you say . . .

"I have the new knee, and the new hip, my prostate is acting up and my blood pressure is through the roof. Besides, my doctor told me I shouldn't do any heavy lifting . . . In fact, I'm getting dizzy just thinking about it . . . Get me my pills, I gotta sit down. Where are my pills?"

When you're in your seventies and they ask you to move it, you just keep going,

(Cupping your ear.) "HUH? . . . WHAT? . . . WHAT DID YOU SAY? I CAN'T HEAR YOU, SPEAK UP! . . . LIFT

WHAT?"

Until they finally give up and say, "Fuck it, I'll do it myself."

Finally, if you're lucky enough to make it to your eighties and someone is stupid enough to still ask you to move it, you answer . . .

"You want me to move that? HA! Who are you kidding, sonny? I can't even move my bowels!"

* * *

SOME HOLLYWOOD OBSERVATIONS . . .

Malibu Barbie

When I lived in Hollywood, I met a girl that was just like that Malibu Barbie doll.

It wasn't so much her looks, but she had plastic tits, her head was hollow, and there was absolutely no chance that I could ever get inside her.

The Reason Hollywood Sucks

I think that the reason that Hollywood sucks is purely a matter of physics.

There are so many "airheads" in Hollywood, all the vacant space between their ears has created a vacuum and, when these empty-headed people constantly turn around in little circles as they talk on their cell phones all day long, it causes a giant whirlpool that sucks everything else down with it . . . such as standards, morals, integrity, quality, decency, self-esteem, reality and values for starters.

Thanksgiving in Hollywood

When I first moved to Hollywood I was desperate to get stage time in whenever way I could so, when I got a call to do a show on Thanksgiving Day at the Laugh Factory on Sunset Boulevard, I jumped at the chance.

Each year the comedy club provided free Thanksgiving dinners to the homeless and they would eat in the showroom while a parade of comedians entertained the diners throughout the morning and afternoon. It was a nice gesture by the club and I was glad to contribute.

After my set, one of the penniless vagrants shook my hand, thanked me, and said "You were great! I loved your act. I used to be a big producer."

I said, "I'm sure you were but, (looking down) unfortunately, now you can't even produce two matching shoes, so I don't think you can help me."

Broken promises in LA

One night, several movie producers came to my showcase at the Hollywood Improv. One of them was currently in the process of casting three comedy movies and indicated that he really liked me and was considering me for a supporting role.

I was really psyched because, even if he was lying (which he was) . . . it was, up to that time, the most significant broken promise made to me had since I had moved to Hollywood!

It felt like I was moving up in the world . . . kind of like getting turned down by richer, better looking women . . . which, coincidently, also happened to me in Hollywood.

In both cases I'd end up going home with either my heart in my hand or another body part, located somewhat lower in my anatomy.

* * *

Lunch with Jesus

I read that someone took a survey and asked people, "If you could have lunch with any person in history, living or dead, who would it be?"

Overwhelmingly, and unsurprisingly, the answer was Jesus Christ.

That's probably the answer I would give off the top of my head without thinking . . . Jesus Christ. Of course, that makes perfect sense.

That choice seemed logical to me, until I gave it some more thought.

Let's be honest . . . having lunch with Jesus Christ would be a very intimidating and extremely awkward situation.

I would be incredibly nervous and desperately wanting to make a good impression on Him, but I just know I would screw it up somehow.

I mean, really, what would you say to Him?

How do you make small talk with Jesus?

"It's very nice to meet You, Jesus. Thank You so much for taking time out of your busy schedule to meet me for lunch, I really appreciate it.

"Uhhh . . . Hmmm . . . (Struggling to break the ice) We've been having some really lousy weather lately, huh?

"What was that? . . . No . . . *NO!* I'm not blaming You! . . . I'm just saying."

(Trying to change the subject.)

"Ummmm . . . Uhh . . . (lost for words) Sooooo, how's Your Mother doing? . . . Is she still 'full of grace?' . . . Good, good . . . Blessed is she among women, that's what I always say.

"Uhhhh . . . Hmmm . . . (Wheels turning) Do you want to order a bottle of wine? . . . Or would You rather get some water and make Your own? . . . Ha ha ha . . . No? Not funny? . . . I'm very sorry. Please forgive me my puns, as I forgive those who use puns against me.

"Hmmmm . . . Uhhh . . . (Awkward silence.) So Lord, I was curious . . . Can you take a bath? Or would you, like, jump in and like, you know, bounce off? . . . Not that You'd *need* a bath or anything. Just wondering . . . Yeah, I know, it was another stupid question.

"What's that, Jesus? . . . Use your name? . . . In vain? . . . Uh, I know I do that sometimes. I-I-I am *VERRRY* sorry about that . . . sometimes it just slips out . . .

"Huh? . . . No, I suppose I wouldn't want everyone to yell out *my* name whenever they stub their toe on the coffee table or blow an easy two-foot putt or watch a last second field goal go wide right . . . I'll try to make a better effort, I promise."

I mean, seriously, what do you talk to Him about?

Jesus knows *everything*.

(Laughing to self.)

"Ya know, there was this one time when I . . . Huh? Oh yeah, You already know that, of course, of course . . . Know all, see all . . . right . . . right . . .

"I was thinking . . . ohhh . . . You know that too, don't You? . . . Sorry, I forgot.

"You even know that I forgot . . . probably before I did.

"Where the hell . . . Ooh, can I say hell? Is that OK in this scenario or is it a no-no? Doesn't matter, where in the world is that waiter? I haven't seen him in quite a while . . . It's not like they're *that* busy, I mean Jesu . . . *Ooops!* . . . Caught myself! That was close! I'm trying . . . I'm trying!

"Yes, the food here is supposed to be very good. I just hope it's better than your last supper.

"I'm sorry, I'm sorry. I'm a comedian, I can't help it . . . OK, maybe I *can* help it, you're right. You're *always* right . . . I

248

apologize. Please forgive me, I know not what I do."

See? Very uncomfortable.

So why would so many people pick Jesus Christ as their dream lunch date?

I think the real reason for picking Jesus is that most people are basically self-centered and they'd want to have lunch with Him for very selfish reasons.

I believe that the majority of people would choose to have lunch with Jesus so that when they die, and its Judgment Day, and they are standing outside the Pearly Gates of Heaven along with tens of thousands of other people who are all trying to get in as well, they want to be able to go . . .

(Waving their arms to attract attention and yelling.)

"YOO-HOO! JESUS! OVER HERE! . . . REMEMBER ME? . . . PAUL, THE COMEDIAN?

"YOO-HOO! OVER HERE! . . . THE OLIVE GARDEN? . . . YOU HAD THE CHICKEN CACCIATORE . . . I PICKED UP THE CHECK. LEFT A GOOD TIP . . . A LITTLE HELP HERE, MAYBE?"

At Catch a Rising Star

CHAPTER 10:
THIS IS IT, THE LAST CHAPTER

Hocus Poke-Us

I hate phony people.

I lived in Hollywood for six years and, as you could imagine, there were an awful lot of phonies in Los Angeles, *especially* the women . . . including the women in my neighborhood who really *weren't* women. In fact, some of the women I met in Hollywood were so fake, there was nothing genuine about them.

For example, I had a one night stand in L.A. once . . .

I met a girl in a bar, brought her home, and we ended up fooling around.

After it was over we were sitting up in bed and I was pretty damn proud of myself.

I said, "Wow, that was amazing!"

Uninspired, she said, "Yeah."

"Sooo, whatta you think? How'd I do?"

She looked at me with a puzzled expression and said, "Huh? . . . I don't get it. What do you mean, 'How did I do?' "

I said smugly, "You know . . . How was my performance? You have to admit, you really seemed to be enjoying yourself. I must be pretty good in the sack."

In a sarcastic tone she said, "Really? You honestly think so? . . . OK, Romeo, let's think about this one for a minute . . .

"When you first met me at the club I was drinking a non-alcoholic beer that I bought with a fake ID and a phony credit card. I was also smoking an electronic cigarette and lip-synching to a Milli Vanilli song.

"If you were more observant, you would have noticed that I happened to be wearing cubic zirconium earrings, a fake Rolex watch, an imitation fur coat and carrying a knock-off Gucci handbag.

"Look at me. I have bleached-blonde hair with extensions to make my hair look longer than it really is, tinted contact lenses that change the color of my eyes, false eyelashes, capped teeth and so much collagen in my lips it looks like I French-kissed a beehive.

"I've had a nose job, a boob job, a tummy tuck, liposuction, a couple face lifts and butt implants, not to mention recently getting a spray-on suntan and a temporary tattoo.

"Even the phone number I gave you was the take-out line for a local Chinese restaurant.

"What *in the world* ever made you think that I was having a *real* orgasm?"

Tattletale

Kids develop tendencies early in life.

For instance, if there's a fight in a schoolyard at recess and a kid runs away in tears, sobbing, it's likely that he's going to grow up to be sensitive or reserved. Perhaps he'll get involved in the arts or become a social worker.

On the other hand, if the kid chooses to fight back and stands his ground, he's probably going to be a leader and become successful . . . Maybe he'll be an officer in the military or even the CEO of a big company.

However, if a kid doesn't fight or run, but responds by yelling out, loud enough for the teacher to hear, "YOU'RE IN TROUBLE! I'M TELLIN'!" you know the whiny little son-of-a-bitch is going to become a lawyer.

Global Smarming

I care about the environment. Who wouldn't?

You'd have to be a real idiot to not care about maintaining the planet that we all inhabit, but some people are just over-the-top, fanatic environmentalists who have been known to shamelessly fudge data when it didn't support their position, yet will hypocritically ridicule sincere doubters as immoral heretics.

If you bother to look, it's not too hard to see the obvious political agenda behind it all.

I first became skeptical when the "Save the Earth" fanatics got behind the whole "global warming" crisis. Why? Because, when I was still in school, I could recall reading various covers of *Time* magazine that warned us "How to Survive the Coming Ice Age" in 1972; scared us with "The Big Freeze" in 1973; and prophesied "The Cooling of America" in 1979. When the glaciers and the penguins didn't materialize according to their dire forecasts, these zealots just changed the cry to "Global Warming!" When the temperatures and the oceans didn't rise as predicted, they again redirected their focus to "Climate Change!"

Something's fishy.

I also learned that, since our planet was formed, variations in both the Earth's axis of rotation, and the pattern of our orbit around the Sun, have caused several Ice Ages, the latest of which occurred about 20,000 years ago. Huge glaciers formed that were often several miles thick, covering most of Canada and the northern United States, including New England.

Those massive sheets of solid ice eventually melted without any help from conventional light bulbs and gas-guzzling Chevy Suburbans.

Yet, we all have to do our part.

But that doesn't mean just me and you alone, just because we are Americans who happen to work for a living. If we want to save the planet *for* the people, it has to be a worldwide effort *by* the people.

So, the way I see it, here's the deal: I will agree to buy one inefficient, more expensive and potentially dangerous energy saving light bulb for each and every 100 automobiles that have a valid motor vehicle inspection sticker in the planet-Earth-sharing countries of India, China, Mexico, Indonesia and the entire continent of Africa . . . combined.

Fair is fair . . . No stickers on the decrepit, smoke-spewing shit-boxes over there? No curly-Q light bulbs here.

I know one guy who is a rabid, tree-hugging environmentalist and he's a real pain in the ass when he starts preaching about it, so I like to give him a hard time and bust his balls.

One day he says, "Paul did you know that our planet is sick?"

I said, "See, I told you Obamacare was a fiasco."

He said, "That's not what I mean. I'm concerned about your carbon footprint."

I said, "Don't worry, I wiped my feet before I came in."

He said, "No, what I'm saying is, do you conserve energy?"

I replied, "I'm a comedian! I only work about 45 minutes a day! . . . Trust me, I expend very little energy."

He said, "No, Paul, I'm talking about the environment . . . For example, do you support fracking?"

I said, "Honesty? I feel if it's something that's done between consenting adults in the privacy of their own home, it's really none of my business."

"No! No! . . . How do you feel about offshore drilling?"

"Like I just said . . ."

"Is everything a joke with you, Paul? . . . I hope you conserve water?"

"I do. I used to order my Scotch with a splash, now I drink it on the rocks."

He said, "That's not nearly enough. Is that all you do to conserve water?"

"No, I pee in the shower."

"That's disgusting!"

"Hey, it saves a flush, Wood-Chip."

"Paul, aren't you concerned about climate change?"

"It's really not a problem . . . I have climate control in my car and central air-conditioning at home. If the climate changes, I can change it back."

"No, seriously . . . Don't you worry about the effects of global warming?"

"No. I'm all for it . . . I say, 'If you can't afford to go to Aruba, just be patient and Aruba will come to you.'"

"Paul, you're pissing me off. Global warming should be our number 1 priority. If we don't do something to stop it, the temperatures in some places could go up almost two to three degrees in the next one hundred years."

I said, "I happen to have different priorities. For example, Iran is on the verge of getting a nuclear bomb. If we don't do something to stop it, the temperature in some places could go up almost 100,000 degrees in one hundredth of a second."

"You frustrate me no end. We all have to do our part . . . Do you at least recycle?"

I said, "Recycle?"

"Yes . . . you know, Paul, finding value in something that's been discarded by someone who no longer has any use for it."

I said, "Ohhhh . . . As a matter of fact, you'll be happy to know that I have been recycling for years!"

He said, "You've been recycling for years?"

I said, "Yes, I only date divorced women. Two people grow apart, end up hating each other's guts and, in comparison, *even I* don't seem so bad. It's all relative. You know what they say, 'One man's trash is another man's treasure.' . . . By the way, how are you and your wife getting along?"

"Stop it, Paul! You're doing this to annoy me. What about wind power? Windmills generate clean power!"

I said, "You could stand in front of one and light up a small city. Just keep on yapping."

"I give up, Paul! . . . Just forget it!"

I said, "Good. Give yourself a pine cone suppository and relax . . . Maybe if you learn to chill a little it will help cool the planet."

The Dancer

My brother's friend, Vinny, used to go out with an exotic dancer.

One day I was in the Golden Banana, a strip joint on Route One in Peabody, Massachusetts where she worked, and I saw the girl sitting alone in a dark corner of the club, crying her eyes out.

I asked the bartender for a couple of tissues and went over to console her.

"Are you alright, Francesca?"

"Oh . . . (sob) . . . hi Paul."

I was very sympathetic. "What's wrong? Why are you crying? What happened?"

Between sobs she whimpered, "Vinny and I broke up."

"Really? I'm so sorry to hear that, what happened?"

"It's his parents, Paul . . . (sob) . . . They said they didn't want Vinny to go out with me because I'm a stripper . . . But I told them, I'm *not* a stripper, I'm a *DANCER."*

"Huh?"

"Why don't his mother and father understand, Paul? They just don't get it . . . I am NOT a stripper, I'm a *DANCER."*

Grimacing, I said, "Um, I'm sorry to disappoint you honey, but I just saw you get naked onstage in front of fifty drunken construction workers and blow out a match with your vagina . . . I'm no expert, but I'm *pretty sure* you're a stripper."

Class Reunions

A couple years ago I attended my 7th high school reunion.

No, really, it was my 7th . . . there was the 5th, the 10th, the 15th, the 20th, the 25th, the 30th and the 35th . . . see, count them, that's seven.

It's very disappointing when you are really looking forward to attending your high school class reunion and you get a lousy turnout.

It's such a letdown when all the close friends and acquaintances that you always hung out with don't show up and you end up spending a significant part of the night speaking to people that you never said two words to in high school.

You'll try to make conversation . . .

"Wow, you haven't changed at all! . . . I think . . . I mean, to be honest, I don't really remember what you looked like back then.

"Ummm . . . Hmmmm . . . Hey! Remember the time we . . . No, that wasn't you.

"Uhhhh, remember the other time when we . . . No, come to think of it, we never really did anything together, did we? . . . Not that I can recall. I might be wrong . . ."

"Well I remember *you*, Paul. I'll tell what I remember . . . I remember the time you totally ignored me for four years . . . and I remember that you never used to invite me to your parties . . . and I remember that you porked my old high school girlfriend . . . That's something I didn't forget."

"Yeah, well, OK, it was nice talking to you too. Let's do this again in another five."

Even when your old friends show up, it's not the same.

I was at one class reunion and I saw this friend that used to be one of those seventies hippie-types who wore tie-dye and moccasins all the time, had long hair past his shoulders and was always wasted.

Twenty-five years later he was dressed up in a suit and tie, had a conservative haircut and spent the night trying to sell everyone insurance.

Later in the night, when things started to get boring, I grabbed him and said, "Hey, a couple of us are going out to the parking lot to smoke a joint. Wanna join us?"

He looked at me like I had two heads.

"Oh no, I don't do stuff like that."

I said, "Who are you trying to shit? I used to *BUY IT* from you in high school! Loosen up."

One girl who looked vaguely familiar came up to me and said, "Paul, do you remember me?"

I said, "I think so."

She said, "I heard you're a stand-up comedian now. Is that true? Are you really a comedian?"

"Yes, I am."

She said, "Honestly? I'm surprised. You weren't funny in high school."

I said, "Really? Well guess what. You didn't put out in high school and now you have six kids . . . Things change, sweetheart."

Jiffy Boob

I am telling you, if you have to get your car repaired, you need to have a mechanic that you can trust because it's easy to get ripped off when you're having work done to your car.

It's not easy. I definitely need to find a new mechanic because I have no confidence whatsoever in the one that I use.

I dropped my car off at his garage one day and told my mechanic, "Do whatever you think it needs."

The guy installed a trailer-hitch and sold me a boat!

With that in mind, let me give you a little consumer advice.

Be careful when you go to those quickie, drive-thru oil change places, because they try to take advantage of you and sell you a lot of unnecessary services that you don't really need.

I went to one of those Jiffy-Speedy-Quicky-Whatever for an oil and filter change and the manager had the nerve to say, "You know, for an additional $39.95 we will align the roof rack, rotate your floor mats and synchronize the windshield wipers."

I got right up in his face.

"Nice try, but I don't think so, pal. You must think I'm really stupid. Well you can try your little scam on some naïve, unsuspecting housewife, my friend, but I want you to know that I'm a savvy guy who happens to know a little something about cars, so you're scamming the wrong man, mister!"

"I apologize."

"Good . . . Now just do exactly what it says here on this coupon I have and calibrate the moon roof, top off the bumper fluid, change the air in my tires, and get me the hell out of here. You got it?"

"Yes sir!"

They're not pulling that shit with me.

* * *

THINK BEFORE YOU DINK

<u>MEN</u>

This whole dating thing was so much easier when we were young, stupid and inexperienced.

Life gets so much more complicated as you get older.

You go through a series of bad relationships, hear horror stories about other people's relationships and become wiser, in general, and less impulsive.

When a guy is in high school or college and has a chance to sleep with a woman, the thought process is simple and to the point . . . if some girl actually will agree to have sex with him, that's all he needs to know. "Let's go!"

Years ago, if you took some girl out for a couple drinks and she invited you up to her place, you would immediately say "Yes!" without any hesitation or concern about the possible implications . . . whether you enjoyed her company or couldn't stand her . . . you didn't care if it was late or what you had to do early in the morning . . . even if you were kinda, sort of, somewhat seeing someone else . . . no matter what she looked like.

It didn't matter how much you might totally regret what you were about to do if you gave the decision any thought . . . you didn't care about the consequences, you'd worry about them later . . . Let's just do this before she changes her mind!

Once you've been through several relationships and have a wide range of experiences, decisions like that aren't quite so simple.

In the fraction of a second between the time that you hear the question, "I had a nice evening. Would you like to come up to my place?" until the time your lips begin to form the answer, the 'mature' adult mind kicks in like a high-speed computer, drawing from your own personal experience . . . all the newspaper articles that you have ever read . . . television shows you've watched . . . news that you've heard . . . rumors that have been passed along . . . gossip that's been spread . . . stories that have been told . . . things that you've been told by your parents, friends, teachers, and coworkers, and . . .

In that fraction of a second, your mind now goes through a scenario such as:

"Go up to her place? That means she wants to sleep with me.

"Is she good in bed?

"If she is, then how did she get so good?

"How many men has she been with?

"How will I measure up to them?

"Does she have diseases?

"If so, are they curable?

"What was her relationship with her father?

"Did she hate him?

"Was she molested as a child?

"Does she have major issues to work out before she can have a normal relationship?

"Was she treated badly by the men she went out with?

"Will she take it out on me?

"What if she wants to get revenge against all the men that hurt her in the past?

"What if she wakes up after we have sex with me and feels guilty about what she did?

"What if she decides to fabricate a story to protect her reputation, denies that she consented to having sex with me and she claims that I got her drunk and took advantage of her or I slipped Rufies in her drink and cries 'Rape?'

"What if she presses criminal charges and the DA's office prosecutes me for something I didn't do?

"She might realize she was wrong to ruin my life, but it's

too late . . . she's in too deep . . . and has to go through with the trial even though she's lying.

"The story will be in all the newspapers.

"They'll televise the court proceedings and my face will be recognized everywhere!

"Woman's groups will be picketing the courthouse with signs that say, 'Castrate him!'

"What if I'm wrongfully convicted on her phony testimony and I go to prison as a sexual offender? I'll be brutally gang-raped by inmates that despise sexual predators like me.

"And even if I'm acquitted or the charges are dropped, no one will ever know the real truth except for me and there will always be disbelievers so I'll be labeled as a pervert for the rest of my life . . .

"My face will be forever associated with date rape . . . and what decent woman would ever go out with me again?

"What employer will hire me if he's afraid there's a chance that I could sexually harass one of his employees and expose the company to a civil suit?

"I'll be a broke, unemployed loner and I'll have no choice but to turn to male prostitution in a seedy part of town to support the drug habit that I'm sure to pick up when I can't cope with the sorry turn of events that ruined my life . . .

"Homeless and solitary, I'll end up eating pizza crust that I picked out of a dumpster and pissing myself in the back of a cold, dark, damp alley, muttering to myself, 'It wasn't worth it, not for a half hour of pleasure.' "

And, by the time your mouth receives these messages from the brain, you chicken out and the answer comes out . . .

"Oh, no thank you. I'm a little tired tonight . . . and, besides, I have to get up early tomorrow. Good night."

And then you go home, fantasize about her, and touch yourself.

WOMEN

And it's no different for a woman who's been around at all. After a pleasant date, he might drive up to your apartment or home to drop you off . . . you two might kiss and then he'll ask you if he can come in.

In the fraction of a second between the time that you hear the question, "I had a nice evening, are you going to invite me in?" until the time your lips begin to form the answer, the 'mature' female adult mind kicks in like a high-speed computer, drawing from your own personal experience . . . all the newspaper articles that you have ever read . . . television shows you've watched . . . news that you've heard . . . rumors that have been passed along . . . gossip that's been spread . . . stories that have been told . . . things that you've been told by your parents, friends, teachers, and coworkers, and . . .

And in that split second . . . just a split second, mind you, that it takes for the message to travel through your ears, into your brain and down to your mouth, your mind may contemplate the following:

"What is this guy, a lady's man?

"Is he trying to use me for sex?

"Does he only like me because he's been drinking?

"Do I only like him because *I've* been drinking?

"If I sleep with him, will he become jealous and possessive or stalk me and harass me with a million phone calls?

"Or, even worse, if I sleep with him, what if he doesn't call at all?

"What if I'm wrong? What if this is the guy I've been waiting for all my life? My Prince Charming . . .

"So, even if he is . . . even if we have five or six or seven . . . even ten or twelve wonderful years together, then what?

"Even if we enjoy each other's company, have fun together,

laugh, travel, dine, dance and spend romantic evenings with each other . . . even if we have a couple beautiful kids together . . . realistically things that are that good never last.

"Eventually the romance will fade, like it always does . . .

"The flowers he once sent for no reason once a week will come every month . . . then on my birthday and Valentine's Day and Mother's Day . . . then he'll even forget to do that.

"Our relationship will begin to go downhill.

"Our lifestyle will regress from the first stage, when we are 'living life to its fullest' . . . to the next stage, which is 'settling into a routine' . . . then to the third stage, which is 'getting stuck in a rut' . . . and, before you know it, you're 'trapped in a living hell!'

"We'll spend the next few years killing time and growing older in a passionless relationship.

"He'll start to get tired of me.

"I'll become more insecure every time I get a new gray hair or gain a couple pounds or get another wrinkle.

"His eyes will start to wander . . .

"He'll want a younger girl and, the next thing you know, the pig will be cheating on me with some big-breasted, mindless bimbo a couple years older than a fetus who can't heat up soup without reading the directions three times.

"I'll be emotionally scarred and won't ever be able to trust another man again, but it won't matter because I'll be damaged goods . . . and what quality single man would want a gray-haired, chubby, wrinkled, divorced middle-aged woman with another man's children?

"I'll probably take my anger and frustration out on the poor kids who'll run away from home and the state will determine that I'm an unfit mother and they'll take custody of my kids away from me.

"That will make me so depressed I'll hit the bottle so hard I won't be able to hold down a job and I'll have to resort to working as a cheap streetwalker in a sleazy part of town to buy more booze.

"I'll be homeless and alone with no husband and no family . . . eating pizza crust from a dumpster and shivering in the back of a cold, damp, dark alleyway, muttering to myself, 'It wasn't all worth it . . . not for five minutes lousy sex and no orgasm.'"

And, by the time your mouth receives these messages from the brain, you chicken out and the answer comes out . . .

"Oh, no thank you. I'm a little tired tonight . . . and, besides, I have to get up early tomorrow. Good night."

And then you go home, fantasize about him, and use your vibrator.

Paranoia Will Destroy Ya

There is a big push on to legalize marijuana. I used to smoke pot, but I started to worry that smoking marijuana was making me lazy and unambitious, so I gave it up.

After I quit, I realized . . . it's not the pot, I'm just lazy and unambitious . . . so I started again.

I'll never forget the first time I tried hooch. It was in high school and some kid said, "Here, Paul, try this" and handed me a joint.

I was reluctant, but he finally talked me into taking a couple hits.

My friend said, "Did you get high, Paul?"

I said, "No, I don't think so but, for some reason, I am *rrrreally* hungry."

The kid gave me a little weed for myself and I walked home to raid the refrigerator, knowing that my father was still at work and my mother was out shopping.

I had my head in the stocked fridge, gleefully contemplating what I was going to munch-out on, when I heard my father yell from the other end of the kitchen, "PAUL, GIVE ME THE POT."

I was totally stunned . . . absolutely taken by surprise.

"D-D-Dad . . . w-w-what are you doing home this early?"

"I got done early . . . now give me the pot like I asked you."

That's when the paranoia kicked in, big-time!

All I could think was, "Oh my God! How does my father know about the pot? . . . Can he smell it on me? . . . Are my eyes all bloodshot? . . . Can he tell I'm high? . . . Am I acting goofy? . . . Did somebody see me smoking it? . . . Did my friend rat me out? . . . How the hell does my father know? *I am soooo fucked!"*

Once more, my dad bellowed, "I am *NOT* going to ask you again, Paul, give me the damn pot!"

No matter how my father knew about the pot, I resigned myself to the fact that I was bagged, fished into the pocket of my jeans and threw a plastic baggie onto the kitchen table.

My father looked at the baggie and said, "What the hell is that?"

I said, "It's the pot."

He said, "You idiot, I brought home a couple of lobsters. I need the big pot in the cabinet next to the refrigerator . . ."

Then he pointed to the baggie. ". . . and, by the way, you're grounded."

Star Trek

I'm not quite sure if TV is becoming more and more ignorant to appeal to a population that is getting dumber or if people are getting dumber because TV is getting progressively more stupid.

I was flipping through the channels and, as I have many, many times, I came across the futuristic *Star Trek* series which is obviously very successful because it has been on TV continuously, in one form or another, since I was a kid.

In fact, there are some fanatics who get into *Star Trek* a little *too* much. I mean, it's nice to have an escape from reality, but when you get to the point that you have "Starship Enterprise" painted on the door of your mini-van, name your first born son "Spock" and crop his ears like a Doberman, it's time to beam yourself back down to Earth, Captain Quirk.

The *Star Trek* series may be extremely popular, but I find it stupid as well, but not for the reasons you may think.

No, I don't have a problem believing that, sometime in the future, people will be traveling across space to distant, far away planets located in other solar systems and meeting all different forms of life in the universe.

This is my problem.

Every single week it's basically the same thing. These intergalactic space travelers from Earth venture across the vastness of outer space to distant universes far, far beyond the reaches of our solar system where they meet all types and variations of alien creatures . . . Creatures with deformed insect-like heads with three eyes on the end of long stalks and weird, mutant foreheads with speed bumps and antennas growing out of them . . . and squirmy tentacles and green-scaly lizard skin . . . some with exposed skeletons.

And yet, somehow, every one of these alien creatures, from remote galaxies located in the distant reaches of outer space, millions and millions of light years away from planet Earth . . . always happens to speak perfect English.

On the other hand . . .

When I lived in Los Angeles, which, believe it or not, actually used to be a part of the United States of America . . . if I left my apartment and walked just three blocks in any direction . . . *NOBODY* could speak *a word* of English.

Hmmmmm . . .

Maybe, if they could outsource my computer's tech support to Neptune or Uranus, I could finally understand what the hell they are saying.

Theory of Relativity . . . II

The economy sucks, times are tough, and just about every person, from time to time, will occasionally think to himself or herself, "You know, if I just made a little more money, *then* I'd be happy and all my problems would go away."

But be content with what you have, because making more money will not necessarily make you happier. Why? Because the more money you make, the more money you will spend . . . sooo, at the end of the month, you're still gonna be tearing out your hair, going *"How the hell am I going to pay all these bills?"*

It's all relative.

Let me explain . . .

For the sake of example, let's say that you're a single guy who has a decent job and makes about $35,000 a year . . . then, BANG! . . . out of the blue, you get a huge raise or a big promotion and now, all of a sudden, you're making $350,000 a year . . . ten times more money! Wow!

Now you're going to save ten times more money, right?

No way . . . You are going to lead a different lifestyle.

If you only make $35,000 a year, you probably live in a modest apartment in a two family house in a so-so neighborhood. Could be better, but it's home.

But, if you get a raise to $350,000, you'll go out and buy yourself a big house in a nice neighborhood . . . maybe on a golf course.

"Why not? It's expensive, but I can afford it. After all, I'm making $350,000 a year now!"

If you're making $35,000 a year, chances are you're driving something like a five year old Toyota Celica with about 80,000 miles on it. It gets you there.

But, if you get a raise to $350,000 a year, you'll go out and buy yourself a brand-new BMW or Mercedes.

"I can't park that rust bucket in my ritzy neighborhood, it wouldn't look right and what would the neighbors think? Besides, I've got it, why not spend it?"

If you're pulling in $35,000 a year, you probably go out with a nice girl.

If you're bringing in $350,000 a year, now you're dating a hot chick.

The nice girl generally makes about $25,000 a year.

The hot chick *COSTS YOU* $75,000 a year!

What do you do in your leisure time?

If your yearly salary is $35,000, you might spend the weekend at a lake, water skiing behind your rich friend's boat.

On the other hand, if your yearly salary is $350,000, now *you're* the asshole driving the boat, pulling your indigent friends around on water skis all weekend.

Conversely . . .

If you're making $350,000 a year and you're losing your hair, you make an appointment to get hair-plugs and write out a check for $15,000.

If you're only making $35,000 a year and notice that you're losing your hair, you buy yourself a hat . . . costs you $15.

If you're making $350,000 annually, you probably belong to a fancy country club and collect fine art.

If you're only earning $35,000 a year, you belong to an Elks Club and collect aluminum cans.

Looking pale? Need a tan?

If you're making $350,000 a year, you call your travel agent and book a trip to the Bahamas. The vacation costs you $2,500.

You're making $35,000 a year and you need a little color?

You go to the Crispy Critters tanning salon, three visits for $25 . . . and then *tell everyone* that you went to the Bahamas.

Making $350,000 and have some serious issues to work out?

Maybe you need therapy.

You go see your private analyst and he charges you $150 an hour.

You're only making $35,000 a year and need therapy? You call your mother . . . "Maaaaaa, nothing's going right!" Costs you nothing but a few tears, a bunch of guilt and a little self-respect.

What's your retirement plan?

If you're making $350,000 a year, every month you invest $5,000 in your IRA.

If you're making $35,000 a year, every month you invest $50 in scratch tickets.

"Come on, baby! Be the one! . . . I'm depending on you!"

Work getting to you? Lots of shit going on at home? Stressed out?

If you're making $350,000 a year, you get a professional deep-tissue massage that costs you about $150 an hour, plus tip.

And, when you leave the message parlor, you think to yourself, "Ahhhhhh, muuuch better . . . I'm so relaxed now."

If you're stressed and tense and you're only making $35,000 a year?

You roll a joint, lock yourself in your computer room, log onto CrankSpankers.com and give it a snap.

Costs you next to nothing.

And when you leave the room, you think to yourself, "Ahhhhhh, muuuch better . . . I'm so relaxed now."

And, either way, at end of month, you'll still be going, *"How the hell am I going to pay for all this shit?"*

See, I told you. It's all relative.

Old Comedians

It has been pointed out to me that many comedians continue working long after workers in most other professions have retired.

Legends like Bob Hope, Milton Berle, Jack Benny, Rodney Dangerfield, Redd Foxx, Henny Youngman, Phyllis Diller and Don Rickles were performing well into their seventies and eighties . . . Hell, George Burns was a hundred years old and still making appearances.

I was asked if this was evidence of the fact that comedy keeps you young.

I said, "No. This is evidence of the fact that comedians have a shitty retirement plan."

QUICKIES . . .

I got athlete's foot so I went to Walgreens to get something to treat it.

I bought some medicated foot powder and, when I got home, I took my shoes and socks off and read the directions on the container.

All the instructions said was: "Apply Liberally."

Apply liberally? Hmmmm . . .

So I shook the powder on my feet while I yelled out, "THIS IS ALL GEORGE BUSH'S FAULT!"

* * *

I learned a valuable lesson from my divorced friends.

If you're a married man, and you want your marriage to last, breakfast is the most important meal of the day.

If you're not home by then, you're in big fucking trouble.

* * *

I want to open up a hair salon.

I don't know anything about cutting hair, but I have a great name for the place . . .

"Who Cut One?"

What do you think?

* * *

I saw a sign that said "Ethiopian Restaurant."

I was confused because I didn't think they had any food in Ethiopia.

How the hell can you have a restaurant when you don't have any food?

I don't want to ask a waiter, "Excuse me, do you have ribs?" . . . and have him lift up his shirt and say, "Yes, I do!"

* * *

One day, a friend of mine was asking me about my girl-friend's ex-husband.

He said, "What does her ex-husband do for a living?"

I said, "He's a contractor."

My friend said, "Really? What does he build?"

I responded, "From what I've seen, I'd say mostly tension and resentment."

272

* * *

There is an ongoing scientific debate about what killed off the dinosaurs.

Since no one can seem to agree, I offer my own theory.

Dinosaurs didn't become extinct.

They got married, bought a house, had kids, promised they'd stay in touch, but got so wrapped up in their own lives that their friends never, ever saw them again.

* * *

I have a friend who is colorblind.

One day I was a passenger in a car that he was driving.

We went flying through an intersection and, horrified, I turned to him and said, "Hey, do you know that you just went through a gray light?"

* * *

When I was an assistant DA I had one office manager who was absolutely terrible . . . the worst ever. She was lazy, incompetent, had a bad attitude and was totally useless.

I told one of my colleagues, "My secretary is horrible . . . She doesn't know her ass from her elbow."

He said, "Then why don't you fire her?"

I said, "Because she has a great elbow."

* * *

One day I told my friend, "My girlfriend hates me so much, I think she's trying to kill me."

He laughed and said, "That's ridiculous, Paul. What on earth would make you think that your girlfriend is trying to kill you?"

I said, "The other day she made me a sandwich and I almost choked on a chicken bone."

My friend chuckled again and said, "Ahhh, you're being paranoid, Paul! Things like that happen all the time. It doesn't mean your girlfriend did it on purpose. Every once in a while you'll get a chicken bone in a sandwich. It's really no big deal."

I said, "It was peanut butter and jelly."

"Oh . . . Well, that's different."

* * *

A language barrier can create a lot of communication problems when things you say are misunderstood or lost in translation.

Take, for example, my trip to Puerto Rico.

I asked a man to take my picture . . .

Apparently, he thought I said, "Take my camera."

Maybe it was my fault.

* * *

I had a date with a girl who makes me feel different than all the other girls I ever met before.

It burns when I urinate.

* * *

I went to the dentist to get my teeth cleaned.

After a while, the hygienist said, "Mr. D'Angelo. Your gums are bleeding. That means you haven't been flossing properly."

I said, "Excuse me, but you don't suppose it has anything to do with the sharp metal pick that you've been gouging them

274

with for the last twenty minutes, do you? . . . I would like to remind you that this is not an autopsy, I'm still alive!"

She said, "But you have plaque."

I said, "Plaque? Forget about the plaque, I'll give you a fucking *trophy* if you stop hurting me!"

* * *

Maybe it's because I'm a comedian, but I often find humor where other people might overlook it.

For example . . . one time I was Christmas shopping in a very busy department store and I was waiting in a long line at the checkout, getting very bored and frustrated.

A man walked up behind us and yelled out to the woman at the cash register, "EXCUSE ME, MA'AM. DO YOU HAVE A LARGE BOX?"

Nonchalantly, she said, "No, that would be Miss Grimes in Customer Service."

I was killing myself laughing and no one else in line knew why.

* * *

I know it happens to a lot of people, but I still can't believe that I actually hit a deer.

I know it wasn't my fault, but I still feel guilty about it.

I was at a petting zoo and he bit me . . . so I smacked him.

* * *

I joined a dating service that promised to fix me up with a woman with similar interests.

They were right . . . the girl I met liked to lift weights and sleep with women.

* * *

They say that you can teach a dog to play Frisbee.

I don't know if my dog is stupid, but I was out there every day with him for weeks and he still couldn't throw that thing for shit!

* * *

My girlfriend made me go shopping with her.

She tried on one dress and said, "What do you think? Is this dress me?"

I asked, "How much does it cost?"

She said, "$250."

I said, "No . . . it's not you. That dress might be a girl with a better job or a richer boyfriend, but it's definitely not you."

* * *

I recently bumped into an old girlfriend who I hadn't seen for a long time.

She said, "What a coincidence that we should run into each other, Paul. I was just thinking of you the other day."

I was flattered. "Really, you were thinking about me?"

She said, "Yeah, I remember I was in the deli section of the supermarket and I saw something that reminded me of you, but I can't recall exactly what it was."

Confidently, I said, "Perhaps you were looking at a big, fat, Italian sausage."

She exclaimed, "Oh no! That reminds me! . . . It was a sign for Beef Jerky."

* * *

The other day I ate in a Mexican restaurant.

Even though I was sitting in a non-smoking section, when they brought out the sizzling fajitas I got a lot of second-hand fajita smoke.

It didn't affect my lungs but, when I got into my car, I had a strange desire to tint the windows and lower the suspension.

* * *

When I was a naïve, innocent little boy, I can recall being totally bewildered when I was listening to a Red Sox game on the radio and the play-by-play announcer said, "Yaz would have scored easily from second base if it wasn't for his base running boner."

I can remember thinking, "No wonder the poor guy couldn't run!"

* * *

I read that one of the world's most notorious international terrorists, the late Osama bin Laden, was actually the 17th of 52 children.

Are you thinking the same thing I'm thinking?

What is it about the 17th kid? . . . They are *ALWAYS* trouble!

* * *

After going out on many dates I found out that I'm extremely allergic to cats.

Well, actually, not just cats . . . I'm pretty much allergic to almost *all* Broadway musicals.

"AHHH CHOOO!"

* * *

I once went out with a girl who insisted that she definitely would *NOT* have sex with me until *after* marriage.

I had no problem with that.

I figured that I could hold out until after the wedding.

I just hoped that, when the time finally came, her husband wouldn't object to our little arrangement.

* * *

The economy is in rough shape and everybody seems to be feeling the pinch.

Even the big country fair that they hold around here every fall has had to cut corners.

They used to have donkey rides and face painting for the kids but now, for financial reasons, they had to consolidate the two.

Now they have ass painting.

* * *

My friend recently bought a pit bull to protect his house.

It's very effective . . .

He hasn't been able to get near the place for two weeks.

It Could Be Worse

People often seem to complain about not having enough when they really should be counting their blessings for the things that they DO have.

Everything is relative.

No matter how bad you have it, there is always someone who has it much worse.

To remind people of this, when I die and I'm lying in that box, I want to be wearing a pin on my lapel that says:

" . . . AND YOU THOUGHT *YOU* WERE HAVING A BAD DAY?"

Dugie and the Hot Dog

My pal Dugie is one of my oldest and dearest friends. We met way back in 1983 when I started out as a prosecutor in Salem, Massachusetts where Dugie was a court officer at the Superior Court.

Dugie is an animal lover and just adores his pets, so I was very concerned a few years ago when his black lab, Missy, was sick. Dugie had been back and forth to the veterinarian's office for a couple days and things weren't looking too good, so I wasn't really surprised when I called to check up on Missy one morning and Dugie was crying his eyes out.

"Dugie, are you alright?"

Between sobs he said, "No, Missy's gone. I had to put her down this morning."

I said, "I'll be right over" and hopped in my car to console my grieving friend.

When I arrived at Dugie's home in Beverly, Massachusetts, my heartbroken friend was looking at photos of his beloved dog on his computer and asked if I could help him print out some pictures for a photo collage in a frame, which I did.

When we were done, Dugie really looked down in the dumps so I said, "We need to get you out of the house. I'm gonna take you to lunch, my treat."

So I got into my car and headed for the Weathervane Tavern in Hamilton with my weeping buddy in an attempt to cheer him up.

As we drove down an isolated stretch of rural roadway that cut through some desolate marshland, we were approaching an attractive young woman walking her dog when Dugie abruptly came to life and yelled out to me, "Pull over next to this woman! Stop the car!"

I said, "Why?"

"Just pull over! Hurry up, stop right here! Stop the car! Pull over, now!"

Based on my experience with Dugie, I was justifiably concerned as I slowed the car down and began to pull alongside the girl and her dog, so I asked Dugie again, "Before I stop, you need to tell me what you plan on doing."

Dugie proceeded to pull a raw hot dog out of the pocket of his pants and said. "I want to give her this."

I immediately took my foot off the brake and punched the accelerator so hard our necks snapped backward.

As our car sped off, Dugie cried out as he looked over his shoulder at the girl, "What the hell are you doing! I told you to pull over! Go back there!"

I said, "Are you fucking crazy? First of all, what the hell are you doing with a hot dog in your pocket? Who carries around a fucking *hot dog* in their pocket?"

Dugie said, "I brought it to the vet's with me for Missy. She loved hot dogs and I was feeding them to her while the doctor was putting her to sleep. I wanted to give it to that girl's mutt. Why didn't you pull over like I told you to?"

I was dumbfounded. "Why didn't I pull over? *Why didn't I pull over,* you ask? What the hell is wrong with you, Dugie?"

"What's the problem?"

"*What's the problem?* You're a real genius, you are. Think for a second, Dugie . . . A mysterious car with two strange men approaches a good looking girl from behind as she walks alone in a secluded area, then suddenly pulls alongside her as an old guy jumps from the car, whips out a long, tubular piece of pink meat from his pants pocket and yells, 'I GOT SOMETHING FOR YOU, HONEY!'

"What could *possibly* go wrong in that scenario? Huh?"

"Ummm . . . good point."

"No shit! Why don't you put a couple of meatballs in your trousers to make it official? I love ya, Dugie, but I'm not sharing an eight by eight cell with you for the next twenty years, you stupid shit!"

Dugie thought about what he almost did and started cracking up so hard that his tears of sorrow turned into tears of laughter.

Mission accomplished.

Early show at Chase House
Salem, Massachusetts - 1987

with
Brad Garrett

with
Jason Alexander

with
Bobby Collins

ACKNOWLEDGMENTS

I would like to acknowledge some people who were most important to the genesis and development of my career in stand-up comedy.

First of all, my earliest influences: my late father, Jack 'Tiger' Murphy and my Uncle Vito. When I was just a little boy my father would get me out of bed (over my mother's protestations) to watch all the comedians on *The Ed Sullivan Show* and I "permanently borrowed" my uncle's Bill Cosby albums, which I listened to endlessly. Two of the funniest men ever, I would often marvel at my father and uncle entertaining people with their hilarious jokes and stories, wishing I could be like them.

I'd also like to recognize my grandmother, Elsie Murphy, who taught piano and worked as an entertainer well into her eighties, because she was the only one who truly understood when I started out; my grandparents on my mother's side, whose hard work, sacrifice and selflessness provided me with a great environment to grow up in and the means to pursue my dreams; and my Uncle Paul, who I never had the honor of meeting but, from whom I have apparently inherited much more than just a name.

I would like to thank my dear friend, Bob Ogan. It was my performance at his bachelor party 'roast' that provided me with the impetus (i.e. 'balls') to sign up for my first open mic.

I would like to thank comedian Steven Wright for inspiring me with his brilliance and originality, plus all the other 'original'

Boston comics, Lenny Clarke, Steve Sweeney, Don Gavin, Mike Donovan, Bob Seibel, Kenny Rogerson, DJ Hazard, Barry Crimmons, Jimmy Tingle, Mike McDonald, Teddy Bergeron, Chance Langton, Denis Leary, Tony V, and more, who set such an incredibly high standard of excellence for those who followed in their footsteps.

I would like to express my gratitude to former Essex County District Attorney Kevin Burke for his patience and understanding, and for giving me the freedom to "moonlight" as an entertainer while I worked as a prosecutor.

In addition, I would like to thank two good friends, who are also outstanding attorneys, for allowing me to associate with them in private practice; Randy Chapman, who inadvertently gave me my start as a criminal defense attorney; and Eddie O'Reilly, who inadvertently inspired me to say "fuck this shit!" and move to Los Angeles.

I want to also acknowledge the late Steven D'Addario. I walked into Stevie D's Comedy Tonight on my lunch break from the DA's office . . . when it was nothing more than a framework of two by fours . . . and announced that I wanted to headline the room when it opened. (Even though I had never done so before.) Stevie promised me that I would, he kept his word, and we had a great run together.

I want to thank Michael Clarke and Barry Katz, the first two Boston-area bookers who gave me the opportunity to work on a regular basis, as well as Paul Barclay of the original Comedy Connection.

I am thankful to owners Jack Gateman and "Sonny" Page, as well as manager Dominic Ventre, who gave me the opportunity to host my own show at Nick's Comedy Stop for many years when the room was always packed and comedy was really fun.

I would like to thank Mike Lacey of the Hermosa Beach

Comedy & Magic Club and Bob Fisher of the Ice House in Pasadena, the only two comedy club owners in Los Angeles that really gave me a fair chance.

I would like to express my gratitude to the Castraberti family, owners of Prince Restaurant/Giggles Comedy Club, and the Wong family, owners of the Kowloon Restaurant/Kowloon Komedy, for their years of hospitality at my 'home' clubs. Also, Ron Sava of the old Grille 93.

I would like to sincerely thank my valued friend, comedian Mitch Stinson, who has expertly emceed each one of my live recordings and has always been there to help when I needed his comedic advice.

Thank you, Lenni!

I would like to thank this book for giving me a renewed sense of false hope.

Finally, I would like to acknowledge comedians Kevin Knox, Bob Lazarus, Rich Ceisler and all my other friends in the comedy community who left us much too soon.

Purchase Paul D'Angelo's
CD's

and DVDs

at www.pdangelo.com

Portsmouth Music Hall - New Hampshire

Johnny Walker Finals
Improv - Los Angeles, California

Made in the USA
Charleston, SC
09 December 2015